SWEDEN

BORNHOLM (Den.)

Baltic Sea

Klaipeda (Memel)

LITHUANIA

Stolp

Gdansk (Danzig)
TO POLAND

Kaliningrad (Königsberg)

EAST PRUSSIA

ANNEXED BY U.S.S.R.

Vistula R.

Niemen R.

W9-BBK-436

Szczecin (Stettin)

FORMER GERMAN TERRITORY NOW ADMINISTERED AND CLAIMED BY POLAND

Posen

Warsaw

Bug R.

Frankfurt-on-Oder

P O L A N D

Lodz

S. U. S.

Neisse R.

S I L E S I A

Breslau

Oder R.

Vistula R.

Prague

Cracow

Lwow

R.

CZECHOSLOVAKIA

CARPATHO-UKRAINE

Linz

Vienna

Bratislava

TRIA

Graz

Budapest

H U N G A R Y

Danube R.

RUMANIA

Germany Between Two Worlds

ALSO BY GERALD FREUND

UNHOLY ALLIANCE: *Russian-German Relations from the Treaty of Brest-Litovsk to the Treaty of Berlin*

GERALD FREUND

Germany

BETWEEN TWO

WORLDS

HARCOURT, BRACE & COMPANY

NEW YORK

DD
259.4
F78

© 1961 by Gerald Freund

All rights reserved. No part of this book may be reproduced in any form or by any mechanical means, including mimeograph and tape recorder, without permission in writing from the publisher.

first edition

Library of Congress Catalog Card Number: 61–7686

Printed in the United States of America

42916

Dedicated
to
MY PARENTS

PREFACE

An American student of contemporary Germany is embarrassed by the depth and variety of strong feelings about his subject in the United States. Except for Soviet Russia and China, United States relations with no foreign country are steeped in greater controversy, or subject to greater waves of emotionalism. Relations with Germany arouse not only the generally well-informed and knowledgeable in foreign affairs, but also vast numbers of Americans who usually abstain from taking positions on international issues.

Radical changes have taken place in the status of West German society in the years since 1945, but relations between Bonn and Washington today are still conducted against a tragic background of wartime animosity and frustrations. This background not only affects government policy, but—more basic than that—contributes to the "climate" in which popular attitudes and expert opinions in America regarding Germany are shaped. The role of individuals and of organized groups, both those who are prejudiced against the Germans and those who admire them and support whatever Germany does, cannot be ignored in analyzing American opinion about Germany. Indeed, the scholar can ignore these forces only at his peril, for unless he is willing to adopt a Germanophilic or a Germanophobic orientation, he may find himself without support and the target of powerful individuals and groups intent either on imposing their own viewpoints on him or on discrediting and possibly suppressing the fruits of his researches.

One keen observer has concluded that many Americans take one of two extreme points of view about postwar Germany: there are those who believe "that Nazism was a disastrous interlude" and that through the very excesses of the disease "the German body politic" has been left "healthier and more immune to the virus than ever before." These Americans consider the West Germans today sterling democrats and the U.S.'s stanchest allies in Europe. The other extreme view applies "a kind of reverse racism to Germany": the Germans can never be trusted; "they are almost congenitally barbarous." Those with this view warn of an imminent resurgence of "Nazism."[1] Both of these extreme views, neither of which gives a fair estimate of the situation in West Germany today, contribute significantly towards the intemperate climate of opinion in America regarding Germany. No single group can be blamed for the emotionalism which clouds U.S.-German relations, but the many thousands of refugees who escaped Nazi persecution or the ravages of war and settled in the United States, and the even greater number of second and third generation Americans who remain sentimentally attached to the European homelands of their forebears, are undoubtedly chief among the forces whose activities account for the prevalence of extremism about Germany in the U.S. today.

This is not the appropriate place for a detailed analysis of such groups and their activities, but they have a bearing on the subject of this book and therefore require some comment.

"I am told," a former Ambassador to Bonn writes, "that more than a sixth of the population can claim one or more German ancestors. Though the vast majority of these Americans were anti-Hitler, they were quite naturally sympathetic with German aims (*and I may remark parenthetically that the political influence of certain groups with such sympathy has been of far more impor-*

1. Kurt P. Tauber, "Over Germany: Shadows from the Past," *New York Times Magazine,* December 27, 1959.

tance in determining United States policy than is usually recognized) ."[2]

The groups Conant refers to and their counterpart, groups that are actively hostile to German interests, rarely come to the attention of the general public. But congressmen, governors, candidates for office, and government officials cannot afford to ignore or to slight them whether they press their interests through lobbies in Washington or on the grassroots level.[3]

The bewildering array of pro-German groups actively trying to influence U.S. foreign policy includes an American public relations firm hired by the Bonn government, a New York based and professionally directed political organization closely related to a number of "captive nations" groups, and a myriad of organizations and lobbies sponsored by official or private sources in the Federal Republic who are interested in gaining favorable disposition of the German assets frozen in the United States during World War II. Of course there are a comparable number of anti-German groups many of whose members are identified in some way or other with countries bordering on Germany. Their own experiences or knowledge of the horrors that Nazism inflicted upon their friends and relations set up an impenetrable psychological barrier to an objective view of postwar German society. Similarly, many of those

2. J. B. Conant, *Germany and Freedom, A Personal Appraisal* (Cambridge, Mass., 1958), pp. 83-84, italics added. According to Dean Acheson, the United States "has received over 6.5 million immigrants from Germany, and today over 5.5 million people are either German born or the children of a German-born parent"; speech at Kansas City, Mo., April 15, 1958.

3. See for example the report of German-American Day celebrations in North Bergen, N.J., attended by Governor Robert B. Meyner, where a resolution was passed calling upon the United States to proclaim "the indisputable inviolability of German rights to the undiminished territories beyond the Oder-Neisse line"; *New York Times,* May 20, 1957. See also the report about the "American Council for the Reunification of Germany," in Chicago, in *Der Tagesspiegel* (Berlin), June 9, 1957, and the speeches of Representative Reece (May 16, 1957) and Representative Machrowicz (August 15, 1957) in the *Congressional Record,* 85th Congress, 1st Session, CIII, pp. 7117-32, and *ibid.,* pp. 14972-78.

whose roots in Germany were painfully severed at some stage of
their mature lives are today unable to look at their former homeland with a real awareness of the changes that have taken place
there. One German who spent the war years in the United States
and has since taken a position in the Federal Republic, recently
said that when he visits his American friends of German origin he
feels like an archeologist rediscovering all the levels of Germany's
recent history. Many German-born Americans, he said, visualize
the country of their origin as if it had not changed since the day
they left it.

In addition to the Germanophilic and Germanophobic individuals and organizations that try to direct American thinking about
Germany, there are other, more complex, individuals who, although
they also may have suffered before they escaped the madness and
terror that swept Europe during the Nazi period, have since resolved to build a bridge of lasting friendship between the United
States and Western Germany. Moved simply by charity or forgiveness, or perhaps by other motives, they seek to join, as it were, their
adopted homeland and the *Heimat* from which they were trans-
planted, but from which they have never been intellectually or,
above all, emotionally divorced. One can certainly sympathize with
the desire of these unhappy people who were uprooted by forces
beyond their power to control to prove to their fellow Americans
that German culture is not totally evil, as some interpreters of recent history and certain intensely anti-German writers would make
it appear.[4] Yet, in their anxiety to cast a favorable light on German
history, some of them gloss over certain unhappy events during the
Weimar period and repress the memory of ugly facts of the Nazi
era. This desperate attempt to set Nazism apart from all German
history that preceded and followed Hitler's rule is probably no less
misleading in its impact on American thinking than the propaganda
of pro- and anti-German organizations.

4. See Michael Kuehl's article, "Die Exilierte Deutsche Demokratische
Linke in USA," *Zeitschrift für Politik* IV (1957), 273 ff.

The dramatic events of the last ten years, during which the whole emphasis in American policy, and in Western policy generally towards Germany, shifted from subjugating a defeated hostile power to cultivating the closest relations with it as an ally, also militated against any but a most immediate and superficial view of the Federal Republic's interests in relations with her allies. The American tendency to "overcompensate," that is, to turn sharply from blind hatred to equally blind love, has been an important factor in German-American relations since 1945.[5] Certain publicists, political analysts, news and picture magazine publishers and editors have put on sustained campaigns to insure that the general public would shift its stereotyped view of Germany from the one extreme to the other. This process has also been fostered by the stationing of large numbers of military and civilian personnel in Germany during the Occupation, and then under NATO. For most American servicemen and their families, the year or more spent in Germany is a happy time. The G.I. from Montana or Georgia does not feel that he has as much in common with the French or British as with the Germans. Like himself, they enjoy tinkering with automobiles, take an earthy delight in downing brimming liters of beer, and share his meticulous devotion to detail and technical perfection. On the whole, Americans and Germans like the same style of living and enjoy the same comforts and conveniences of daily life. The average German appears to pay no more attention to the political issues of the day than does the average Illinois factory worker or the Kansas farmer; he is equally disdainful of arguments about first principles and equally indifferent to public affairs. Thus the surface impressions Americans gain in Germany are mostly gratifying reflections of home and of their own way of life.

But American servicemen and government employees in Germany ensconce themselves in colonies replete with every feature

5. See the article by Hans W. Gatzke, "The United States and Germany," *Current History* (January 1960), pp. 6-10.

of American community life. Their excursions beyond the confines of the army camp, or the restricted "Little America" residential area, do not bring them into contact with the dull routine of life which might give them both a more realistic and a less favorable impression of West German society. Like tourists, they bring home a picture of Germany which features the precision wares of the camera and automobile industries, colored slides of Berchtesgaden, and fond memories of evenings spent in beer halls. The accumulation of these experiences retold in letters and conversations has had an impact on American thinking which should not be underestimated. The picture they present may be misleading, for if these Americans had to live in Germany indefinitely they might miss the neighborly spirit, the coöperation, and the feeling of community that have played such an important role in their own upbringing.

The climate of thought about Germany in the U.S. today is, however, also produced by more deliberate and experienced individuals than the innocents returning from service abroad. Particularly those who contributed to the rebuilding of West Germany after 1945, under whose guidance and occasional tutelage the West German regained sovereignty, have a vested interest in the political fortunes of the Federal Republic. These are the handful of former Occupation officials who regard themselves as the Founding Fathers of the Federal Republic, who enjoyed wielding unlimited power over the conquered Germans after the war, and are reasonably sure that it is due to the expenditure of their energies and the exercise of their talents that the West Germans deserve a place in the sun today. And since their duties had to do entirely with Western Germany, they restrict their conception of Germany to the territories encompassed by the Federal Republic and the western sectors of Berlin. Though they do not deny the injustice of partition, their stress on the contemporary situation projects the identification of Germany with the Federal Republic into the indefinite future. In view of the undiminished desire for reunification that exists in Germany (a subject which will be considered in detail in subsequent chapters), the influence of these self-styled Founding Fathers of the Federal Republic can and has misled the thinking of the American people. Even more dangerous, it can mislead Germans to believe that Americans who profess themselves dedicated to improving mutual understanding with the Federal Republic tend to hold back American sympathy and support for the cause of German unity.

The "miraculous" recovery of the West German economy also made a deep impression on American thinking, especially in the business community. Professor Ludwig Erhard's Free Market Policy, which has encouraged private initiative and competition and rejected socialization, comes close to representing the American ideal of a successfully functioning capitalist system. The West Germans have also earned American admiration for running their economy with a minimum of inflation and labor-management strife. Many American businessmen look with envy at a country in which the workers refrain from pushing demands for higher wages and benefits and are as docile, generally, as those in West Germany. And American business is also profiting from the successes of the West German economic system. Well over a hundred United States firms have plants in the Federal Republic for the production or assembly of their products, and there are an equal number of German corporations that are controlled by American interests. In addition, numerous U.S. and West German companies have interlocking relationships based on the exchange of patent rights for shares in German firms, or for cash royalties.[6] These partnerships have also contributed to the idealized picture Americans have of the West German economic system. Americans admire German ingenuity and technology; they respect the efficiency of the German worker and believe that he likes to work hard. Members of the American business community, in particular, are under the impression that West Germany's economic recovery revealed the

6. *Christian Science Monitor,* December 4, 1957.

strengths of the capitalistic system and proved that socialist programs are unnecessary, if not useless.

In recent years the notion has spread that Western Germany is becoming a replica of the United States, that—as the phrase goes—Germany is becoming "Americanized." This is not the first period in which Americans have been led to believe that German society was becoming a reflection of their own. An American President once gave the Germans credit for making "an attempt to reproduce in Europe some of the best features of our own Constitution, . . . The local governments of the several members of the union are preserved, while the power conferred upon the chief [executive] imparts strength for the purpose of self-defense, without authority to enter upon wars of conquest and ambition. . . . The adoption of the American system of union," the President continued, "under the control and direction of a free people, educationed to self-restraint, cannot fail to extend popular institutions and to enlarge the peaceful influence of American ideas." These were President Ulysses S. Grant's comments on the union of the German states in 1871.[7]

American institutions and ideas probably have a greater impact on Germany today than in 1871, but we are no more justified in speaking confidently of the "Americanization" of Germany today than President Grant was in referring to "the adoption in Europe of the American system." An illustration of the way Germans view the United States may reflect the mistakes which many people on this side of the Atlantic make in looking at contemporary German society: The American dramatist Thornton Wilder has gained truly phenomenal fame and popularity in the Federal Republic. His plays are performed everywhere; he has received the most coveted prizes the German intellectual world can bestow. When he visits

---

7. Cited by Jeanette Kein, *Forty Years of German-American Political Relations* (Philadelphia, 1919), p. 33, and quoted by Fritz Epstein in a speech entitled "Germany and the U.S.A.: Basic Patterns of Conflict and Understanding," at the University of Kansas, 1957.

the Federal Republic Wilder is acclaimed as a great genius; newspapers hail him as a philosopher and the masses listen to him and discuss with great solemnity his opinions on subjects ranging far and wide beyond the world of literature. Now, Wilder is undoubtedly a great writer; perhaps a genius. Americans can be proud of his successes. Nevertheless, the spectacle of an American writer receiving such widespread and lofty acclaim in Western Germany is bound to arouse one's curiosity. Why should Thornton Wilder, an American writer, be singled out by the Germans not only as the outstanding dramatist of the day, but as an expert on social and political problems—as a veritable prophet who can lead them out of the wilderness? Answering this question, more than one German has replied that Wilder, because of his great intellect, his intense seriousness, his humanitarian concerns, and his fastidious manner, is a true European! "It is rare," they say, "to find an American who is so possessed of the best European virtues." This is indeed a revealing response, and one which reflects a mistake that Americans, on their part, are prone to make in generalizing about the Germans.

It is not unusual, for example, to hear Americans distinguish among Germans of their acquaintance, calling some "good Germans" and others "bad Germans." Frequently the "good German" is one who is actually atypical, in whom are found few traces of that complex of attitudes, beliefs, and mannerisms which are associated with German intellectual proclivities and behavior. The German who is liked, the "good German," does not fit the stereotype; he is fancied to have American virtues. And if he bears some or all of the earmarks of that flexible and easy-going type that actually exists in America, despite Hollywood's caricatures, then the "good German" is an "Americanized" German.

The point is that what Germans and Americans dislike about each other is what they do not understand, because they cannot find a reflection of it in their own character or in their society. Conversely, what they most like about each other are those qualities that reflect their idealized image of themselves. The widespread impression that the Germans have become "Americanized" seems, then, to be the result of increased contacts between the two populations and the Americans' discovery that many Germans are remarkably like themselves.

Perhaps Americans and Germans do have more in common than they thought. One can welcome the realization of this and the friendships for which it is responsible. Yet it is possible that some of the facile generalizations made in each country about the other may be no more valid than the ill-fitting stereotypes which used to be so popular. One must, in any event, reject the rationalized and sentimentalized conception of the Germans as a people who erred in the past but who have now latched on to the right way of life by becoming "Americanized." Such misconceptions obscure the real dynamics of modern Germany and the issues of her frightening existence between two worlds, which are the focus of attention in this book.

ACKNOWLEDGMENTS

This book was started in 1957–1958 on a research fellowship at the Council on Foreign Relations in New York, and was completed at Haverford College, where I was a member of the faculty.

I am indebted to those American and West German organizations whose library, research, and secretarial assistance proved most helpful to me. I also wish to acknowledge the invaluable assistance given me by numerous government officials on all levels, and by politicians, journalists, academics, and other friends in the United States, Great Britain, and the Federal Republic of Germany. Most of them must remain anonymous, some by their choice, others by mine.

My special gratitude goes to those officials of the Department of State and the *Auswärtiges Amt* who gave unsparingly of their time, experience, and good judgment for my benefit. The names of two of these may be mentioned since they no longer hold official positions: Theodor von Kessel—a brilliant diplomat, prematurely retired, whose advice has too often gone unheeded; and Axel von dem Bussche, who, like his gracious wife, Camilla, has a passionate desire to establish Anglo-German and U.S.-German relations on a sound footing, and who proved to be the best and most helpful of friends.

Among the private American citizens to whom I am most indebted for help and encouragement are George S. Franklin, Jr., John C. Campbell, and Charles E. Nelson, who has been a very patient and helpful friend.

I alone bear responsibility for the opinions and judgments in this book.

The last and most heartfelt expressions of gratitude are reserved for my wife, Jane, whose loyalty and sympathetic understanding helped me through this work and attendant worries, and for our son, Jonathan, who received less attention during his first two years of life than he deserved because of his father's preoccupation.

GERALD FREUND

Stamford, Connecticut
December 1960

CONTENTS

Germany Between Two Worlds

One

■

BACKGROUND OF THE ISSUES

Germany exists between two worlds: both respect and fear her, would dominate or bind her if they could, and would use or exploit her; but much as they might wish to, they cannot afford to ignore her. Just as Germany lies between East and West, no longer prostrate but her future still undecided, the German people coexist with their own two worlds: that of the recent past which they have neither understood nor assimilated, and that of the future, with which the present interlude seems to have only the remotest connection.

The Germans fascinate the Western world. The eruptions in bursts of ruthless power of these gifted and highly productive people, many of whose pioneer ancestors helped to populate the North American continent, have both intrigued and repelled the Western mind. Innumerable books, studies, articles, journals, tracts, and critiques have concerned themselves with the Germans, these unhappy people who have made so many creative contributions to Western life, but whose extraordinary moods and ambitions have also shaped much of the tragic history of the twentieth century. Unfortunately these many volumes have not produced a high level of understanding of the Germans, largely because of the intolerant climate of thought and opinion produced by the bloodshed and frustration of two world wars.

All Americans were affected in one way or another by the major wars of our time. What is often forgotten is that the fervor of the war spirit in 1914-1918 was much greater than anything the United States experienced during World War II. In the earlier conflict, hatred of the unfortunate Kaiser and his warlords inspired an enthusiasm for battle that spilled over into a frenzied desire for vengeance against the German people as a whole. Many Americans viewed World War I as a crusade against the godless Hun to whom Christian ethics had no meaning. The fanaticism of those years resulted in the scandalous persecution, often unpunished, of numerous Americans, sometimes for no better reason than that they happened to bear German family names.

The distorted popular American image of the Germans lingered on long after Versailles. The harsh attitude on reparations of the British, and especially of the French, produced in certain intellectual circles in America a mild sympathy for Germans in their attempt to create a democratic republic,[1] but it was the apathy of the masses longing for the return of normalcy that determined America's postwar role in Europe. During the postwar depression, and later in the midst of a booming economic expansion, the American people refused to be troubled by postwar problems. The United States had been instrumental in winning the war; it was willing to give loans to Germany but that, as far as most of the country was concerned, was a sufficient contribution to a lasting peace. Americans gave very little encouragement to the fledgling Weimar democracy, perhaps assuming that when the Kaiser, Ludendorff, and their foremost lieutenants had been driven into exile and after their political institutions had been overturned, democracy in Germany would flourish of its own accord. Subsequent events proved, however, that the Nazis had only to place a tombstone on the grave of German democracy, for the Weimar experiment was doomed at birth by a lack of support both within the country and abroad.

The frenzy of Nazism awed and appalled the American people; its ideology was completely alien to anything in the experience

1. Conant, *Germany and Freedom,* p. 80.

of most of them. The complex of emotions and grievances that gave the movement its driving force was never really understood in America, except by a handful of imaginative individuals. They tried, in vain, to make others aware of Germany's impending conflict with the democracies. When the fighting started in Europe, most Americans unhesitatingly took sides with the Allies. Feeling ran high not only against the Nazi leaders, but also increasingly against the German people as a whole. Although the enthusiasm for battle against the enemy did not reach the fever peaks of 1914-1918 (which is extraordinary in view of the incomparable atrocities committed during World War II), America's active participation in the fighting after Pearl Harbor destroyed the last vestiges of objectivity in considering the situation in Europe that had made the outbreak of hostilities virtually inevitable.

Thus, from before Versailles until after Pearl Harbor the climate of thought in America, and the attitudes of Americans regarding Germany, ranged from disinterest to loathing. Genuine concern and knowledge—the prerequisites for a clear understanding of Germany's interests and grievances—were at no time sufficiently widespread in the United States to provide the basis for a real understanding between the two countries.

If one tries to recall today the reasons why the United States went to war in 1917 and 1941, and if one contemplates the results of those bloody conflicts, one can begin to account for the continuing frustration Americans suffer when they have to contend with the vexing problems of central Europe. The Kaiser's armies were defeated and Nazism was crushed. But the causes of liberty and peace suffered one setback after another, despite the sacrifices that were made for them. Even those who regarded the world wars not as efforts to "make the world safe for democracy" or to fashion a new balance of power, but simply to destroy German power in Europe and in the rest of the world, could not view with satisfaction the outcome of these struggles. The revival of German power since 1945 has only embittered those who are convinced that the Germans are the unregenerate black sheep of Western civilization.

Since 1945, however, American official policy toward Germany has undergone rapid and radical changes. The policy of Unconditional Surrender, now the subject of much retrospective criticism, was followed in the early postwar period by Allied occupation policies designed to prevent the resurgence of Germany's power, both economic and political. The exponents of a punitive peace were a powerful influence in framing British, French, and American policies. The "pastoralization" of Germany as envisaged by the Morgenthau Plan was not attempted, but steps were taken to prevent Germany "from ever again becoming a threat to the peace of the world." These included not only the destruction of German arms and armament potential and the elimination of all Nazi influences, but also the calculated holding back of German production and the imposition of military occupation for an indefinite period.[2] Although, in theory, the war was fought against the Nazi government, the policy of Unconditional Surrender implied that all the German people shared in the "collective guilt." No German party, sect, or organization, and in the opinion of many, no German individual, could be considered guiltless of the unspeakable crimes committed in the name of the Nazi government, and therefore nothing less than "an entirely renovated Germany, male and female," was to be readmitted into the family of nations.[3]

2. Directive of the United States Joint Chiefs of Staff to the Commander-in-Chief of the United States Forces of Occupation Regarding the Military Government of Germany (JCS 1067), April 1945. *Documents on Germany Under Occupation 1945-1954,* ed. B. R. von Oppen (London, 1955), p. 16.

3. See *ibid.,* pp. 15-18. The quotation is from Lord Vansittart, *Bones of Contention* (New York, 1945), p. 13. Occasionally Allied statesmen made more conciliatory remarks about the German future, but these did not change the prevailing atmosphere. Cf. President Roosevelt's address before the Foreign Policy Association, October 21, 1944, in which he said that the Germans might "earn their way back into the fellowship of peace-loving and law-abiding nations," but did not specify how.

Until that day, Germany was to be subjected to control. There were disagreements among the Allied nations about the use of Allied discretionary powers, and a lack of coördination in planning the future development of the German territories.[4] But the British, American, and Soviet governments were in full accord on the simple principle of imposing total foreign control, without making any provision for the continuation of a responsible German government. The decision to exercise supreme authority in Germany, "including all the powers possessed by the German Government, the High Command, and any state, municipal, or local government and authority," was tantamount to abolishing the German state for an indefinite period.[5]

That was fifteen years ago. But the German policy that prevailed then did not last long. Germany soon became the focal point of the struggle for power in Europe between Soviet Russia and her wartime allies. The task of rebuilding the European economy, of which Germany was a vital part, and the need to elicit from the Germans an active contribution to the military defense of the non-Communist world, forced the Western allies to compromise, and, finally, to revamp their conception of Germany's future.

The events leading to the dissolution of the Occupation in 1955 and to the creation of the Federal Republic have often been re-

4. For contrasting American views of the reasons why no detailed agreements on political and economic occupation policies had been reached before the cessation of hostilities in Europe, see Philip E. Mosely, "The Occupation of Germany: New Light on How the Zones were Drawn," *Foreign Affairs*, XXVIII (July 1950), 580 ff.; and Walter L. Dorn, "The Debate over American Occupation Policy in Germany in 1944-1945," *Political Science Quarterly*, LXXII (December 1957), 481 ff. Also see the publisher's introductory note to the translation of Dorn's article, *Vierteljahrshefte für Zeitgeschichte*, VI (January 1958), 60-61, and 61-62, n. 1.

5. "Arrangements for Control of Germany," June 5, 1945, quoted by John C. Campbell, *The United States in World Affairs, 1945-1947* (New York, 1947), pp. 167-168. On the legal status of Germany during the Occupation, see *World Polity*, the Yearbook of the Institute of World Polity, I, published for Georgetown University (Utrecht/Antwerp, 1957).

counted.[6] To justify yet another detailed review there would have to be new information superseding what has appeared in the best accounts to date. Lacking the confidential information that governments clutch to their bosoms during the years of its usefulness, one must patiently await the efforts of those who will be able to write about this period with the benefit of more data and a greater historical perspective. Nevertheless, certain of the developments since 1945 will bear mentioning here, and will be considered at greater length in discussions in the following chapters.

As early as September 6, 1946, Secretary of State Byrnes, replying in Stuttgart to Molotov's bid for Germany's favor (July 10, 1946), indicated that the United States was considering a more positive German policy, one that emphasized constructive efforts. Competition for Germany's allegiance in the East-West struggle was under way, although Byrnes insisted that it was not "in the interest of the German people nor in the interest of world peace that Germany should become a pawn or a partner in a military struggle for power between the East and the West."[7]

Efforts to reach a settlement of Germany's future status in accordance with the Potsdam agreements were unsuccessful. Following the indefinite adjournment of the Council of Foreign Ministers on December 15, 1947, the American and British governments established the German Bizonal Economic Administration (February 9, 1948). Together with the French government, they arranged a six-power conference in London (without the Russians), which decided to establish a West German government (June 1, 1948). On June 16, the Soviet representative walked out of the Allied Kommandatura, thereby breaking the last link in the four-power government of Berlin. Two days later, the British, French, and American authorities announced a currency reform in the

6. For example, see the recent study by E. Davidson, *The Death and Life of Germany* (New York, 1959).

7. Campbell, *U.S. in World Affairs, 1945-1947,* pp. 194-198.

Western zones and in their sectors of Berlin. With this step Western Germany was started on the road to economic recovery.

For all practical purposes, the division of Germany was complete by the end of 1948. Both halves of the country were precipitated along divergent courses of development. The Soviet authorities consolidated their control of the Eastern zone under cover of an East German regime dominated by the *Sozialistischen Einheitspartei* (SED), a fusion of parties dominated by the communists. The West German *Länder* were authorized to summon a constituent assembly, the Parliamentary Council, to draw up a temporary constitution, or Basic Law, which entered into force on May 24, 1949. Meanwhile, the Soviet blockade and the Allied airlift which prevented the Communists from taking over Berlin (June 24, 1948-May 12, 1949) focused Western attention on the beleaguered city. By their dramatic resistance, the Berliners won the sympathy and admiration of Germany's former enemies in the West. The combined efforts of the United States and Great Britain in the airlift helped to produce among their peoples an increasingly favorable attitude towards all of Western Germany. In West Germany the effect of the blockade and of the airlift "was to raise Western prestige and reduce Soviet influence" and to "align almost the entire political leadership of West Germany on the side of the West."[8]

Elections to the German Federal Republic's first *Bundestag* were held in August 1949; the new parliament held its opening session on September 7. Simultaneously, the former military occupation was converted into a contractual relationship. The enactment of the Statute of Occupation gave a new legal status to the Allied authorities in Western Germany. The "Petersberg Protocoll" (November 23, 1949) was the first of a series of agreements between the new Bonn government and the Western allies. They granted the Germans economic dispensations, in exchange for

8. W. P. Davison, *The Berlin Blockade, A Study in Cold War Politics* (Princeton, 1958), pp. 281, 306.

various pledges, one of which was to "maintain the demilitarization
of the Federal territory," and to "prevent the re-creation of Armed
Forces of any kind."[9]

Reconsideration of West Germany's military status did not lag
far behind the changes in the country's economic and political
situation. In December 1949 the West German Chancellor, Konrad
Adenauer, said that the defense of Germany rests with those "who
disarmed us." He foresaw, however, that the Federal Republic
would have to participate in its own defense and stated the terms
of his consent. "If our people are forced to take a hand at some
unforeseen time in the defense of Europe," Adenauer said, "then
we could do so only on the basis of equal rights and within the
framework of a European army."[10]

The outbreak of the Korean War during the summer of 1950
produced something very much like a panic in West Germany, and
in the United States. The fear of a similar attack on Germany, where
the situation seemed to resemble that of divided Korea, brought
the project of German rearmament formally onto the agenda of
inter-Allied discussions. In July 1950 the Federal Republic was
admitted as an associate member of the Council of Europe, and in
September the North Atlantic Council, meeting in New York, declared that West Germany should be permitted to contribute to an
integrated European defense force. Two months later the Council
of Europe approved West German participation in a European
army, on the basis of equality. A European Defense Community
treaty was negotiated and signed, but the entire project was de-
molished when the French National Assembly voted against ratification on August 30, 1954. By that time, most of the limitations
on West German sovereignty were being removed and both Washington and London were taking the view that German rearmament
was not only desirable but necessary. According to Chancellor

9. *Department of State Bulletin,* XXI (December 5, 1949), 863-64.
10. Quoted by Richard P. Stebbins, *The U.S. in World Affairs, 1949*
(New York, 1950), p. 220.

Adenauer, it was "thanks to the initiative of the British Foreign Minister of the time, Eden,"[11] that the London and Paris treaties of October 1954, providing for the restoration of West German sovereignty and for the accession of the Federal Republic to NATO —which had been rushed into the breach left by the defunct EDC —were hurriedly negotiated and signed. Less than ten years after the Unconditional Surrender of 1945, a West German government had been established, sovereign except for restrictions on the manufacture or possession of certain types of armaments, the so-called ABC weapons.[12]

In succeeding years renewed attempts were made to reach an East-West agreement on Germany, but without significant progress. The first Eden Plan was proposed at the Berlin Conference (January 25-February 18, 1954).[13] Later attempts to negotiate a settlement of the reunification problem at the "summit" meeting and the meeting of foreign ministers in Geneva (July 18-23 and October 27-November 16, 1955), also failed. The Soviet leaders insisted that withdrawal of foreign troops from Europe and the signing of a nonaggression treaty must precede German reunification. "Having despaired of getting a satisfactory German settlement through negotiations with the Big Three," the Russians "were prepared to wait until a chance developed for extracting more favorable terms directly from the Bonn government."[14] On their part, the Western powers stubbornly insisted on free, all-German

11. Bundestag foreign policy debate of March 20, 1958; Protocoll of 18. Sitzung, p. 842. Cf. J. B. Conant, "The Federal Republic of Germany, Our New Ally," lecture at the University of Minnesota (February 24, 1957). Conant insists that "Dulles deserves a large share of the credit for . . . this diplomatic miracle."

12. *Final Act of the Nine-Power Conference,* Cmd. 9289 (London, October 1954), pp. 6-8; *Documents Agreed on by the Conference of Ministers,* Cmd. 9304 (London, November 1954), pp. 41-42. Some of these curbs on West German arms production were lifted in 1958-1959; see below, p. 157, n. 34.

13. See the discussion of disengagement proposals in Chap. 8 below.

14. H. W. Barber, *U.S. in World Affairs—1955* (New York, 1957), p. 63.

elections as a means of achieving reunification. They and the Bonn government also maintained that a reunited Germany must be free to join military alliances, meaning NATO. It was clear that West German territory and Bonn's military contribution were indispensable to NATO and that, for the West as for Soviet Russia, German reunification was at most a secondary objective at the Berlin and Geneva conferences, to be sought for or to be accepted only as a means of gaining advantage in the East-West struggle.

The stalemate has continued to the present day. The Soviet government now claims that it is fulfilling its responsibility for the achievement of German unity by urging the Pankow and Bonn governments to join in a confederation. The Federal Republic rejects this scheme, which would mean accepting the East German government as an equal, competent to represent the interests of the seventeen million people in the Eastern zone.[15] The United States and its allies reiterate their demand for free elections as the instrument of reunification. They insist that a united Germany be free to commit itself to military alliances. This solution, which would result in the exclusion of Communists from the new government, is wholly unacceptable to the Pankow regime and to Moscow. They will not agree to united Germany's membership in NATO.[16]

The dangerous and uneasy East-West stalemate in central Europe has acted to increase the friendly ties and to enforce the mutual interdependence of the United States and the Federal Republic. Chancellor Adenauer's visits to Washington have been public demonstrations of West Germany's reliance upon the United States for her defense against overt aggression, and the American government, on its part, has used these occasions to show its respect and

15. See *Manchester Guardian*, July 29, 1957, and *New York Times*, August 9, 1957, for Grotewohl's and Khrushchev's speeches asking for a German confederation. Also see *Süddeutsche Zeitung*, September 10, 1957, for the text of Moscow's note to Bonn on reunification.

16. Text of *Four-Power Statement on German Unity* (Berlin Declaration) in the *New York Times*, July 30, 1957. For the Soviet reply to the statement, see *ibid.*, August 3, 1957.

affirm its support for Adenauer's leadership in Germany and Europe. Relations between the United States and West Germany have been put on a normal footing. In October 1951 the state of war was officially terminated; in June 1953 the 1923 Treaty of Friendship, Commerce, and Consular Rights was revised; and in October 1954, during Adenauer's second visit to Washington, a new Treaty of Friendship, Commerce, and Navigation was signed.[17]

Marshall Plan funds, and other forms of American economic aid, made a major contribution to West Germany's spectacular economic recovery. The United States also gave the Federal Republic equipment and other support to help build up its military establishment. Symbolic of America's partnership with Adenauer's Germany have been the President's frequent public assurances of continued support for the creation of a united Europe, for German reunification, and for other West German aims. The American administration in 1953 made no secret of its desire to see Adenauer and his government returned to power, and expressed the same attitude, somewhat more subtly, just before the German federal elections in September 1958. President Eisenhower, his Secretary of State, Dulles, and the British Prime Minister, by frequent personal communications, most of which have never been made public, reassured the West German leader of the friendship of his most powerful NATO allies and of their support for the objectives of West Germany's foreign policy.

On the surface, then, the relationship that has grown up since 1945 between West Germany and her allies, especially with the United States, appears to be friendly and realistically based on common interests and aims. One of the two principal purposes of this book is to examine the realities of West German relations with her principal allies, both official and unofficial, to determine to what extent the interests motivating the policies of the powers in these relationships are similar or divergent, and, if the latter, to consider

17. Text in *Department of State Bulletin,* XXXI (November 8, 1954), 681-683.

the prospects for harmonizing them. Since a nation's social structure and domestic political processes affect the reliability of its foreign policy, current and prospective development of democracy in West Germany must be one area of inquiry. Another will have to be the Federal Republic's economic interests and their interrelation with those of her European neighbors, with special reference to their implications for American trade interests and prospects. A third area of inquiry is mutual defense. Without attempting to reconcile conflicting military strategic doctrines, we shall try to define West Germany's role in NATO and to examine the implications for the West generally of the Federal Republic's rapidly increasing military strength and viability. Bonn's policy in eastern Europe, inclusive of the *Deutsche Demokratische Republik* (D.D.R.), will have to be investigated in order to gauge its effect on American and Western aims and interests.

The second major purpose of this study is to discuss the principal issues confronting American, West German, and other Western governments in Europe. The division of Germany and the achievement of reunification in acceptable conditions are the key problems, but they are inextricably bound up with other crucial issues such as the "reduction of East-West tensions," control and reduction of armaments, the reunification of East and West Europe, and the safety of Berlin. Each of these general issues raises specific questions for discussion. Is German unity desirable? How dangerous is the indefinite continuation of partition? Can Germany be unified by peaceful means on a basis that satisfies the German people, Russian and American interests, and the interests of Germany's neighbors? Can NATO survive if Bonn withdraws or if a reunified Germany is excluded from the organization?

These questions lead in turn to others: Can tensions be reduced by any means other than the resolution of specific East-West disputes? Do proposals for military and political "disengagement" in Europe hold out hope for securing peace on the Continent? Would the Soviet Union conceivably withdraw her divisions from

East Germany for a price the Western powers could afford to pay, or would Moscow require in exchange an intolerable weakening of the West's defensive posture?

Proposals for new political policies must be attuned to the rapidly changing weapons technology and the exigencies of strategic doctrines. It is possible that a "disengagement" policy might have been feasible from the Western standpoint three or four years ago, but that the development of long-range missiles has radically changed the West's defense needs. What are the implications of the new weapons for proposals to create denuclearized or neutral zones in Europe? How much flexibility is desirable, how much can there be in Western policy in view of the need to maintain a strong defensive posture?

Simultaneously with the consideration of proposals to overcome the uneasy and dangerous stalemate in Europe, attention must also be given in the following chapters to the requirements of western European and Atlantic military and political strength and unity. For as long as there is no let-up in the armaments race, no concrete evidence of a lessening of the potential Soviet threat to West Germany, Europe, and the United States, and no progress toward solving the major East-West disputes in central Europe, the NATO powers must continue to make efforts, and possibly more and better efforts, to deter possible aggression and to defend themselves against it. A number of complex problems must be overcome if the West is to be strong and unified: decisions have to be made about emplacing strategic deterrents, about the number of nations that are to possess these weapons and their responsibilities, and about the machinery for controlling and firing the weapons. Apart from the strategic deterrent, there must be a reëxamination of the manpower and weapons NATO requires to prevent or repulse acts of aggression short of an all-out attack. Even the scope of NATO's activities is in dispute. Should it be a purely military defensive alliance, or also take on political and economic functions? And in this connection, what are the opportunities and dangers of western European unification through the Coal and Steel Community, the Common Market, and Euratom? What are the implications for Western defense of the split between the Common Market Six and the Free Trade Area Seven?

These are among the questions discussed in the following chapters, leading to a conclusion that summarizes the challenges that confront the United States and the West in Germany, and, in relation to Germany, in Europe. Also, in the final chapter, consideration is given to the merits and drawbacks of alternative courses of action which the United States and the West can pursue in meeting and responding to those challenges in order to achieve the aims of Western policies.

Two

■

WEST GERMANY: A NEW SOCIETY?

Two governments in Germany purport to speak for the German people, but the United States and its major allies recognize only the government of the Federal Republic and have no relations with the government of the German Democratic Republic at Pankow. Discussion of U.S.-German relations must therefore be restricted to the relationship between Bonn and Washington, and to developments within West Berlin and Western Germany.

The fact that the Western powers recognize the Soviet military and civilian administration as the only governing authority in Eastern Germany, and the additional fact that the Pankow regime has been accorded recognition only by members of the Communist bloc and Yugoslavia, must be accepted as political realities. Political realism also requires that the Federal Republic, which the Western powers insist is "the only government qualified to speak for the German people as a whole,"[1] be distinguished from "Germany." The Federal Republic is not Germany. The West German state was sponsored by the United States and its major allies when Soviet Russia proved unwilling to permit the creation of a unified German state on conditions acceptable to them. The Basic Law of West Germany, and declarations by the Bonn government, the United States, Great Britain, and France, assert that

1. *Four-Power Statement on German Unity* (Berlin Declaration) of July 29, 1957. For text, see *New York Times,* July 30, 1957.

the Federal Republic is a temporary institution, to be replaced at the earliest possible time by a united German state representing all the interests encompassed within yet undetermined boundaries.[2] The relationship between the United States and West Germany is temporary, pending the unification of Germany.

This is more than an academic distinction. It has practical application in considering the development of the German society with which the United States has relations today. That society comprises only a segment of the German people whose new institutions and habits of community life will be subject to change if Germany is reunified, the nature of the change depending on the timing and means used to achieve unity. The division of Germany is a political reality which restricts studies of contemporary U.S.-German relations to the relationship between Bonn and Washington. It limits, also, the significance of such studies to the indefinite period until reunification. Theoretically, that could be only a matter of months; it is more likely to be a matter of years, or even decades.

However impermanent a feature of the European scene the Federal Republic may be, its contributions to the organization and life of the Continent are already a matter of record. The creation of a stable West German state so unlike previous German societies that it appears to have no connection with the good, and bad, traditions of the German past, was a great accomplishment not only for the Germans, but also for the Western governments who helped them to construct it. The latter, it is true, were not moved by generosity or altruism in rehabilitating the Germans and admitting them as equals in the community of nations. The Federal Republic was the product of the Cold War, of the need to strengthen and unify the West in the face of Communist aggres-

2. Article 146 of the Basic Law states: "This Basic Law shall cease to be in force on the day on which a Constitution adopted by a free decision of the German people comes into force."

sion. But its origin in political expediency has not checked its rapid strides toward stability and influence, nor lessened its impact on the life of the Continent. And West Germany's social organization and institutions of government will have a profound influence in the future as well. Even if a unified Germany is not constituted on the precise pattern of the Federal Republic, as many West Germans hope, the social and political institutions that have evolved since 1945 will certainly influence the society and government of a unified German state.

The creation in little more than a decade after the war of a free, democratic German republic—which in 1945 was unimaginable, and would have been so even if the world had then found itself in a tranquil era—was an amazing accomplishment. The pace of international life is so hectic in modern times that even great achievements of this sort are soon forgotten. Unless one keeps in mind how little time the infant republic has had for its development, one may perhaps lose sight of its accomplishments in the glare of its weaknesses and shortcomings. The defects of a political system attract the attention of foreign observers, and tend to obscure its less obvious strengths. This is especially true of West Germany today. Europeans and Americans have bitter memories of the crimes and acts of aggression committed by Germany under the aegis of a system which once had the support of her masses. They are, therefore, intensely sensitive to shortcomings of the West German society, which keep alive the fear that history will repeat itself. They raise doubts about the ability of the German people to uphold civil liberties and to eliminate from their national character the political irresponsibility which made the brutal Nazi system possible.

These fears and doubts explain why Americans and Europeans are so interested in the way Germans look at their recent past, as revealed by the results of polls and other investigations. It is a common view that if the West Germans repent their past behavior,

their democracy today is on a sound footing, but if they have
repressed or forgotten the recent past then democracy has not
taken hold and has little chance of eventual success. These common
generalizations are based on two false assumptions. The first is
that the ability to face the past with resolute honesty must go hand
in hand with the successful practice of democracy. In an individual, self-examination and self-criticism are commendable qualities, but a whole people rarely, if ever, exhibits them. Democracy
is a process involving the utilization of institutions for peaceful
self-government by a society of free peoples. Democracy may
benefit from accurate assessments of the past; it is not a function
of an historical viewpoint.

The second erroneous assumption is that a people can contemplate their past and form attitudes toward it which are un-
affected by subsequent events. Only if the Germans could see themselves, and their country, as they were in the Nazi era, untouched
by the events of the postwar period, could they make sound judgments of their past behavior. Only a judgment so formed could
indicate how far the democratic spirit has permeated contemporary
West German society. Sixteen years now separate the Germans
from the Nazi era, and every week and month of this period has
been crowded with difficult personal experiences and events of
national importance.

Even without this complex background, attitudes toward the
past would still not be reliable indicators of the health of the West
German society. It is, for example, not possible to draw from the
apparent failure of the Germans to feel "collective guilt" for the
Nazi atrocities meaningful conclusions about the future behavior
of the West German state, or even to foretell future relations
between Germans and Jews. A sense of guilt or shame is a matter
of individual psychology; it cannot be imposed by outside forces.

The Nürnberg trials and denazification procedures of the victor
powers were probably the best possible devices under the circumstances. Certainly they were more justifiable than killing the major

Nazi offenders on sight, and more practical than establishing new German courts to try them, the alternatives suggested at the time. But by taking matters into their own hands, the victors denied Germany "a chance to settle her own moral scores within her own boundaries."[3] And the purging qualities of the shattering defeat in 1945, the closest Germany had come to revolution, were quickly dissipated by the events that followed.

Attempts by the occupying powers to make the Germans feel and admit collective guilt were thwarted when the victors sought the friendship and allegiance of the vanquished. As the East-West struggle in Europe took shape, the Western powers were forced to coöperate with the Germans in restoring order and stability, and in efforts to repel Communist aggression, as in the Berlin airlift operation. The Germans, finding themselves the object of Western entreaties and beneficence, could hardly have been expected to intone a litany of *mea culpa*. And after the Federal Republic had been created, acclaimed, and invited to join as an equal with the free nations of the world, the Germans could not be expected to engage in mass self-recrimination.

The major events of the postwar period are elements in the complex background of West German society that have affected its attitudes toward the past, and these elements alone indicate that sweeping judgments of Germany today cannot be based upon an awareness of these attitudes. The personal fortunes and misfortunes of individual Germans throughout this hectic period have also played a role in forming their attitudes. Because they have personal experience with the problem and know how complex it is, most Germans—however tempted they may be to purge their country's name—have not made generalizations about Germany's past. They have left this practice to outsiders and have suffered the descriptions of themselves in imperious silence.

3. Margaret Mead, "Comment on 'Germany's New Flagellants,'" *American Scholar* (Spring, 1958), p. 179.

Many thoughtful Germans, including members of both major political parties in the Federal Republic, will admit in private conversations that nothing like a general reëxamination or evaluation of the Nazi period has taken place in West Germany. They do not underrate the attempts of the Occupation powers to reëducate and "democratize" the German people, nor the later efforts of the Bonn and *Länder* governments and of the publicly owned radio corporations, the newspapers, and the educational authorities to develop a clearer understanding of the history and significance of the Nazi period. But even those reëducation programs which had a modicum of success in publicizing the details of Nazi machinations and recalling the public response did not spark a general reëvaluation of the Nazi experience. Most Germans today condemn Hitler and his cohorts for starting the war and bringing the country to defeat and ruin.[4] The excesses of Nazism are damned, and few Germans today would exchange the benefits of their new life for the excitement aroused by the misguided idealism of the 1930's.[5] But to support the contention that Nazism has been "repudiated," or any similar generalization, there would have to be evidence that the Germans have faced the facts of their prewar history. Many Germans would be among the first to say that there is no such evidence. There has been no general effort to understand the brutal and degrading system which the country once supported, and few individuals have acknowledged their responsibility in bringing the Nazis to power, or in forwarding their mad ambitions. Fred Luchsinger of the *Neue Zürcher*

4. See the results of the polls taken by the Institut für Demoskopie, *Jahrbuch der Öffentlichen Meinung 1947-1955*, pp. 135-137, and *ibid. 1957*, p. 142.

5. *Ibid. 1957*, pp. 277-279. The polls cited in footnote above, and referred to elsewhere in this book, are useful indices of the state and direction of West German public opinion, but are not mathematically precise measurements of public thought. German inhibitions in expressing opinions, above all political opinions, publicly are reflected in the results of even the best polls.

Zeitung, who is probably the best informed foreign correspondent in Bonn, has written that "German public opinion in the widest sense has cowardly evaded facing not only the problem of anti-Semitism, but also that of the 12 years of Nazism, with the result that these issues still have not been settled."[6] This is not to say that most Germans are unrepentent Nazis, or that the present West German system is only an interlude before the reappearance of totalitarianism. It simply means that the West Germans have not come to grips with the nation's past.

There are good reasons why such an *Auseinandersetzung* has not taken place and why it may never occur. For one thing, the Nazis did not inculcate new characteristics in the German people. They rather took advantage of their patriotism, and perverted existing characteristics such as the idealism which in German philosophical thought is bound up with the "historical and moral worth of the nation."[7] The Germans naturally find it painful to recall how their idealism and good intentions were taken advantage of—how they were duped by Hitler and his associates. Their desire to repress or forget these memories is not necessarily unhealthy. Indeed, to want to put a distance of years between themselves and painful events that would heavily burden their consciences was not only natural, it has had salutary results. It has prevented the Germans from unleashing again, as after the Treaty of Versailles, a torrent of self-pity and rage such as Hitler later took advantage of for his own ends. A similar situation might have arisen after 1945. Theodor Heuss, the first President of the Federal Republic, recalling the condition of his country after the surrender, said "the people were exhausted and starving; the attitude of many towards the victorious powers was 'Do what you like with us.' At that time the reproach was heard . . . that the

6. *Neue Zürcher Zeitung,* December 27, 1959.
7. Wilhelm Hoffman, *Nach der Katastrophe* (Tübingen & Stuttgart, 1946), p. 63.

Germans were sorry for themselves. There was something in that."[8]

The life of the average German in the early postwar period, when food, clothing, and fuel were often unobtainable, was a day-to-day struggle for survival. He could not contemplate the past; the future seemed hopeless. Had the broad mass of the Germans at this time borne the self-imposed stigmata of guilt, an aggressive reaction might have swept the country some years later. As it was, the exigencies of the Cold War led the Western powers to institute a currency reform and to include West Germany in the European Recovery Program. The subsequent revival of their economy fostered a more optimistic spirit and a new self-respect among the German people. They still suffered from the shock of the total collapse, in 1945, of their military power, their institutions of government, and their economic life. But a brighter future now beckoned to them; they applied themselves to the tasks of reconstruction with new vigor, concentrating on material welfare to the virtual exclusion of other goals.

For many middle-aged, and older, Germans the years after 1948 offered the first real opportunity to enjoy the fruits of their labors. They gained wealth and spent it on themselves; they cultivated hobbies and took up games—such as golf, which now enjoys a new vogue. They did not want to recall the unhappy past, lest it embitter the joys of their newfound prosperity. Even those Germans who were not convinced that the Nazis were scoundrels, and that they themselves had been fools to tolerate them, could not escape the facts of Germany's defeat and destruction. Because a repetition of such madness was unthinkable, examination of its causes seemed unnecessary.

This attitude prevails, especially among West Germans ranging in age from the early forties to the late sixties. This is the genera-

8. Address given before a Joint Meeting of Congress, Washington, D.C., June 5, 1958. Text in the *New York Times,* June 6, 1958.

tion which produced the architects of the new West German state; it includes the Federal Republic's leaders in government, business, and the professions. They are intent on safeguarding their achievements. They do not want to be reminded of the Hitler regime or have their children learn about the role their elders played in it.

There are few survivors in German public life of the still older generation which came to maturity in the "good old days" of Kaiser Wilhelm II. But those few, Chancellor Konrad Adenauer above all, took a stern view of the Nazi upstarts in 1933, and were in opposition to the Third Reich. They were not deterred by defeat, or distracted by the succeeding economic "miracle," from the resolute condemnation of their country's past behavior, which they continue to voice to the present day.

Germans now between the ages of twenty-five and forty are too young to have had any part in bringing Hitler to power, although many of them served in the armed forces during World War II. Their education was dominated by Nazism; only a few of them had any experience of the Weimar Republic. By 1945, however, they were old enough to form mature judgments about the kind of life and the ideals to which they had been educated, and young enough to think anew and adopt new ideals. Some of them were too shocked by defeat or too disillusioned by their experiences to respond courageously. They withdrew (some would say escaped) into materialism, adopting an *"ohne mich"* attitude toward all political questions, past and contemporary. But some in their late twenties and early thirties have faced up to questions about the past—which their elders failed to ask—and have repudiated Nazism and all it stood for. These young people infused a new maturity and sense of purpose into university life after the war. They have consistently upheld the deeds of the anti-Nazi resistance, and are today prominent in civic education groups that are trying to inculcate a new sense of political responsibility in the West German people. Five or ten years from now many of these young men and women may be the leaders of the German community.

There is also, of course, a vocal minority that actively disclaims German responsibility for the outbreak of war and tries to minimize the atrocities committed by German authorities. In the hate-sheets of extremist organizations, whose total circulation is small, but also in some of the widely read, illustrated weeklies, this minority tends to counteract the contribution made by the respectable press toward an understanding of Nazism.[9] The extremists have launched shrill accusations against Allied wartime policies, especially those which emerged from the Quebec, Yalta, and Potsdam conferences, and venomous attacks on Franklin D. Roosevelt. Their propaganda of self-justification has cited the Suez invasion of 1956 as proof that the behavior of the Nazis was no worse than that of the democracies.[10]

Statements such as these have a strong impact on the country people who are more ignorant and gullible than their urban cousins in political matters.[11] It is important not to exaggerate the effects of this propaganda which, so far, do not seem to be widespread. One should not assume that every German who reads such travesties of the truth is an unregenerate, or a budding, Fascist

9. The most effective of these are reprints of documents, such as the Protocoll of the Reichstag debate over the Enabling Law (*Frankfurter Allgemeine Zeitung*, March 21, 1958) and Hitler's speech to representatives of the German press (*ibid.*, May 21, 1958). Professor Walther Hofer's pocket-book selection of Nazi documents (*Der Nationalsozialismus— Dokumente, 1933-1945*, Frankfurt, 1957) has had a wide circulation and is another constructive contribution to German discussions of the Nazi period.

10. An excellent example of this type of propaganda is the episode from Admiral Karl Dönitz's apologia published under the title "Ich lege Rechnung" in the German illustrated *Quick*, May 10, 1958. The publisher's introduction asserts that "Here, for the first time, Germany learns from an authorized source what really happened during the last days of the Third Reich, between Hitler's death on April 30 and the imprisonment of the last national government on May 23."

11. For example, see the breakdown of poll results in the *Jahrbuch der Öffentlichen Meinung 1957*, pp. 278-279.

any more than he would condemn all American and British readers of their national scandal sheets as adulterers or sadists.

The foregoing description of attitudes toward Germany's recent past displayed by various age groups is valid, not so much for the masses as for the small percentage of the West German people who comprise the informed leadership, the *Oberschicht*. These are the people—irrespective of party affiliation—who are in power today. It is likely that they will be succeeded in their governmental, business, and professional positions by those who also have had the advantage of prolonged formal education. Hence their views of the past and their conception of the future they are helping to shape are of the greatest interest.[12]

In short, some Germans have faced the Nazi past and repudiated it; others have attempted to justify it. But most West Germans have repressed their memories of the Hitler regime and are likely to continue doing so, at least until their future is more secure. They do not want forgiveness, rather help in forgetting. In a possible future awakening to historical facts, in less troubled times when the Germans have put more distance between themselves and the ugly past, there may be a reappraisal which will, moreover, be more dispassionate than any that could have been made in the years since 1945. The resulting self-judgment may assign blame with greater honesty than after World War I. If such a reappraisal does take place, the Germans may strike a balance between condemnation of the excesses of Nazism and approval of some of its political accomplishments.[13]

12. A recent book by Karl W. Deutsch and Lewis J. Edinger (*Germany Rejoins the Powers*, Stanford, 1959) includes a pioneering study of elites in West Germany and their role in Bonn's foreign policy. See especially Chap. 9 and Appendix III.

13. In July 1956, 1066 West German males between the ages of 17 and 27 were asked "What do you think: was national socialism a good or bad idea?" 33 per cent answered that it was partly good and partly bad ("*Teils, teils*"); 22 per cent said it was a bad idea; 16 per cent said it was a good idea, and 29 per cent did not give an opinion. *Jahrbuch der Öffentlichen Meinung 1957*, p. 149.

◆

The Federal Republic's young people have been the subject of much study both at home and abroad. The present generation of school children, university students, and professional apprentices has been excluded from the foregoing discussion (1) because their attitudes toward the past—assuming that they can be identified—are not based upon personal experiences of Nazism or even, in most cases, of the war, and (2) because they constitute the only generation that has been brought up in the new postwar society. Young people up to the age of twenty-five can have no responsibility for the past; they are a product of the new Germany. Their style of life, their attitudes, and their interests reflect both the failures and the accomplishments of the Federal Republic. For this reason their political knowledge and their outlook are of genuine interest in gauging the future development of German society.

An unusual psychological distance separates these young West Germans from those twenty-five to forty years of age. Members of both generations are aware of this gap and comment upon it. It seems to have been caused chiefly by the older generation's keen recollection of the 1945 catastrophe, an experience which most of the youth do not share. In 1945 the young soldiers were profoundly shocked by the defeat and collapse of the nation; some of them were deeply affected by the revelations of the full scope of the horrors perpetrated on subject peoples by the Nazis. They suffered the national catastrophe as deeply as their personal misfortunes. They reacted—especially those who were intellectually inclined and thoughtful—with a resolute determination to recast German society in a new mold. They were more prepared to experiment with new social and political institutions than Germans had ever dared to be; they welcomed the introduction of novel educational techniques by the Western occupying powers (which was resented by older and more tradition-bound Germans). They wanted to take an active part in German and European politics in order to help bring about decent human relations, more equal social opportunities, and higher standards of living.

In contrast, even the oldest among today's youngest generation were old enough only to be bewildered by the destruction of all around them in 1945. Although they suffered directly from the hardships of life in the immediate postwar period, they were too young to have meaningful recollections of the social and political system that preceded the Occupation, and were too immature to think constructively about the kind of society that was to grow out of the rubble. For the children of that time, the adolescents and young grown-ups of today, the Occupation was chiefly a negative experience and is still associated with the suffering of cruel winters without sufficient food, heat, or shelter. Many of these young people still carry a burden of insecurity from their pre-adolescent years when they were forced to toil for their food, and this manifests itself in a craving for material plenty which today directs their attention to achieving secure jobs and high incomes. At no time has today's West German youth sought the kind of social revolution for which its older brothers and sisters longed in the years immediately after the war, but which they could not bring about. The sober young men and women in the German universities today are indeed Western-oriented in that they recognize Germany's cultural ties with the West. But they give no evidence of the fervent desire for common citizenship and for a European homeland, which moved some of the previous generation of West German university students to the symbolic act of breaking down frontier barriers. At home, in their schools and churches, the young people put emphasis on order and stability—not the jackbooted precision and blind obedience exacted by the Nazis, but rather a regularity and a quietude which are more dull than dangerous. This reaction to the terrible disorder and instability after the war has been strengthened by the fear of renewed war and subsequent social chaos.

◆

In some *Länder,* courses in civics instructing students in the history and development of democratic institutions in Germany are somewhat successful in arousing their interest in politics and their sense of civic responsibility. But the Federal Republic's educational system as a whole cultivates the quietist tradition which is symptomatic of the entire society. To some extent, the schools suffer from defects which are found also in other Western countries. The Federal Republic's school facilities are inadequate. The failure to train teachers during World War II produced a postwar shortage which forced the *Länder* authorities to reinstate those teachers who had been expelled in the initial denazification procedures. The high average age of the school teachers in 1957 (as many as half were over fifty) is undoubtedly one reason for the slow development of modern teaching techniques. It may also explain the resistance in the *Länder* to giving instruction in recent history and current political developments. The inadequacies of the teaching staffs may also explain why the classroom atmosphere is in most schools intellectually stifling, and why there appears to be no spirit of coöperation between teacher and taught. One observer has remarked that "the German school is a place to work hard in for as long as may be necessary; it is not a place to live in or even play in."[14]

The children's knowledge of recent history is restricted to what their parents and teachers have been willing to divulge about the fate of the Weimar Republic and the experience of the Nazi years. Despite all the discussions of how this subject should be approached with the young, and the good intentions of most educational authorities, and the liberal tone of the resolutions of the legislatures of some of the *Länder,* what the youth knows about the Hitler regime is pitifully inadequate.[15] Teaching the history of

14. George C. Allen, "Germans at School," *The Listener,* August 15, 1957, pp. 235-236.

15. For example, see the results of a poll of 12-year-olds in a small south German town: "Zwölfjährige geben Auskunft über Hitler," *Der Bürger im Staat* (May 1959), p. 63.

the Nazi period is, of course, a difficult task. The teacher who tells her seventh grade pupils that they are too young to judge the merits of the July 1944 plot on Hitler's life, when one of her charges asserts that his father said the members of the resistance were all "traitors," is undoubtedly doing a better job than the teacher who insists that all Storm Troopers were "gangsters," and who punishes the boy who complains that his father was not a gangster. Nevertheless, many West German children are leaving school today with a thorough knowledge of the *Niebelungenlied* but with little or no acquaintance with the events of 1926-1945. Now that the problems of teaching recent history are actually being discussed, perhaps a more satisfactory job will be done in the future, especially as young teachers take up their work in the classrooms.

There is, also, much discussion in the Federal Republic of the need to combine the best of Germany's intellectual tradition with a better understanding of the right relationship between teachers and pupils. Educational exchange programs with other Western European countries may make a significant contribution toward adoption of a more flexible curriculum and modern teaching techniques in West Germany. Looking ahead, there are grounds for hope that over the next ten to fifteen years some of the basic difficulties in German education will be recognized and solved. Up to now, however, the school and university systems have been, and are still, in many respects deficient. The craving for security and stability, which is characteristic of the entire society, is reflected in the kind of education they provide.

University curricula remain, on the whole, rigidly circumscribed, retaining their old emphasis on legal and philosophical studies. The study of recent history and politics is relegated to several excellent, but largely ignored, *Hochschulen*. A handful of imaginative professors have striven with only partial success to introduce political science and the other social sciences into the university curriculum against stiff opposition from the other faculties who give no sign of yielding.

For the privileged few who are able to gain a place at a university[16] the available *Stipendia* (scholarships) although recently increased are still barely adequate to provide for living expenses. The need for better university facilities and for more adequate scholarship funds is especially urgent in view of the continued flow of refugees from the East—half of them under twenty-five years of age—who want to continue their education in the Federal Republic.[17]

In the social life of the universities there has been an unfortunate resurgence of the *Korporationen* (fraternities), and these are now striving to recover their former position as privileged centers of student activity. It is true that they include only thirty per cent of the students, and that some of them have dropped the most reprehensible of their customs. But in many dueling has been reintroduced, particularly in those controlled by the alumni, *die Alte Herren*. It is doubtful whether the latter, mostly civil servants and businessmen, are worth the attention of the university student in Germany today. But the fact that a dueling scar has again become a mark of distinction indicates that the ideals of those who once led Germany to power and then to ruin have taken hold again in some youthful circles.[18] Many students, and most educational authorities, are hostile to the fraternities, but efforts to break their power have been blocked by court action and by pressure

16. No more than half the approximately 4 per cent of young West Germans who pass the *Abitur* continue their education at a German university.

17. See the chart entitled "*Die Fluchtbewegung aus der Sowjetzone u. Ost-Berlin*," published by the Federal Minister for Expellees, Refugees and War Victims (Bonn, 1958).

18. See Arthur J. Olson, "The Dueling Scar Reappears in Germany," *New York Times Magazine*, August 18, 1957.

from *die Alte Herren,* some of whom are among the leading citizens of the Federal Republic.[19]

The revival and support of the reactionary *Korporationen* by responsible adults who have ostensibly turned their backs on the useless traditions and on the romanticism which these fraternities typify is only one of many examples of the bewildering contradictions which confront the youth of the Federal Republic. The ambiguities of adult behavior are a problem for youth everywhere, but when these concern basic social and political convictions, as they do in the Federal Republic, they pose major problems for a younger generation that is trying to shape its own political attitudes. This is especially true at a time when, in a country whose democratic institutions are not deeply rooted in experience, democratic convictions are encountering their greatest challenge.

The problems that bewilder West Germany's youth are often no less confusing for their elders. The Federal Republic is a young country. Still in the early stages of its development, it is exposed to swift and sweeping changes. To this situation no German, regardless of age or experience, is adjusted. Major social and political problems, most of them inextricably bound up with foreign political events, continue to plague the young Republic. No amount of simplification, to which Germans as well as some foreign observers are prone, can solve these problems or wish them away. To understand the forces that are shaping the political convictions of the Federal Republic's youth one must try to appreciate the problems which face the entire society. A study of the challenges which face the Germans in creating a happier and more secure life for themselves may throw some light on the kind

19. *New York Times,* July 15, 1957. According to the *Verband Deutscher Studentenschaften,* there are 23 *Korporationen* today to which 38,260 West German students belong. The dueling fraternities have a membership of 14,250, or 11 per cent of the whole student body. There are 132,220 *Alte Herren* who are active members of the fraternities. See the report in the *Süddeutsche Zeitung,* August 22, 1957.

42916

of German society the United States will be dealing with in the future.

The ideological struggle of the world today, and the polarization of military power, have strongly affected the internal affairs of the Federal Republic as well as its international relations. The progressive development of mass communications, rapid transport, and the introduction of weapons of overwhelming destructive capacities, have brought it about that events in the far-flung corners of the globe—a revolution in China, a speech in Moscow, a battle at Suez, or a riot in Little Rock—are certain to have an impact on both the Federal Republic's posture toward the outside world and on its internal social structure, its institutions of government, and its economic organization.

The Germans seem to realize that they are no longer masters of their fate and that neither they nor any other European people can base a constructive philosophy or style of life simply on national traditions or racial characteristics. They understand, also, that the recent transformation of national societies resulted not only from man's desire to live in closer contact with his fellow men, but also from irreversible changes in his struggle for control over his environment. They know that both voluntary and involuntary changes have caused national societies to become less independent, but they are not reconciled to the new situation.

Germany's dependency upon the outside world has been emphasized time and again by many of Bonn's leading political figures. They have urged their people to seize the opportunities offered by the new internationalism with courage and with a sense of responsibility. The response of leading individuals in West Germany's academic world, especially in the scientific community, has also been farsighted. The Federal Republic's assumption of rights and obligations as a partner in the Western community of nations would seem to indicate that the country as a whole has approved and followed the advice of its leaders. But this conclusion is not altogether justified. In fact, until now, the voices of those who are trying to instill an understanding of the country's new position in international life have been crying in the wilderness. They are more admired than understood. The West Germans appear only to feel that they can no longer avoid being intimately affected by decisions and actions taken elsewhere in the world; they do not as yet understand why this change has taken place, nor do they appreciate its implications. The Germans are not alone in this failing. It is, indeed, a curious fact that nations, such as the United States and Canada, which previously lived in a kind of isolation, now have a keener understanding of what it means to live in the modern world than some of the European countries which, for centuries, have lived side by side with neighbors who could not be ignored.

Provincialism characterizes the Federal Republic's outlook on the rest of the world. Take for example the news coverage of the press, even the major newspapers, or the various radio stations. Prominent and thorough coverage is given to foreign events only when these have an obvious and direct impact on the Federal Republic's immediate interests; otherwise neither the news media nor the general public as a whole concern themselves seriously with what is happening in the rest of the world. By comparison, even secondary newspapers and radio stations in the United States, which have yet to be accused of overemphasis on world affairs, appear to be enlightened.

Another example of provincialism can be found in attitudes toward the so-called backward areas of the world. Commercial circles, and members of the educated and leading *Oberschicht,* display an increasing awareness of the importance of these areas to the future of Europe. But despite the great increase in West German trade with Africa, Asia, the Middle East, and Latin America, the German people still tend to think of these areas as a hinterland of Europe. They make the blithe assumption that central Europe retains its former predominant importance. In that area, they believe, the battle between Communism and democracy will be fought to a decisive end. This outdated attitude toward the underdeveloped countries is shared by other Europeans who are unable to reconcile themselves to the decline of their colonial empires. In the Federal Republic it is the result chiefly of "the lack of a clearer world political awareness in the public mind."[20]

The failure of the West Germans to comprehend fully their place in the modern world has intensified the insecurity which they suffer because of their exposed position on the front line of the East-West struggle. It is reflected in the abject pessimism, almost fatalism, with which many of them regard their future. They live only for the present, preoccupied with the pursuit of creature comforts, paying less and less attention to the needs of their children and even, in some cases, feeling guilty for having brought them into the world. The intense insecurity that underlies this unhappy state of mind cannot be attributed entirely to the slow progress of the West Germans toward political maturity during the postwar years. The trouble goes farther back. But the present emphasis on material welfare, and the rush to the churches for spiritual solace, paradoxical features of German postwar behavior, and the arid state of the arts in the Federal Republic,[21] are all symptoms of the despair and lack of self-confidence which result from failure to understand the challenges—and opportunities—facing Germany today.

The slowness of Germany's spiritual reawakening and of the recovery of her creative drives, in contrast with the "miraculous" economic reconstruction, has limited the scope of foreign policy

20. Theodor Steltzer, lecture at the Bremen Club on March 13, 1958, entitled "East-West Relations in the Current World Political Situation." In this lecture, Steltzer, who is acting president of the German Council on Foreign Relations, gives a critical and often brilliant picture of German thinking today in the field of international politics.

21. Architecture is an exception. It has flourished in the midst of the reconstruction building boom.

activity. So far, the Germans are still reacting to outside influences more than they are utilizing their power to serve their own interests. The extent to which Bonn will be able to seize the initiative in foreign policy in the future will depend, in part, upon the maturity of the West German people, but also on their awareness of the limits of constructive national action.

Few Germans, and fewer outsiders, can conceive of West Germany without Konrad Adenauer, its first Chancellor and chairman of the CDU government party. Adenauer is recognized as the founding father of the Federal Republic, the commanding figure in West Germany, and the outstanding statesman of postwar Europe. Since the death of Kurt Schumacher, the leader of the Social Democrats (Germany's oldest political party, which had probably suffered more at the hands of the Nazis than any other), Adenauer has dominated the political scene without being seriously challenged.

Schumacher's death in 1952 left a gap in the SPD which has not been filled and which even Willy Brandt, the new leader of the party, may not be able to fill. The lack of a serious challenge from the major opposition party, and the absence of men of equal stature and political ability in his own party, have confirmed Adenauer in the autocratic ways which have made him the most hated, as well as the most admired, individual in West Germany. America's enthusiasm for Adenauer's efficient leadership of his country under a constitutional government, in partnership with the West, has added to his prestige and emboldened him. But it has discouraged those Germans who have been unobtrusively engaged in building up democratic practices and traditions among the general public. Adenauer's successor will probably not be able to inspire Americans with the same confidence. Hence many of them may be disillusioned about the Federal Republic when power is no longer being wielded by a familiar and reliable figure in Bonn. Some Americans may even display an "exaggeratedly hostile reaction which would be no more justified and no less dangerous than unconditional approval."[22]

The implications for U.S.-German relations of a change of government in Bonn cannot be ignored.[23] It is not impossible that the great and perhaps exaggerated identification of the U.S.-German alliance with Adenauer's leadership may exact in the future a costly loss of American confidence. The United States cannot escape responsibility for helping to make it appear that Adenauer is virtually indispensable to the Federal Republic. Yet the tendency in West Germany, found chiefly among supporters of opposition parties and those who have no party allegiance, to blame the United States for the growth of a leadership cult around the figure of Konrad Adenauer is both unfortunate and unjustified. It is unfortunate because blaming the Americans and other foreigners, convenient whipping-boys, for seeming to make democracy in the Federal Republic dependent on one man prevents the Germans from identifying the real weakness in their political system. They remain unaware of the real problem of leadership which confronts them. The criticism is unjustified because the cult of Adenauer is, first of all, a German problem that can be solved only within the country.

The tendency to build up a strong chief executive, to follow the leader, has a long history in Germany. Other peoples, also, have been known to set a father figure on a pedestal in the hope that his magic charm will sweep away all their ills. But the practice is clearly more hazardous in a country which is not far removed from the time when it idolized a ruler to the extent of granting him absolute powers. This is not, however, a reason for demanding that the Germans, going to the opposite extreme, should choose a calm, undramatic, chairman-of-the-board leader, the kind that the British have been known to elevate to the position of prime minister. In

22. Richard Hiscocks, *Democracy in Western Germany* (London, 1957), p. 7. Gatzke, "The United States and Germany," p. 10.
23. See below, pp. 42-43, 68-70.

1953 and again in 1957 this alternative to the reëlection of Adenauer was clearly rejected by a majority of the West German people.
The Germans prefer dynamic leaders who exude wisdom and inspire confidence, who have a flair for the dramatic while embodying
the finest parental virtues. They share these preferences with the
peoples of other democracies; in Dr. Adenauer the Germans have
undoubtedly made a better choice than some.

Like other strong executives, Adenauer has made the most of
the powers vested in his office, and the strong support of public
opinion has enabled him to wield with enormous authority his
power as Chancellor and party chairman. However, the Republic's Basic Law (*Grundgesetz*) did not intend that the Chancellor
should exert his power capriciously, but only in conformity with
the guide-lines it had established. Moreover, although Adenauer
is respected for his achievements in restoring the country's sovereignty and reconstructing its economic life, and is honored for
his outstanding personal qualities, there are limits to the obeisance
paid him. He is held in respect, not affection; admired, not loved.
Most West Germans revere him because of his age, not because
they think he is incapable of mistakes or because they always agree
with him. Indeed, some of the greatest admirers among his closest
associates think that democracy in the Federal Republic will be
strengthened when the Chancellor is replaced by a less domineering
personality.

But there are some members of Adenauer's own party, as well
as members of the opposition and independents, who chafe under
the Chancellor's tight-fisted control of the government. They do
not realize that only because Adenauer's rule has been strong and
effective, because he could be relied on to safeguard the nation's
security and welfare, are they able to afford the luxury of criticism
and grumbling. Without the "Old Fox" at the helm it is doubtful,
for example, that members of the Bundestag would have dared to
rock the ship of state with radical ideas—such as the SPD's proposed plebiscite on the stationing of atomic weapons in West

Germany—aiming more often to gain party political advantage than to solve the country's problems. Some West Germans lament that a new German state was not allowed to develop more slowly, to experiment with new forms of social organization, and to base its government on a gradual evolution of political thought. They too often blame Adenauer—and Bonn's Western allies— for the restoration of old patterns of authority and for the continued partition of the country. They fail to identify the major cause of Germany's frustrations: Soviet Russia's threats of aggression and her intransigence at the conference table. The real alternative to the independent and wealthy Republic which Adenauer helped to fashion out of mutilated Germany after the war was something which all Germans would have found less desirable. For had there not been a falling out of the major wartime allies all of Germany might today still be under military occupation. Under such conditions little or no progress could have been made toward the creation of a free society.

Some Germans, especially intellectuals who support the CDU, believe that Adenauer's greatest contribution has been to demonstrate that an orderly and efficient conduct of democratic government is possible. Many conservative businessmen in the Federal Republic attribute this success entirely to Adenauer and are, therefore, still skeptical of the efficiency of the democratic process. But there can be no doubt that the discipline of the government coalition and the effective functioning of the government bureaucracy during the last ten years have been a valuable experience and have established high standards for any future German government— and that Konrad Adenauer deserves a great deal of credit for this success.

But there is another aspect of the cult of Adenauer. The successful operation of free institutions under the leadership of one exceptionally strong, dedicated man has exacted a price in the failure of the citizens in general to gain political experience through participation in the democratic process. For all too many Germans, democracy means merely voting at the general and *Länder* elections, leaving the rest to the Bundestag and, far more, to the executive branch of the government. The Germans have been told, and they believe, that to cast the ballot is a duty, an obligation. But they seem hardly conscious of other obligations and responsibilities that should be fulfilled by citizens of a democratic state. Public indifference to political parties and institutions and to government policy has a long history in Germany. Twelve years of Nazi rule deprived the people of experience in operating their own government and left them indifferent to the ideals of democracy. This handicap they might have overcome after the catastrophe had they not devoted themselves primarily to raising their standard of living and had the government, under Adenauer's leadership, not persisted in cultivating the belief in the wisdom of government as long as it is successful.

Modern Germany has no tradition of neighborliness and community action such as has been handed down to Americans from pioneer and frontier days. The general failure of the parent-teacher associations, which American occupation authorities introduced into West Germany, was owing to the lack of community spirit. Where such associations are still active in the Federal Republic today they are usually supported and encouraged by resident Americans. But most of them dissolved because German parents—and teachers—believe that what happens in the schools is the responsibility and concern of the school authorities alone. This pattern of behavior is similar in other areas of the German society.

German apathy toward politics, the propensity to leave the responsibility for political decisions to elected leaders and appointed officials, has been encouraged—certainly not discouraged—by Adenauer's government and especially by his own example. His domineering behavior and apparent intolerance of the views of others in his own party, in his cabinet, and in the government generally—what one author has called Adenauer's "well known authoritarian habits"[24]—have helped to persuade most citizens to leave the business of government to the bureaucracy. Most officials, in turn, leave the issues, especially of foreign policy and defense, to Chancellor Adenauer and prefer to be left in peace to cultivate their own garden, "growing red tape."[25] Many stories about Adenauer's autocratic behavior are apocryphal; but whether or not they are correct in every detail, they characterize his relations with those associated with him in government. Typical of such stories is one concerning a CDU member of the Bundestag who, when asked if he ever disagreed with the Chancellor, replied: "When he is not present, sometimes; when he is there, never!"[26]

Despite their grumbling, most Bonn officials admire Adenauer. They know that they add to their own prestige by telling stories about him, even if they seem to reflect badly on themselves. On the highest level, however, men who consider themselves possible successors to the Chancellor talk about his highhanded dealings and occasional personal cruelties with a deep resentment. The listener is apt to conclude that Adenauer chose as cabinet members men who consider their association with him indispensable to their future careers, excluding others who, enjoying independent means of support, have the courage to protest, even to resign, if they do not agree with him.

Whoever succeeds Adenauer will not have the same authority as his predecessor. His government may, therefore, not be as effective, and the Federal Republic consequently may prove a less

24. John H. Herz, "Political Views of the West German Civil Service," in H. Speier and W. P. Davison (eds.), *West German Leadership and Foreign Policy* (Evanston, 1957), p. 111. Hiscocks says that Adenauer is "authoritarian in character, though not authoritarian in conviction, and is too concerned to achieve his political objectives to care greatly about the means employed to do so." (*Democracy in Western Germany*, p. 7.)

25. Herz, "Political Views of the West German Civil Service," p. 134.

26. *Ibid.*, pp. 111 ff.

dependable ally. But there can be no doubt that a change of chancellors in Bonn could hasten the establishment of democratic practices in West Germany, provided that Adenauer's successors conduct the business of government more openly than he has done, giving adequate information and according proper respect to the Bundestag committees—especially in foreign and defense affairs.

Major efforts at political education on various levels are being made in the Federal Republic today. Countless bus loads of children and tourists pour through the endless corridors of the Bundestag. Excellent instruction is provided by the Evangelical academies, by similar Roman Catholic institutions, by various political institutes and university *Hochschulen,* and at community centers such as Haus Rissen near Hamburg. The Bonn government supports these efforts and works "to strengthen and disseminate the democratic and European idea in the German people" through the liberally financed *Bundeszentrale für Heimatdienst* (Federal Office for Homeland Service) which publishes and distributes a variety of propaganda material.[27] In addition, each *Land* has its own programs for political education. There are also international projects, such as the Wilton Park courses, which have been given in an English country house since the war, and the annual Anglo-German Conference at Königswinter.[28] These educational efforts, combined with memories of the bitter defeat and national disgrace suffered under Nazism, have led to a general acceptance of free institutions and to a slow but continuous growth of sentiment in favor of democracy. The progress that has been made in promoting democratic ideals inspired Ambassador Conant's judgment that

27. Hans Wallenberg's pamphlet, *Report on Democratic Institutions in Germany,* New York, 1956, lists the *Bundeszentrale für Heimatdienst* under the heading of "Forces Against Subversion" (pp. 19-26), suggesting that it is primarily engaged in combatting the D.D.R.'s espionage and propaganda activity.

28. Hiscocks discusses the various forms of political education in the Federal Republic; *Democracy in Western Germany,* pp. 244 ff.

"the spirit of free Germany, today, is the spirit of a people who have turned their back on the Nazi past."[29]

But the rejection of Fascism does not guarantee the success of democracy. Democracy in the Federal Republic will succeed only if its citizens individually are prepared to shoulder the burden of political responsibility and to participate in the routine of caucuses and elections. The chief influence on their political attitudes is not the teaching of schools and organizations, but the activity of politicians. So far, their example has not encouraged the citizen either to show greater concern for political decisions, or to display the *Zivilcourage* necessary to insure the defense of individual liberties. There have been instances of community action instigated by a handful of courageous citizens in defense of the entire society's freedom. The most famous of these, the "Schlüter case," occurred in Lower Saxony, where the Rector, Senate, and students of Göttingen University protested effectively against the appointment as Minister of Culture of an unqualified individual with a Nazi past. But the number of West Germans who are vigilant and prepared to act to preserve their liberties is all too small.[30]

The general public, apathetic in political matters, tends to look to organizations for salvation. This dependence upon leaders, and on the machinery of government, to maintain free institutions and

29. Conant added: "This is not only my considered judgment but that of many American observers, both official and unofficial, who have lived in Germany during the past five years." (*Germany and Freedom*, p. 10.)

30. In June 1956, 2000 West Germans above the age of 18 were asked: "Suppose that a new National Socialist party made an attempt to gain power, how would you react?" 3 per cent replied that they would welcome such a party and would support its efforts. Another 9 per cent said they would welcome a National Socialist party but would not help it. 21 per cent replied that they would not care one way or another, and 15 per cent gave no response. 27 per cent disapproved of a new National Socialist party but would not oppose it. Only 25 per cent said they would do whatever they could to prevent such a party from coming to power. See the *Jahrbuch der Öffentlichen Meinung 1957*, pp. 277, 279.

civil liberties gives rise to the danger that the Germans will attribute all their political failures and shortcomings to "the parties" and "the system." They conceive of democracy as an ideal and as a state of being rather than a process. The majority rule and the practice of tolerance towards minorities, both vital to democratic procedures, have been accepted in the Federal Republic. But the art of compromise, which is also essential in the democratic process, has not been sufficiently practiced. Compromise runs counter to the mainstream of German political thought, for the Germans are idealists; they do not like halfway houses. Democracy is an imperfect system; as fallible as the humans who practice it. It requires compromise and the reconciliation of groups representing conflicting interests and selfish aims. German disdain for this essential feature of the democratic process is exemplified by the following quotation from a West German commercial journal, which, at the same time, professes a devotion to democratic principles:

While it is a blessing of democratic government that political and economic projects have to stand the trial of public discussion before they can be realized, the deplorable reverse side of this system is that great ideas lose their impetus when they are the subject of bargaining by groups of interests, which only apply the yardstick of their own benefit and their own risk.[31]

It will take time and experience before the West Germans—and especially the intellectuals among them—realize that "selfish" interests competing for power and benefit are characteristic of a free society. Only when this is understood will compromise become an acceptable practice. Meanwhile, in West Germany, feuds among political opponents and pressure groups will continue to be more embittered than in the Anglo-American countries. They represent a regrettable tradition in German political life which Chancellor Adenauer, not alone among Bonn's political warriors, enjoys. Political feuds, however, produce deep rifts between the parties and

31. From "Pressure Groups Are Wearing Down an Idea," *Wirtschafts-dienst,* No. 7 (July 1957), p. 9.

intense intraparty discipline which appears not only in the voting behavior of the Bundestag deputies but also in *fraktion* (party caucus) meetings. Political infighting takes place behind the scenes, rarely in the open. In the CDU, major policy decisions are made by Adenauer and a handful of trusted advisors; in the SPD, at least until the party conference of May 1958, political and policy decisions were taken by hard-shell members of the party hierarchy, the functionaries. Such procedures give rise to much talk of skulduggery and political stabs in the back, most of which is probably accurate.

Individuals who dare to oppose the CDU leadership in public—few Bundestag deputies ever do—risk expulsion from the party, and ostracism. For example, Gustav Heinemann wanted to remain in the party although he felt conscience-bound to oppose the government on the rearmament issue, but he had to resign. Most SPD members, also, keep from criticizing their party leader in public; they refrain, however, not out of fear of personal consequences but in order to give the party an appearance of solidarity. On the other hand, the most important of the smaller parties, the FDP and the former BHE, have been torn with strife on occasion, which has resulted in divisions, embitterment, and resignations. They, also, have suffered from lack of experience with the art of compromise and from continued striving for absolute solutions.

Bonn is not Weimar; that is obvious.[32] Weimar was conceived in defeat and national humiliation. It was subject to the pressures and dictates of military officers and nationalists who were anti-republican to the core. Bonn was the outcome of the postwar dissension among Germany's conquerors; its military component has been successfully subordinated to civilian control. Neither monarchical nor Communist nor Fascist extremists have been able to

---

32. *Bonn ist nicht Weimar* is the title of a book by a Swiss, Fritz René Allemann (Cologne-Berlin, 1956), the most widely quoted foreign correspondent in West Germany. Although this book is probably the best study of postwar Germany, it has not been translated into English.

play a significant role in the administration or in framing its policy. Bonn's weaknesses and successes are its own; no comparisons or analogies with Weimar can detract from Bonn's successes. The strength of the Federal Republic lies not only in its booming economy, although this has provided an ideal background for the establishment of democratic procedures. A sound foundation for democracy has been provided perhaps first of all by the shining example of its aging first President, Theodor Heuss, a great liberal and intellectual who has set a high standard for the successors to his office. The prestige and immense authority of an antimilitarist and antitotalitarian Chancellor has shown all Germans that an efficient government can operate under democratic institutions. Adenauer, moreover, almost singlehandedly restored the moral worth of Germany in the society of free nations.

The integration of expellees and refugees from the Eastern territories into West German society has been a great achievement; if the Federal Republic contained a seething mob of malcontents demanding revenge and the reconquest of their homelands, its institutions of government would be endangered from within, and its foreign policy would be subjected to pressures much more violent than can be exercised by the few fanatic refugee groups in West Germany today.[33] In recent years, moreover, two fundamentally democratic parties, the SPD and CDU, have established their predominance in the Bundesrepublic and in most *Länder*. A steadily growing percentage of the West German people have been willing to give their allegiance to either one or the other; the minor parties, all but the FDP and the DP, have been excluded from the Bundestag. The leading trade union organization, the *Deutsche Gewerk-*

33. For the demands of certain extremist refugee groups, see the *New York Times*, April 11, 1957. The Südetendeutsche, among others, combine a moderate demand for the right to return to their homeland and for self-determination with talk of a new Greater Germany, including all the Eastern territories annexed or conquered by Hitler as of September 1939. This they say is necessary to relieve "overpopulation" in the Federal Republic; *Informationsfunk der Bundesregierung*, Bonn, May 27, 1958.

schaftsbund (DGB), has also become one of the fundamental
pillars of the new democratic society. It has resisted encroachment
by Communist influences, and has repulsed efforts to misuse it
for political purposes, such as the suggested general strike against
atomic armaments.[34] Because of its contributions to the education
of the German people in democratic practices, the DGB has been
called the most important democratic potential in German society.[35]
The democratic institutions and practices in the Federal Republic
are not steeled against a political or an economic crisis—the Republic has experienced neither since its founding—and there has
been as yet no change in the party in power, the acid test of a
democracy. It takes more time than the Germans have had since
1945 to build sound democratic traditions. They must overcome
important shortcomings in their political practices before the
Federal Republic can be described as a mature democracy.

West Germany's youth today reflects the uncertainty that plagues
the whole society. Born to insecurity, the nation's young people
are uncertain about the development of their own country and its
institutions. They fear the impact of the dangers of life in central
Europe. There are, of course, differences among them, but they
have most often been described as a skeptical generation.[36] Their
skepticism does not take the form of doubt, but rather of distrust.
They do not so much question the norms of the present as they fear
their lot in the future.[37] They seek good jobs and material welfare.
Even those few who take political jobs do so because politics offers
a career, not because of enthusiasm or idealism. Having no ideals

34. *Neue Zürcher Zeitung*, March 25, 1958.

35. Otto Kirchheimer, "West German Trade-Unions: Their Domestic
and Foreign Policies," in Speier and Davison, *West German Leadership and
Foreign Policy*, p. 191.

36. *Die skeptische Generation* is the title of a sociological study of
German youth by Helmut Schelsky (Düsseldorf-Cologne, 1957).

37. Ulrich Sonnemann, "Die alles nur nicht skeptische Generation,"
Frankfurter Hefte, XIII (May 1958), 337.

for which they would make sacrifices they are not likely to be taken in by any form of demagoguery. Even the conventional flamboyance of political speakers is badly received by audiences of young people in West Germany. They, therefore, are "more threatened today by the inroads of a pervasive cynical materialism than they are by any extremist nationalist tendencies."[38] But they are not so much content with the materialism rampant in the Federal Republic as puzzled to find alternatives to which they can devote themselves. The past, insofar as they know about it, offers no inspiration. Sullen rebellion against their elders because of their silence about Nazi atrocities inspired many who participated in pilgrimages to the burial place of Anne Frank. Thus, ironically, they attempted to atone for something for which they have no responsibility.[39] The rebelliousness of West Germany's youth has been mitigated by the close family ties enforced during the early postwar time. Where rebellion exists, it lacks even those minuscule sparks of originality found in Britain's "Angry Young Men" and America's "Beat Generation." For example, the motives of most of the German youths involved in the rash of anti-Semitic incidents that started on Christmas Eve 1959 in Cologne and spread throughout the Federal Republic, the rest of Europe, and to other continents, were only vaguely political; "the majority seem to have acted out of a need to shock."[40] Pilgrimages to concentration camp mass graves cannot be equated with the daubing of anti-Semitic slogans on synagogue walls, but the fundamental motivation of these demonstrations seems to have been substantially the same. Neither was primarily political or principally the result of feelings one way or the other about Jews. Both were essentially acts of rebellion designed to

38. George F. Kennan, *Russia, the Atom and the West* (New York, 1958), p. 48.

39. See Norbert Muhlen's article, "The Return of Anne Frank," *New Leader,* August 5, 1957, pp. 12-14.

40. Ernest Jouly, "German Youth and German History," *Commentary,* April 1960, p. 313.

shock, and the youth chose to convey their feelings through symbols and issues out of the past.

The sullen and suspicious demeanor of West Germany's youth is especially evident in its political attitudes. Many of them will say that "politics should be left to those who understand something about it." This reflects perplexity and frustration more than personal irresponsibility, for beneath the exterior of unconcern "there is a strong interest in world affairs, especially in those that have some bearing on their own prospects."[41] Despite this interest, the youth are no more willing than were their elders to commit themselves to full participation in the political life of their country. An overwhelming majority of Bonn's young people declare themselves in favor of democracy, but for many democracy simply means "absolute personal freedom and the absence of all compulsion: to do or not do as one pleases."[42] They are what the Hamburg sociologist Helmut Schelsky has called "unpolitical democrats." In this respect they differ markedly from their contemporaries in East Germany who are intensely interested in politics but who have not found a system—either democratic or Communistic—to which they are willing to entrust their future welfare and freedom.[43]

The future of this generation of young Germans in the West is in doubt. It is too sober, temperate, and calm to be swept away into political excesses. It may, indeed, remain dull and lacking in self-confidence, enslaved by its fears, too apathetic to make any major contribution to a German or European society. But given inspiration and an appeal "that carries the ring of real vision, of conviction and of seriousness of purpose,"[44] these young people who are today so bewildered and troubled may yet be infused by a creative spirit which seems to be utterly lacking in their society

41. Schelsky, *Die skeptische Generation*, pp. 453, 457.
42. *Ibid.*, p. 451.
43. See the brilliant article by Thilo Koch about the ideological alienation of East Germany's youth from the West in *Die Zeit* (Hamburg), June 12, 1958.
44. Kennan, *Russia, the Atom and the West*, p. 48.

today. If they are working to undertake the responsibilities of citizenship, they may help to establish on a firm basis in West Germany the institutions of free government.

West Germany's youth is still unformed in its outlook on the future; its political attitudes have still to be shaped. In this respect, too, the young people typify the society of which they form a part. Industrious and personally ambitious, they are still surrounded in politics by an aura of suspended animation. A keen observer of the German scene since before World War I put it well when he described contemporary West German society as one "in which all is not yet there." This concern is shared by the brilliant correspondent of the *New York Times,* Flora Lewis, who expressed it in another way:

There has scarcely been anything to remind people that history is a continuous process, a play drawn on a developing theme and not a series of vaudeville skits in which the same actors may keep reappearing but without the least connection between their successive roles. That air of having just been born, with no past at all, is by far the most disturbing quality of the German atmosphere now. It is a ghostly feeling of levitation from time, of unreality, where the worst thing to be feared is not what is happening, but the thud that will come when solid ground is hit once more.[45]

How Germany will develop cannot be predicted. Major steps in the direction of establishing democratic habits have been taken, but the future depends largely upon the direction and inspiration of German youth. A definite statement about the success or failure of democracy in West Germany would be premature. "Underrating the difficulties of democracy is no service to the democratic cause. Rather it encourages the self-deception of anti-democrats, who are only too ready to accept a low estimate of a system they dislike, and discourages true democrats, who are aware of present imperfections and of the path that has yet to be travelled."[46]

45. Flora Lewis, "A Motto on the Cemetery Wall," *The Reporter,* June 11, 1959, p. 35.
46. Hiscocks, *Democracy in Western Germany,* p. 294.

Three

■

ADENAUER, WEST GERMAN POLITICS, AND FOREIGN POLICY

In the years since 1945 few West Germans have shown an intelligent or persistent interest in foreign policy. Preoccupation with the struggle for survival was forced upon them in the initial postwar period. The currency reform of June 1948 made it possible for the Germans to work productively—"All of us suddenly had forty marks thrust into our hands," one German recently recalled, "and we started to work again—to live again"—but the miracle of economic recovery, the *Wirtschaftwunder,* consumed their energies; it left no time to contemplate problems which seemed to have no immediate bearing on their welfare as individuals. The Germans, in addition, had had little experience in conducting their own political affairs. They had more often been subjects than citizens. Years of Nazi rule followed by foreign occupation discouraged independent thinking about questions affecting the entire community. However much they were concerned about the future of their homeland—Would the country be peaceful? Could it be reunited? Would it join the East or the West?—the German people did not feel competent to make decisions, or powerful enough to implement them. This feeling of impotence, and the resultant willingness to accept authority, have gradually lessened with the development of West German independence and self-confidence, but they are still characteristic. The feeling of helplessness is reinforced in other ways. It is encouraged by the paternalism of the

Roman Catholic church, chiefly because of its excellent organization and direction a more potent force in West Germany today than Protestantism or anticlericalism. It is encouraged, too, by the West Germans' unhappy memory of their earlier political enthusiasm. They believe that they have suffered enough; they do not want to burn their fingers again. They feel incapable of solving the nation's problems and they do not want to try. Chancellor Adenauer has successfully discouraged, except among some intellectuals and the opposition parties, all potential criticism of the government's foreign policy, and he has persuaded most people that the country's foreign relations are in capable hands. *"Der Alte"* will decide these problems for us, they say.

Party leaders, civil servants, and industrial groups participate in the formulation of foreign policy from time to time, but it has been stated without exaggeration "that Adenauer exercises not only the strongest single influence on the formation of West German foreign policy but, in fact, the dominant influence."[1] The Chancellor has made foreign relations his special province. He devotes most of his working time to international affairs and exercises probably a more effective control over the implementation of policies than do individual leaders in any other NATO country.

Historical circumstances account in part for the Chancellor's all-powerful role in the Federal Republic's foreign policy. The gradual devolution of authority from the Occupation powers to the West German government gave Adenauer the opportunity to accumulate power. With every Allied concession the Chancellor personally assumed greater responsibility for the exercise of German sovereignty, for it was to him that Germany's Allied guardians looked for reassurance that the new freedoms would not be abused.

The pace of restoring sovereignty to West Germany was stepped up after the outbreak of the Korean War in June 1950, when the

1. Samuel L. Wahrhaftig, "The Development of German Foreign Policy Institutions," in Speier and Davison, *West German Leadership and Foreign Policy*, p. 56.

British, French, and American governments became convinced of the need for a German contribution to the defense of Europe. In exchange for rearmament, Adenauer made demands which amounted to the annulment of the Occupation Statute and acceptance of West Germany in "the Western camp of freedom" as an equal.[2] Convinced that, under Adenauer's leadership, the Federal Republic would be closely associated with the West, and realizing that the Germans would rearm only upon the Chancellor's urging, the Allied powers began discussions leading to the termination of the Occupation. The process initiated by the Petersberg Protocoll of November 1949, and continued with the revisions of the Occupation Statute in March 1951 (authorizing Bonn to establish a Foreign Ministry and to enter into direct diplomatic relations with other countries "subject to the prior approval of the Allied High Commission") culminated in the Contractual Agreements of May 26, 1952. These agreements, also known as the Bonn Convention or Treaty of Germany, restored sovereignty and gave Bonn full authority over its external affairs, except for certain rights retained by the Allied powers which concerned the stationing of forces in Germany, the status of Berlin, the unification of Germany, and the signing of a peace treaty with the reunited country.[3]

With every step along Germany's road to independence, Adenauer's responsibilities increased. Repeatedly he descended from the Petersberg clothed with more of the authority previously exercised by the Allied High Commission. Acting as his own foreign minister for four years, even after 1955 when he appointed Hein-

2. See Adenauer's speech of January 14, 1951, *New York Times,* January 15, 1951.

3. For these agreements, see *Documents on Germany Under Occupation, 1945-54* (London, 1955), pp. 439-442, 549-554, 616-627. The Contractual Agreements, because of the defeat of the EDC Treaty in the French National Assembly, did not come into force until May 1955, after the ratification of the Paris Treaties of October 1954 which provided for the Federal Republic's admission to NATO (see *London and Paris Agreements,* September-October 1954, Washington, 1954).

rich von Brentano to this post, the Chancellor personally made all important foreign policy decisions, leaving only most day-to-day matters to his subordinates.

A second circumstance that explains the unusually wide scope of Adenauer's activities in foreign relations is the break in the continuity of Germany's political institutions and traditions. West Germany's Basic Law gives the executive responsibility for directing foreign policy, with some parliamentary participation. It also provides certain guide lines for the conduct of policy. Because these are somewhat contradictory, it has been argued that the Federal Republic's international agreements will not be binding on a unified Germany. It has been held, also, that unification is not a foreign policy issue in the traditional sense, and should not, therefore, be left exclusively to the national executive.[4] But the Chancellor's authority has not been weakened by these disputes; if anything, it has been strengthened. Rising above political arguments, he has provided the strong leadership needed, thereby creating a body of constitutional precedent which his successors will inherit. After the defeat of Nazism, the nonpolitical institutions that survived 1945 could offer no guidance in foreign affairs. The Chancellor, with his strong personality and amazing vitality, has virtually compensated for this lack. He embodies dignity, strong will, and firm resolution, qualities which both the German people and the Western powers regard as symbolic of West Germany's return to international society. Adenauer's great prestige, without which he could not have undertaken this task, has gained immeasurably from the generous personal support he has received from British, French, and American governments over the years—especially from the Eisenhower administration and, specifically, from the former Secretary of State, John Foster Dulles.

Adenauer's control of his country's foreign policy has had overwhelming public support. The elections of 1953 and 1957 have endorsed the major features of his policy—the unification of west-

4. Wahrhaftig, "German Foreign Policy Institutions," pp. 23-25.

ern Europe and the commitment of West Germany to NATO. As chief of his party in the Bundestag he has dominated both the foreign policy formulation and its tactics. As party chairman he has controlled patronage, decided who the candidates for office will be, and in what constituencies they will run for election, and determined how the party's finances would be used. He has no difficulty impressing his point of view on members of his party, both in and out of the Bundestag.

A third and equally important factor has been the triumph of the government's economic policies, which has assured its success at the polls and its widespread popularity. Prosperity has blunted the attacks of political extremists who in hard times might have made a more successful appeal to nationalist ambitions. And because the German voters associated their prosperity with the Chancellor's pro-Western policies, the Social Democrats and Free Democrats could not embarrass him by insisting that reunification should take precedence over other political issues.

The role played by the SPD is a fourth factor in Adenauer's ability to dominate West Germany's foreign policy. The SPD has opposed the government's foreign policy, although—as the Chancellor knows—it is as anti-Communist and Western-oriented as the CDU. The SPD has not challenged the Federal Republic's democratic institutions, and has not made use of them in a way that has seriously threatened the Chancellor's power. Though Adenauer has had no reason to fear the Social Democrats, he has been able to use their opposition to his foreign policies to enhance his diplomatic bargaining position, exacting concessions from the United States, Britain, and France on the ground that these would help him to defeat the SPD.[5]

The Chancellor, in short, has taken advantage of historical circumstances and of German political conditions to dominate Bonn's

5. Hans Speier, "Introduction: The German Political Scene," in Speier and Davison, *West German Leadership and Foreign Policy,* p. 3.

foreign policy. In the Cabinet, only Foreign Minister von Brentano and Defense Minister Strauss appear to be involved in foreign affairs, and even they often are not consulted by Adenauer before he decides on a course of action. The Minister of All-German Affairs, Ernst Lemmer, in his frequent speeches on matters of foreign policy sometimes—like his predecessor, Jakob Kaiser—diverges from Adenauer's rigid position on relations with the People's Democratic Republic, the D.D.R.,[6] but the Chancellor rarely calls on him to help frame policies; Lemmer was appointed chiefly as a sop to the refugee groups and others who put reunification above Bonn's ties to the West. The Minister of Finance, Franz Etzel, is in a similar situation. Formerly Vice-President of the Coal and Steel Community (the Schuman Plan), Etzel until 1959 was clearly Adenauer's choice to succeed him as Chancellor. But Brentano and Minister of Economics Ludwig Erhard, after the 1957 national election, blocked Etzel's appointment as chief of the projected European Affairs Ministry, and it is doubtful whether behind the scenes he has been able to exercise an important influence on foreign affairs.[7] Indeed, Etzel's docile acceptance of the Chancellor's foreign policy leadership, and the assumption that he would permit Adenauer to dominate in this field from the presidential palace, was a major factor in Adenauer's short-lived decision to step aside in favor of Etzel in the spring of 1959.[8]

When Brentano in 1955 first took charge of the Foreign Ministry he was thought to have great influence with the Chancellor. He was expected to wield considerable power in foreign affairs and at that time was considered the leading candidate to succeed Adenauer. Since 1955, however, Brentano has not shown much independence and his standing with the Chancellor and in the CDU generally has declined. Brentano's failure to control the con-

6. For example, see Lemmer's interview with the *Süddeutsche Zeitung*, February 20, 1958.

7. *Der Tagesspiegel*, August 11, 1957.

8. See below, pp. 107-108.

duct of foreign policy is explained, in part at least, by the close relation between Adenauer and the former Undersecretary of the Foreign Ministry Walter Hallstein, who acted as the Chancellor's chief agent in that ministry until 1955 and continued to report directly to him even after Brentano took charge. Hallstein's unusual prerogatives were well illustrated in October 1957 when he precipitated the break in diplomatic relations between Bonn and Belgrade, even before Brentano, who was searching for a less drastic reaction to Yugoslavia's recognition of the Pankow regime, was reconciled to this step. Hallstein, however, is only one of a small group of the Chancellor's personal advisors, which includes Cardinal Frings, Herbert Blankenhorn, formerly Bonn's Ambassador to NATO and now to Paris, State Secretary Franz Thedieck, Dr. Hans Globke, the Chancellor's most trusted assistant, and the banker Robert Pferdemenges. These men seem to enjoy the Chancellor's confidence more than do professional administrators like Brentano.

Although Brentano's position is ambiguous, there is no suspicion of his loyalty to the Chancellor. He is staunchly pro-Western, and, despite the fact that he "is known to have privately, little hope that Germany can ever be reunified as a military ally of the Western powers,"[9] he has firmly rejected all proposals for German neutrality. Adenauer undoubtedly takes information furnished by the Foreign Ministry into account, but he is said to be dependent upon other channels—notably on the intelligence service headed by ex-General Gehlen—for interpretation of world events. This service, built up with American support during the Occupation, has since become Bonn's official foreign intelligence agency.[10]

9. Gaston Coblentz, in the *New York Herald Tribune,* May 7, 1956.

10. Although this organization has played a most important role in West Germany since the war, little is known about it or about its mysterious chief General Reinhard Gehlen. Hiscocks (*Democracy in Western Germany*) and the authors of *West German Leadership and Foreign Policy* do not even mention the organization. But cf. Brian Connell, *A Watcher on the Rhine* (New York, 1957), pp. 221-223.

Because the Foreign Ministry is largely ignored in important policy decisions, and also because of its antiquated personnel procedures and methods of reporting, it has failed to attract outstanding talent and many of its most capable minor officials have suffered frustration. For all these reasons, the Ministry has not attained high stature in Bonn, especially in comparison with the rapidly expanding Ministry of Defense. The calibre of the Foreign Ministry's personnel nevertheless is probably much better than it appears. Not until they have more scope will a sound judgment of their abilities be possible. Since the winter of 1957-58, Brentano has been fighting a battle for greater authority within his Ministry, but the struggle has cost him what little popularity he had left in the CDU. He defeated Blankenhorn's attempt to succeed Hallstein (which Adenauer is said initially to have approved), thereby sparing himself the agony of having another undersecretary with closer personal ties to the Chancellor than his own. Brentano appointed instead an affable and industrious administrator, Albert van Scherpenberg, whose main task has been to carry through the reorganization of the Ministry announced in January 1958. Brentano's appointment at that time of two additional undersecretaries and a new chief of personnel, and his misguided attempt to curb newspaper criticisms of foreign dignitaries by the so-called *Lex Soraya*[11] unleashed a storm of criticism and plunged his prestige to a new low. The attacks on Brentano in the Bundestag are, at least in part, veiled criticisms of the government's foreign policy, for CDU deputies do not dare to make them openly.[12] In the autumn of 1959, Adenauer once again humiliated his Foreign Minister by causing one of the undersecretaries whom Brentano had brought into his Ministry only a year before, Dr. Herbert Dittmann, to be "exiled" from Bonn to a Latin American embassy. The transfer of

11. The law was introduced in the Bundestag but not enacted after the Shah of Iran had protested vigorously the publicity given by the West German press to his divorce of Queen Soraya, who is of German parentage.

12. *Christ und Welt,* March 6, 1958; *Frankfurter Allgemeine,* March 11, 1958.

Dittmann is one in a series of changes in the Foreign Ministry in recent years which can be attributed to the same three causes. The first and most important is policy differences with the Chancellor. Adenauer was angry with Brentano for expressing independent ideas in the planning period and during the conference of Foreign Ministers in the spring and summer of 1959, and particularly displeased with a section of the Ministry which strongly favored closer relations with Poland and Czechoslovakia, a project for which he has little enthusiasm. Adenauer wants "men who are willing to execute his instructions unreservedly."[13]

Second, when it became apparent that there would be a series of high level meetings in 1959 and 1960, Adenauer decided to take charge of the preparations for these personally. The Foreign Ministry was to continue functioning simply as "a technical organ, with nothing else to do but to carry out instructions which the Chancellor, sitting in high council by himself, decides a few houses farther down the road."[14] At times not even the texts of letters from Premier Khrushchev and President Eisenhower, which Adenauer regarded as "personal," were communicated to the Foreign Minister.

Third, leading Foreign Ministry officials have been transferred or retired because they no longer want to serve a government, at least not in Bonn, which does not value their expert advice. Some of the leading figures in the West German Foreign Service who now serve abroad in prominent and obscure embassies are away from Bonn at least partly by choice, hoping for fruitful professional careers in the post-Adenauer era if they are not too closely identified with the government's policies during Adenauer's remaining period in office.

◆

13. J. Emlyn Williams, "Bonn Foreign Office Jarred," *Christian Science Monitor,* October 21, 1959.

14. *Ibid.* In this section of his article Williams is referring to conclusions drawn by the *Süddeutsche Zeitung.*

The man who stands to benefit most from the decline of Brentano's star is Franz-Joseph Strauss; his supporters in the Bundestag have made Brentano's life uncomfortable. Strauss's rise to power has been meteoric. Entering the Cabinet as minister without portfolio, when he had just turned thirty-eight, he subsequently headed the Atomic Ministry and today, at forty-five, is in his fourth year in charge of the Ministry of Defense. His remarkable and controversial character promises to keep him at the center of attention in the years to come. He is highly intelligent, witty, enormously energetic, quick to grasp new ideas, an expert debater, and very, very ambitious. Strauss has been accurately described as "the second most powerful and the single most distrusted man in West Germany."[15] His power is derived from a number of sources, but he is distrusted for only one reason: he is suspected of wanting to be Germany's "strong man." Others around the Chancellor are also ambitious, but they are less blunt. Not afraid to let it be known that he wants to be Chancellor, he is feared by many, distrusted by most, but ignored by none.

Strauss seems to have a great deal of freedom of action in the Defense Ministry, within the framework of Bonn's commitment to NATO. His is undoubtedly the most dramatic Cabinet position. A great deal of attention has been focused on West Germany's rearmament effort, especially since March 1958, when the Bundestag decided to equip the Bundeswehr with "the most modern weapons," meaning nuclear arms.[16] He has devoted his outstanding abilities to the task of re-creating a German military power. Obviously fascinated with his work, he insists that he has "the soul of a civilian,"[17] though in fact, he exercises more control over military activities, and has gained more respect from military per-

15. R. H. S. Crossman, "A Talk with Franz Josef Strauss," in the *New Statesman,* April 12, 1958, p. 460.

16. See below, Chaps. 5 and 6.

17. Ernest Leiser, "Germany's Would-Be Strong Man," *New York Times Magazine,* June 1, 1958. Cf. Flora Lewis, " 'Franz-Josef'—German Question Mark," *ibid.,* May 1, 1960.

sonnel, than any civilian defense minister in the Weimar Republic. Whatever the Chancellor may think of Strauss personally, he seems to rely upon his knowledge and his judgment, not only in military affairs but in some political matters as well. Behind the scenes, Strauss has used his influence in the selection of personnel. In the Bundestag, he has taken a leading role in defending the government's foreign and defense policies. His interventions in the March 1958 foreign policy debate, for example, probably saved Adenauer from at least a rhetorical defeat.[18] But despite his speeches, there is much doubt about Strauss's own views on German foreign policy. He is today a strong advocate of Bonn's political and military ties with the West, especially with the United States, yet, on one occasion, Strauss risked the Foreign Minister's temper and the Chancellor's wrath by proposing a five-point plan that ran counter to NATO policy in that it accepted, in principle, a disengagement of forces in central Europe.[19] His principal purpose may have been to attract attention, for he all but repudiated the plan when speaking on an American television program some weeks later. By that time, however, the plan had been widely discussed. The Defense Minister's challenging of Brentano's responsibility for foreign policy on this and other occasions aroused much speculation. Many people were reminded of a similar situation in 1956 when Theodor Blank resigned as chief of the Defense Ministry after being criticized by Herr Strauss—who later replaced him.[20]

Such incidents lend credence to the charge frequently levelled against Strauss, that for him policy is secondary to the fulfillment of his own ambitions. He has built up a powerful position within the CSU, the Bavarian branch of the government party. Without the Bavarian component, the Christian Democrats would not have a majority in the Bundestag. The CSU likewise could not form a

18. Deutscher Bundestag, *Protocoll,* 18-21. Sitzung, pp. 861 ff., 1003 ff., 1107 ff.

19. *Der Tagesspiegel,* February 22, 1958; *Die Welt,* February 25, 1958.

20. *Christ und Welt,* March 6, 1958.

government alone. There is no indication of a rift between the two organizations, but the CSU does exercise a good deal of power within the Christian Democratic Union (CDU/CSU) and Strauss will certainly use this leverage to the full in advancing his own interests.

Strauss is fearless—he is one of the very few Germans who have not been afraid to disagree with the Chancellor face to face—yet he is probably more cautious than many people believe. He seems to have sensed the danger of involvement in the Erhard-Adenauer controversy in the spring of 1959 and, unlike most leading CDU/CSU members, he did not support either side. He was rewarded for his discretion by a strengthening of his own chances to succeed Adenauer, while the candidacy of both Erhard and Etzel suffered. He may realize that at present he is too young to have a real chance of succeeding Adenauer; still, if he is not driven by his own impatience, or by his admirers, to compete for the Chancellorship in 1961 or before, he could have an important voice in deciding who will replace Adenauer, take another Cabinet position for himself, and wait for a chance to fulfill his greatest ambition some years later, when he would have a better chance of success. Some of Strauss's intimates believe this is his plan. They say that he covets the post of Foreign Minister as a steppingstone towards becoming the first Chancellor of a reunited country.

Article 59 of the Basic Law which provides that the Bundestag and the Bundesrat must approve international treaties gives the legislature the right to participate in the most important decisions on foreign policy. In these questions, however, there has been no test of strength between the executive and legislature such as frequently occurs in the American system. The government's solid majorities in the Bundestag, and usually in the Bundesrat,[21] have virtually precluded a defeat on matters of vital importance. Ade-

21. For the role of the Bundesrat in foreign affairs, see Wahrhaftig, "German Foreign Policy Institutions," pp. 39-41.

nauer can always be certain of obtaining legislative approval of draft treaties because the members of the majority coalition do not oppose their leaders in these matters, in debate or in voting, and only rarely in party *fraktion* meetings. In foreign policy matters the Bundestag acts chiefly as a forum, providing a platform from which the government can announce and explain its decisions. The debates, the most important of which are broadcast to a nationwide audience, are alarming to the uninitiated. Discussions are hectic, marred by personal insults hurled back and forth, and by *Zwischenrufe*—the time-honored practice of interrupting the speaker who has the floor with supporting or derogatory ejaculations. At times major demonstrations have taken place, chiefly for the benefit of the radio audience. (This is the negative side of broadcasts whose useful purpose is informing the general public.)[22]

Both the first chairman of the Bundestag's Foreign Affairs Committee, Eugen Gerstenmaier, who is now President of the Bundestag, and his successor, Kurt Georg Kiesinger, continuously urged that the parliament should have a more important role in the formulation of foreign policy and, above all, have insisted that the Bundestag committee should be kept currently informed of the government's actions in foreign affairs.[23] Under Gerstenmaier and Kiesinger, the committee did not gain power to initiate or control foreign policies, but the committee on occasion was consulted and brought into the confidence of the government. The committee meets frequently—though not often enough to satisfy the deputies —with members of the Cabinet and officials of the Foreign Minis-

22. For example, when Fritz Erler (SPD) deliberately provoked the assembly by comparing a speech given by Defense Minister Strauss to one by Joseph Goebbels during World War II, the CDU/CSU bellowed their disapproval and left the Bundestag chamber in a body; Deutscher Bundestag, *Protocoll,* 18. Sitzung, March 20, 1958, p. 880.

23. Kiesinger's successor as chairman of the Foreign Affairs Committee, Professor Furler, has been more tractable to Adenauer's wishes and does not seem to want to strengthen the role of the committee in foreign policy formulation.

try. At times, the Chancellor has even consulted leaders of the opposition on issues of foreign policy. Such conferences, however, are sporadic; the Foreign Affairs Committee has not been able to establish a clear right to be informed or to be consulted by the government before it acts. And on the occasions when the Chancellor actually consults leading deputies, he does so "to advance policies which he has already enunciated"; he gives them an audience to discuss "techniques in the presentation of policies to the Bundestag and the German people" which have already been adopted.[24] The Chancellor even insists on dominating the Bundestag's procedure on foreign policy questions. On the other hand, to back up his authority at major international conferences, as on his trip to Moscow in 1955, Adenauer has included leading members of the Bundestag in the government's delegation.

The first Federal President, Theodor Heuss, who according to Article 59 of the Basic Law "represents the Federation in its international relations," has not participated in the formulation of foreign policy to any significant extent. Heuss was occasionally consulted by the Chancellor and by leaders of the opposition parties, and performed ceremonial duties. His public pronouncements were usually restricted to intoning Germany's moral responsibilities in the modern world, but there was one noteworthy exception. The President's traditional New Year's message in January 1958 pointedly praised the former American diplomat George F. Kennan, at a time when the Adenauer government was attacking his controversial BBC lectures. Heuss also endorsed the practice of secret diplomacy in phrases that were widely interpreted as calling for a "more active" West German foreign policy.[25] Heuss himself never tried to exercise authority in the foreign relations field and

24. Wahrhaftig, "German Foreign Policy Institutions," p. 30.
25. Heuss's speech is in the *Bulletin Des Presse- Und Informationsamtes* (Bonn), January 3, 1958. Excerpts from the speech are in the English language *Bulletin,* January 7, 1958.

quite understandably took offense when Adenauer, in declaring himself a candidate to succeed the President, insisted that the powers of that office would permit him to control the Federal Republic's international relations. The Chancellor had apparently forgotten that, at the very first meeting of his cabinet in 1949, he had emphasized to his ministers that President Heuss, to whom they had just been formally introduced, exercised no political authority whatsoever. In his April 1959 statement the Chancellor was apparently influenced by a memorandum prepared for him by subordinates who sought to persuade him to take over the President's office by exaggerating the difficulties that might be caused if the SPD candidate, Carlo Schmid, were to gain the office. Eventually Adenauer was able to secure the Presidential post for Heinrich Lübcke, his Minister of Nutrition—thereby assuring that whatever authority the office might carry in the foreign relations field would not be exercised.

The Constitutional Court at Karlsruhe has been involved only indirectly in foreign policy. It upheld the government's ban on the Communist party in West Germany. It also ruled against the holding of referenda in the *Länder* on foreign policy issues, thus thwarting the SPD's attempt to embarrass the Federal government on the stationing of atomic weapons in West Germany. In a country where legalistic thinking often prevails, this decision, which had the effect of confining political decision-making to the political arena, was especially significant.

In Bundestag debates and in election campaigns, members of the Social Democratic and Christian Democratic parties almost always adhere strictly to the positions taken by their leaders on major issues of foreign policy. This apparent uniformity of party views, which has been a characteristic of the West German system from the beginning, does not mean that there are not genuine differences of opinion within the parties. These differences do exist and are a center of controversy in struggles for power among leaders and factions, struggles which have an important bearing on Bonn's future policies since the parties decide who will be in the positions to take stands on foreign policy issues.

From 1949 to 1959 it was extremely difficult to gain any insight into the struggle for power within the Christian Democratic Union. Chancellor Adenauer had not designated a successor and did not indicate that he would do so. Powerful elements in the party never participated openly in party deliberations; they had no occasion to. Whom the financial and industrial powers of the Ruhr favored to succeed Adenauer remained a mystery; but there was never any doubt that they would have an important voice in the decision. Competition among ministers and groups of Bundestag deputies for the succession had been hectic. Because of the Chancellor's intolerance of the efforts of individual deputies to differentiate themselves from other members of the party in order to enhance their own standing, few tried to attract attention in this manner. Their private views on foreign policy have not often come to light. When they have, they have usually been couched in such subtle language that the general public, and even other politicians, often fail to grasp their meaning. When a deputy has put forward a proposal that goes beyond his party's official stand, it has often been difficult to determine whether it represents a genuine difference of opinion or is merely a self-seeking venture (e.g., Franz-Joseph Strauss's plan for a demilitarized zone in Central Europe which was discussed earlier). Certain Christian Democrats took advantage of the Chancellor's absence from Bonn early in 1958 to present their own plans for reducing tensions and achieving German unity. Vice-Chancellor Ludwig Erhard, long considered the most likely successor should Adenauer not complete his term of office, was left in charge of the Cabinet during this period and was unable to restrain the activities or coördinate the statements of his colleagues. When the Chancellor returned to Bonn he imposed discipline and reasserted his authority with

lightning speed and efficiency.[26] Some experienced foreign observers in the West German capital felt that the dissension within
the CDU during the interim gave a foretaste of a hectic battle
for the Chancellor's mantle in the event of his sudden demise. The
events of the late winter and spring of 1959 verified these fears.
The sharp debate and divisions in the CDU following Adenauer's
reversal of the decision to step down as Chancellor was only a
mild foretaste of the bitter contest for the succession that is likely
to follow his death or retirement. Should the Chancellor live long
enough to appoint his successor, the battle that will follow his
retirement will be even more hectic than if he should suddenly die.

Behind the attention-seeking maneuvers of certain Christian
Democratic leaders there have always been real disagreements
about emphasis and about the conduct of the tactics of foreign
policy. Dr. Eugen Gerstenmaier, the President of the Bundestag
and the leading Protestant layman in the CDU, would like Bonn
to play a more important role in determining the policies of the
Western allies. He has advocated new tactics in pursuit of German
reunification.[27] He opposed the Chancellor's abrupt rejection of
the Rapacki Plan for a denuclearized zone and made it clear that
he does not object in principle to a "disengagement" of military
forces in Europe. He has defended the basic tenets of the government's pro-Western policies, at the same time advocating a more
flexible handling of major issues. Among the significant number
of Christian Democrats in the Bundestag and in the bureaucracy
who look to Gerstenmaier for guidance and leadership, some do
not do so because of his views on foreign affairs, but because they
believe that if given the opportunity, he would curb the influence
of the Roman Catholics in the CDU. The loose-knit group around
Gerstenmaier, whose sentiments are frequently echoed by the
weekly *Christ und Welt,* has not made itself felt as a powerful

26. See *Die Zeit,* March 6, 1958; *Die Welt,* March 7 and 12, 1958.
27. See the interview with Gerstenmaier in *Der Spiegel,* March 12, 1958.

faction within the party; nor is it likely to do so while Chancellor Adenauer remains in command.

Only very rarely has the Chancellor been persuaded by people who disagree with him to revise his attitude or to adopt different tactics. An incident at the Paris NATO conference in December 1957 was exceptional. On the eve of the conference, Felix von Eckhardt, the chief of Bonn's Press and Information Office, and Herbert Blankenhorn persuaded Adenauer to insert in his speech several sentences giving the most sanguine interpretation to the letters recently received from Bulganin and calling for renewed diplomatic efforts to reach agreements with Moscow.[28] Taken by themselves the sentences were harmless, but coming in the wake of the Sputnik successes and George Kennan's eloquent plea for a reassessment of Western policies, they seemed, to some, in conflict with the principal purpose of the conference, which was to strengthen NATO by adding IRBM's and other nuclear weapons to Europe's defenses. The swift and largely hostile reaction of important American, Swiss, and other newspapers made Adenauer's speech a minor sensation.[29] Just what the Chancellor had in mind remains uncertain. His remarks may have been simply a tactical maneuver to gain stronger support in the Federal Republic and increased prestige elsewhere in Europe. But there may have been more to it. One of those involved in this episode has said that, if Soviet leaders had reacted favorably to the Chancellor's remarks, he would have sent von Eckhardt to Moscow as his special representative. If this account is correct, Blankenhorn and von Eckhardt had indeed exerted a powerful influence on Adenauer. But Moscow gave no sign of a positive reaction, not even in the press or radio. Moreover, a number of CDU deputies led by the Bundestag

28. *Bulletin,* December 1957.

29. Members of the German delegation in Paris suspected that the strongly worded editorial denouncing the speech which appeared in the Paris edition of the *New York Herald Tribune* on the following day had been arranged by Secretary of State Dulles.

majority leader, Krone, immediately complained to the Chancellor that his speech had puzzled and confused the party. West Germany eventually supported the crucial NATO decision to agree, in principle, to the stationing of American nuclear missiles in western Europe, and the Chancellor made no further attempt to initiate new East-West talks.

Kurt Georg Kiesinger is another ranking CDU member known to disagree with some aspects of the government's foreign policy. He, however, has registered his dissents publicly only once. In March of 1958 he stormed out of a CDU *fraktion* meeting after being attacked by Krone and Adenauer for his role in postponing a foreign policy debate. The quarrel was ostensibly over procedure, but, in reality, it concerned the new approach to reunification which Gerstenmaier had proposed some days before the debate was scheduled to take place. Kiesinger and Fritz Erler, a leading defense and foreign policy expert of the SPD, are known to agree privately on many of the issues that come to their attention on the Foreign Relations Committee. But in Bundestag debates they appear as bitter critics of each other's ideas. The explanation is not hard to find. Erler and Kiesinger are probably equally far from agreeing with the positions taken by their respective parties. They can admit this privately, but party discipline prevents their doing so publicly.[30]

There is evidence of genuine differences of opinion over foreign policy within the CDU, quite apart from the utterances of attention-seeking individuals. Under the present Chancellor these differences, which have rarely come to the surface, have not had a significant effect on the formulation and conduct of policy. It is conceivable, though very doubtful, that Adenauer's successor will also be able to exercise such effective control. To do so he would have to control the party machinery, and there are strong reasons for believing that CDU leaders will not again permit a

30. Kiesinger is now Minister President of Baden-Wurttemburg.

Chancellor to dominate the party chairmanship as well. It seems probable that more people will become influential in deciding the course of Bonn's foreign relations and that the issues involved will become a more important factor in domestic politics. This likelihood does not suggest the advisability of a change in the present Western attitude toward the Federal Republic, but it does call for a greater effort to understand the interests and ideas of individuals and groups suppressed today which may find expression in Bonn's future policies. No major alteration in the basic orientation of West Germany's foreign policies need follow a change of government leadership, but the resolute manner in which policy is being conducted today, which leaves nothing to be desired from an American or Western standpoint, is likely to disappear in a more turbulent political atmosphere. Bonn's policies may become more unstable when Adenauer is no longer in control.

Disputes over foreign policy platforms have played a major role in the struggle for power among the warring factions in both the Social Democratic and the Free Democratic parties. Although the leaders of both opposition parties have tried to weld their respective members in the Bundestag into a united front on every major issue, they have been less successful than Chancellor Adenauer in keeping dissenting opinions from public attention. This is particularly true of the FDP. The FDP was the only small party outside of the government coalition able to overcome the five per cent clause,[31] and to obtain Bundestag seats in the 1957 election. Internal conflicts in the party have prevented it from following a clear line in foreign policy. One group consists of remnants of the old National Liberals. Headed by Reinhold Maier, chairman of the FDP until 1959, their strength is centered in Baden-Wurttemberg. They are in general accord with another,

31. The Federal German election law for the 1957 national election provided that parties had to win at least 3 constituencies or obtain 5 per cent of the total votes cast to obtain seats in the Bundestag.

and by far the most dynamic group, the so-called Young Turks in North Rhine-Westphalia—Willy Weyer, Wolfgang Doering, Erich Mende, who is now chairman of the party—and join with them in criticizing Adenauer's and Brentano's "inflexibility." On specific issues, the Liberals and the Young Turks are often far apart. They have repeatedly clashed, for example, over suggestions by Weyer and Doering that political relations should be established between Bonn and Pankow.[32] A third group centered in Lower Saxony has outraged the Liberals by flirting with unregenerate Nazis in the *Land* government.

In the FDP the Liberals are becoming less and less important. The Dusseldorf group, the "Young Turks," has virtually taken control of the party; their ideas will increasingly dominate its policies. Since the FDP's break with the government coalition, Mende, Weyer, and Doering have been more and more critical of the CDU's policies, and of the Chancellor. They are supported by segments of light industry and other business interests, especially those firms anxious to do more business with China and other Communist countries, and by Protestants who fear the Roman Catholic "black peril" in the Christian Democratic party as much as they fear the "red peril" in the SPD. With this backing, the Dusseldorf group has followed a line in foreign policy more nationalistic than that of any other major party, resembling somewhat the independent policy of Gustav Stresemann in the Weimar Republic.[33] Hopes of building a mass party—hopes which the Liberals do not share—have suffered disappointments. At present, the FDP is losing support even in North Rhine-Westphalia where it is the best organized political group. The FDP polled only 7.1 per cent of the vote in July 1958 as against 11.5 per cent in the North Rhine-Westphalian state elections in 1954. These indications of decline suggest the eventual exclusion of the FDP from the Bundestag, perhaps in the 1961 elections if the Christian

32. *Neue Zürcher Zeitung,* March 31, 1958.
33. *Die Zeit,* August 22, 1957.

Democratic Union remains united and capable of attracting most of the North German Protestant conservatives and retains its right-wing reactionaries. A major economic setback might drive them into the "Young Turks" camp, or even further to the right. If the decline of the FDP accelerates, sentiment for rejoining the government coalition might revive, splitting the party wide open. On the other hand, there is some chance that the Dusseldorf group will try to postpone the party's extinction by pushing nationalist policies beyond the pale of reason. Thus far the ambitions and frustrations that drive Mende, Weyer, and Doering have been tempered by their somewhat reluctant recognition of the importance to West Germany of her ties to the United States and to other Western countries.[34]

The Social Democrats, from Kurt Schumacher's leadership in the early years of the Federal Republic until 1960, opposed the government's foreign policy unswervingly and with a bold united front. They opposed German rearmament, and when they were defeated on that issue they opposed the draft. Subsequently, they campaigned against the stationing of atomic weapons in West Germany. The Social Democrats also opposed, at first, West German participation in the plans of the six nations comprising the European Coal and Steel Community for political and economic unification. They have persistently criticized Adenauer's government for putting rearmament and programs of European economic integration ahead of the reunification of Germany and policies aimed at reducing political tensions in Europe. They have demanded the reëstablishment of political relations with East European countries, the creation of a demilitarized zone in central Europe, efforts to negotiate political settlements, and a security treaty for all Europe to replace the Warsaw Pact and NATO.

Despite this record, the SPD—all but an insignificant element in the party—is by no means antidemocratic, or pro-Communist,

34. Cf. Terrence Prittie, "Germany's 'Young Turks,'" *The Listener,* May 24, 1956.

or even anti-American. In fact, it is one of the bulwarks of German democracy. As a whole, it has a strong Western orientation; most of its leaders are fully cognizant that the Federal Republic has depended on its political, economic, and military ties to the West for the maintenance of freedom and security, and they believe that this goal has been achieved at the cost of German unity. Many Social Democrats, furthermore, hold Western policies partly responsible for the intensity of the East-West conflict. Not until 1960, when it focused attention exclusively on the national elections of 1961, did the SPD temper its criticisms of Adenauer's foreign policy.

These generalizations describe the broad lines of Social Democratic opposition to Adenauer's foreign policy, but they fail to reveal the differences of opinion that exist among the party's leaders. These are important factors in the struggle for power among the functionaries, the party bureaucrats, and the "liberal" politicians. The outcome will decide not only the position the SPD will take on foreign policy in the future, but also the party's role in German politics.

The tempo of the intraparty struggle for control was stepped up after the SPD's severe defeat in the 1957 Bundestag elections. Until then Erich Ollenhauer, the kindly and unpretentious SPD party chairman, had successfully reconciled the warring factions, maintaining party unity. But the qualities that made Ollenhauer useful to the party—his mild temperament, his ability to compromise and to reconcile conflicting interests—made him unacceptable to the electorate as a potential Chancellor. He does not have the powerful personality that the German people want in a national leader. The party reforms agreed upon at the SPD Congress in May 1958 paved the way for the replacement of Ollenhauer as the party's standard bearer at the party's Congress in November 1960 before the 1961 national election campaign. Power within the party has shifted from the functionaries, who have been Ollenhauer's chief source of support, to the active politicians who represent the SPD in the national and *Länder* governments.[35] For a time the question of who would replace Ollenhauer remained unanswered. The decision was bound to have strong implications for the party's future political orientation. At the 1958 congress Carlo Schmid, a Deputy President of the Bundestag, a scintillating intellectual with a big reputation in middle-class circles, received a few votes for the party chairmanship. Fritz Erler, a Vice-Chairman of the SPD's Bundestag *fraktion,* and the Bavarian Waldemar von Knoeringen, one of the party's Vice-Chairmen, also were possible candidates. Schmid, Erler, and von Knoeringen are leaders of the party's "liberal" wing which has steadily fought against the party bureaucrats' ideological conceptions of domestic and foreign policies. They have opposed also extreme left-wing elements in the party. Most aggressive of the SPD's leaders is its alternate Vice-Chairman, Herbert Wehner. Energetic and conscientious, Wehner is something "rare in the SPD: a full-blooded politician—not an easygoing, unimaginative bureaucrat but a strong imposing personality"[36] who enjoys political combat, something most intellectuals in the party find distasteful and in which they are not effective. His political past—he was once a member of the Communist party—and his stand on issues of domestic and foreign policy, have made Wehner vulnerable to attack as a radical. His speeches on social and economic topics are often reminiscent of the SPD's Marxist past, something the party is trying to, and will have to, overcome if it is going to attract more than a third of the voters. Wehner has been one of the sharpest critics of Bonn's adherence to NATO; he has declared himself favorable to political conversations between West German and East German officials, if these will help to achieve reunification. His rise to power in the party might still lead the SPD further away from election victories, and,

35. See F. R. Allemann, "German Socialists Reorganize," *New Leader,* June 16, 1958; also *New York Times,* November 24, 1960.

36. Allemann, *op. cit.*

at the same time, to the advocacy of tactics in foreign affairs that not only differ sharply from those of the Adenauer government, but also are more radical than those proposed by the "liberal" leaders of the SPD.[37]

At the opposite pole from Wehner on many foreign policy issues in the SPD is Willy Brandt, the popular young Mayor of West Berlin, Like Schmid, Erler, and von Knoeringen, Brandt is in full accord with the Federal Republic's basic Western orientation, but he, in addition, has supported West German rearmament and Bonn's military ties to the West. From his vantage point in the embattled city of Berlin, Brandt knows from first-hand experience the need for military preparedness against the threat of Soviet aggression. Because of this stand, and also because of his un-dogmatic approach to economic and social problems, he is un-popular with many members of the party. His personal attractive-ness and leadership ability have gained him a strong following throughout the country. Following Brandt's electoral success in the December 1958 mayoralty election in Berlin he became a leading contender for Ollenhauer's position and probably the most effective candidate the SPD could nominate for Chancellor. In July 1960 Brandt was chosen by the SPD executive to lead the party and this decision was endorsed at the SPD party congress in November.

Two trends were discernible in the SPD's reëxamination of principles and policies following the party's third consecutive national election defeat, in 1957. One, a desperate reaction to the party's prolonged opposition status, was a trend toward radicalism in both domestic and foreign policy. Had this reorientation been adopted, the party would have been condemned to certain defeat again and again, as long as the Federal Republic enjoys economic

---

37. Allemann (*ibid.*) is less critical of Wehner, calling him "a bogeyman of the German Bourgeoisie," and asserting that Wehner "is a 'radical' per-haps only in the sense that he places the problem of German reunification in the center of his political activity."

prosperity. The other trend led toward less dogmatism in social and economic questions and to a more moderate foreign policy position. At the Bad Godesberg party congress in the autumn of 1959, the party adopted a revised and liberalized platform which broke with the SPD's Marxist past. Nationalization of key industries and a planned economy were no longer insisted upon. The foreign policy platform was revised under the able leadership of Carl Mommer, a deputy chairman of the SPD who like Brandt, Erler, and Schmidt is one of the liberal—one of the "modern"— leaders of the party. Following the break-up of the Paris Summit Conference in May 1960 the SPD released a new foreign policy declaration which brought it a step closer to that of the CDU. The statement proposed a "joint stocktaking" aimed at constructing a bipartisan foreign policy, a suggestion intended to curry favor with the electorate in preparation for the 1961 elections.[38]

Since 1957, then, the struggle for supremacy among the warring factions in the SPD has been won by the liberal, nondogmatic wing. The final outcome of this struggle for power will determine whether the SPD is to become a real rival to the CDU, and its potential successor in office, or whether it is to become an embittered splinter group doomed to perpetual opposition. Since the SPD is today the only party, in addition to the CDU/CSU, within striking distance of gaining a majority, the outcome of the Social Democrats' intraparty struggle will determine what kind of a political system the Federal Republic is to have. Should the SPD remain incapable of winning a majority and forming a government, the Christian Democrats will be in power indefinitely, unless and until a new party can challenge their control of the Bundestag.

◆

38. The declaration proposed bipartisanship on the following basis: 1) Agreement that Berlin should be defended at all costs; 2) Acceptance of West German membership in NATO; 3) Acceptance of the need for a strong defense establishment; 4) Agreement that nothing would be gained by raking over old arguments on foreign policy. *New York Times,* June 6, 1960.

The existence of two or more parties, each of them capable of gaining sufficient electoral support to form a government, is an essential feature of a democratic parliamentary system. In order to play the role of an opposition party the SPD must further reorganize. Successive defeats in elections by increasingly large margins have created the danger that in desperation the party will be driven into a radical position from which it will not be able to compete effectively for power. The tactics of the Christian Democrats, and the speeches of the Chancellor himself during national election campaigns, have increased this danger. During the 1957 election campaign, for example, Adenauer told a Nürnberg audience: "We are absolutely determined to see to it that the SPD will never come to power. Why have we taken this stand? Not—believe me—because of party political hatred. That is not the reason. We reach this firm decision because we believe that an SPD victory will lead to the downfall (*Untergang*) of Germany."[39] Of course the SPD responded in kind, likening Adenauer to Hitler and spreading other lurid propaganda.[40] But the Chancellor's demagogic attacks on the party's integrity (". . . the SPD will lead us to communism"), and his masterful cultivation of the German people's already overdeveloped respect for success, threaten to push the Social Democrats toward more and more desperate maneuvers. An example was their ill-advised 1958 campaign "Against Atom Death." If the party is going to be saddled with radical leadership, it will indeed "never come to power."

For this reason alone, the strong trend toward the Christian Democrats and the Social Democrats in the Bundestag and recent *Länder* elections, at the expense of the smaller parties, does not—as is generally assumed—necessarily herald the adoption of a two-

39. *Der Spiegel,* September 11, 1957.
40. See the SPD poster reproduced in *Die Zeit,* July 25, 1957; also the report in the *Manchester Guardian,* July 13, 1957

party system in the Federal Republic.[41] The trend away from
smaller parties is unmistakable, but this does not insure the existence of two parties either of which is capable of taking power.
The Social Democrats' percentage of the total votes cast has increased since 1949, but only slightly.[42] The party will not attract
more than a large minority of the votes unless it is led by moderate
liberals such as Brandt, Schmid, and Erler and offers a nondogmatic program. But the SPD's ability to stave off radicalism also
depends, in part, upon the Adenauer government's tolerance of
opposition.

The establishment of a two-party system also hinges upon
the Christian Democratic party's ability, in the long run, to con-
tain its diverse Protestant, Catholic, liberal, conservative, and
reactionary groups, and its individual voters. This will be tested
only after the commanding figure of Konrad Adenauer, the party's
unifying symbol and chief integrating force, is no longer present.
Most members of the party expect it to hang together, but even
today some CDU leaders do not exclude the possibility of either
a Protestant and left-wing group splitting off, or of a right-wing
group breaking or drifting away, perhaps to form a new party
with remnants of the FDP. Much also depends upon the election
laws. These have been revised before each Bundestag election, to
the disadvantage of the small parties. In the 1953 and 1957
elections, the ballot, which combined popular with proportional
representation, militated against the splinter groups. If, as is likely,
at the next general election, in 1961, the five per cent clause is

41. The CDU/CSU and SPD together polled 60.2 per cent of the popular
votes in the Bundestag elections of 1959, 74 per cent in 1953, and 84 per
cent in 1957. In the state elections in North Rhine-Westphalia, which has
about one-third of the total West German population of more than
50,000,000, the CDU/CSU and SPD polled 75 per cent of the votes in 1954
and 89.7 per cent in 1958.

42. SPD percentages of the Bundestag election votes were 29.2 (1949),
28.3 (1953), and 31.8 (1957). In the North Rhine-Westphalia elections, the
SPD gained 34.5 per cent in 1954 and 39.2 per cent in 1958.

retained, or as is unlikely, if a single member constituency system is adopted, all parties except the Social Democrats and the Christian Democrats may be excluded from the Bundestag, and, eventually, from most *Länder* diets.

The small parties, chiefly rightist groups, do not today play a significant political role in Bonn, nor have they done so over the years since the founding of the Federal Republic. In the most recent national elections not even the largest of these organizations, the BHE or Refugee party, claiming to represent the interests of more than eleven million expellees and refugees from the Eastern territories, was able to muster the necessary five per cent of the vote. Excluded from the Bundestag, the BHE has steadily lost national support, despite its nationalist propaganda.[43] Pressure groups demanding that the refugees be allowed to return to their "homelands"—including the Sudetenland—are still active and are a political force all parties must reckon with. On the other hand, most refugees have found new jobs and homes in West Germany. Their children, in particular, are being fully integrated into the new society, and although they, like their elders, back the demand for reunification with Eastern Germany, many do not share their parents' nostalgia for the "homeland" beyond the Oder and Neisse. Votes of the outcasts show divided interests, distributed in even greater numbers among the major West German parties. In the event of an economic crisis many refugees, probably the first to suffer, would intensify their demand for *Heimatrecht* (the right to a homeland). But even so a political party such as the BHE based exclusively on Germany's territorial grievances would have little success in the Federal Republic.

The only neo-Nazi party still contesting national and *Länder* elections is the DRP (*Deutsche Reichspartei*), successor to the SRP (*Sozialistische Reichspartei*) which was banned in 1952. The

43. The BHE demanded the restoration of Germany "from the Saar to the Memel." *Manchester Guardian*, April 27, 1957.

DRP received only one per cent of the votes in the September 1957 elections and, even in Lower Saxony where it has been concentrating its efforts, it remains a tiny minority.

The virtual exclusion of radical rightist groups from the struggle for political power is due, first of all, to West Germany's great economic prosperity, secondly, to the success of the CDU/CSU and to a lesser extent of the FDP in attracting as members and voters those who might otherwise have fallen prey to extremist propaganda and nihilist dogmas. Germany's political innocents, who either were duped by Nazism or docilely accepted the Hitler regime, have not so far been fooled again. They have latched on to the new respectability as represented by the major parties and by the Adenauer government. They have had good reasons for doing so. They are enjoying prosperity; the new Federal Republic has established itself as a powerful and respected nation, and in Chancellor Adenauer they have found a leader whom they can trust and follow, whose ardent anti-Communism reflects their own feelings. The Chancellor's condemnation of SPD's Herbert Wehner, who serves, for the bourgeoisie, as the personification of the Bolshevik menace in West Germany, increases their confidence in his judgment. Whatever their reasons for supporting him, many Germans have learned, from the anti-totalitarian Chancellor and from their association with the Christian Democratic party, to understand and prefer democratic practices. They have seen that democracy is not only respectable; it can also be successful. Fascism by contrast spells defeat and catastrophe. Those who in this generation would revive Nazism can make no real appeal to the people. For this reason it is safe to say that, "if there should be another right radical movement of any significance in free Germany, it would in no way associate itself with the Hitler past, or revive the Nazi slogans."[44] It would, nevertheless, be a mistake to ignore or to underrate the innumerable reactionary and Fascist groups and the more militant vet-

44. Conant, *Germany and Freedom,* p. 14.

erans' organizations which continue to bombard the West German people with nationalist and racist pamphlets, books, and newspapers. Of no political importance today, should a major economic or political crisis occur, they could have a disturbing effect on the climate of opinion and could weaken the society's resistance to other forms of extremism. "The danger in Germany does not at present lie with anything that can be called 'neo-Nazism.' The danger lies with a restoration of those élites, attitudes, myths, and drives that once before proved to be fertile soil in which, in periods of crisis, the weeds of Nazism luxuriated."[45]

Leaders of both the SPD and CDU, as well as some unaffiliated intellectuals, have occasionally proposed the formation of a Great Coalition (CDU/CSU-SPD) government, or at least the development of a bipartisan foreign policy. Chancellor Adenauer has never supported these suggestions. The bitterness of party hostilities in recent election campaigns has reduced the chances that, barring a national emergency, either will be adopted. The failure of these projects is no loss to the society. For in coalition governments, the allocation of responsibility is often not clear to the electorate; people do not know whom they should hold accountable for the conduct of national affairs. The same is true of bipartisan policies. Even in mature democracies, bipartisanship tends to restrict the dissemination of essential information to the voting public, because of the exclusion of issues of foreign policy from public debates. This situation is just the reverse of what is needed in the Federal Republic where, at present, the individual does not have sufficient interest in, or take enough responsibility for, public affairs. West Germany does not suffer from an excess of political opposition but rather from a general failure to understand the vital function that an opposition should perform in a democracy. Whatever the value of a united foreign policy front in external relations, it could not begin to compensate for the loss

45. Tauber, "Over Germany: Shadows from the Past."

of the educational value of having two or more major parties debate issues and compete for power. Instead of suppressing the opposition in a coalition government or in a bipartisan arrangement, those who wish to strengthen democracy in the Federal Republic should encourage opposition parties to carry out their function with a greater sense of responsibility and accord them the respect and the honored place that they deserve.

Foreign policy issues have figured prominently in Bundestag debates in both national and *Länder* elections, principally because the parties in opposition have not been able to find other issues on which to base their campaigns. Unprecedented national prosperity and the promise of continued gains have made the government's economic and social policies virtually immune to effective attack. The SPD and FDP's criticisms of foreign policy have not succeeded either. The decisive issues for the vast majority of voters have been economic welfare and the personalities of the candidates; on both counts they have repeatedly favored the CDU.

Adenauer could most probably have won the 1953 and 1957 elections on personality alone, although these were no mere personality contests. He was a strong and successful leader; no one could rival him in stature. The SPD, making the mistake of repeated personal attacks on Adenauer, only pointed up the shortcomings of those who have been pitted against him, and therefore strengthened his chances of reëlection. The Social Democrats must also still convince the general public that their party is no longer a slave to the dogmas of the class struggle. The CDU's 1957 campaign slogan, "No Experiments," invented by Erich Peter Neumann, the head of a polling institute and one of Adenauer's personal advisors, was carefully chosen to fit the mood of the German public and to arouse their fears about the SPD. The slogan echoed the fear that the SPD would endanger the nation's welfare by nationalizing its industries and by other social "experiments." It called attention to the same danger in the Social Democrats' foreign policy proposals.

The impact on the German public of major domestic and foreign events in the months preceding the September 1957 elections illustrates the key importance of economic and personality issues. Neither the Hungarian revolution nor the Suez crisis caused significant changes in the voters' party preferences. These events may have been responsible for the shift toward Adenauer among the four per cent of West Germans who had completed at least a high school education, but the preponderant trend in public opinion toward support of the SPD seems to have been motivated primarily by rising consumer prices.[46] By May 1957 a contrary trend favoring the CDU had appeared and was given additional impetus by the passage of an act reforming the Federal pension system, a measure benefiting vast numbers of West Germans, not only the direct recipients of aid—whom the government in individual letters thoughtfully informed of the boon—but also their families, relatives, and others who previously may have had to contribute to their support. The Christian Democrats showed spectacular gains and drew steadily away to win an unprecedented absolute majority.[47] Polls are never a precise indicator of the voters' sentiments if only because several months before an elec-

46. In October 1956, in reply to the poll question, "Which party best represents your views?" 39 per cent of the respondents favored the CDU/CSU, 40 per cent answered SPD, and 21 per cent named other parties. In December 1956 the replies were: 39 per cent CDU/CSU, 45 per cent SPD, 16 per cent for the rest. Other figures and analyses of trends in public opinion were shown to this writer at the Allensbach Institut für Demoskopie in March 1958.

47. At the end of April 1957, 40 per cent of those polled (see above, n. 46) supported the CDU/CSU and 40 per cent the SPD. In May it was 43 per cent CDU/CSU, 38 per cent SPD; in June, 42 per cent CDU/CSU, 39 per cent SPD; in July, 47 per cent CDU/CSU, 37 per cent SPD; in September, 50 per cent CDU/CSU, 32 per cent SPD. The elections on September 15th gave the CDU/CSU 50.2 per cent and the SPD 31.8 per cent of the votes.

tion—even before the start of a political campaign—people do not express their preferences as they do just before, and on, election day. Polls can, however, be reliable indicators of political trends; the one cited in these paragraphs was remarkable in that it came within two-tenths of a per cent of the actual election results.[48]

While economic and social prospects and personality factors have decisively affected the fortunes of West Germany's political parties, foreign policy issues have had their own importance. Life on a divided continent, subject to the constant threat of atomic annihilation, has produced among the West German people a deep anxiety and an overriding concern with survival. The fact that under Adenauer the Federal Republic has not been involved in a war has contributed to the people's confidence in his leadership, a confidence which his untried and unimpressive opponents have not inspired. Most West Germans realize that none of the major parties would willingly sacrifice their freedoms and the nation's security, and yet the active propaganda support given by Moscow and Pankow to the Social Democrats made it appear that this party would further the aims of the Communists in Europe. At the same time, the United States and other West European nations left no doubt that they would welcome Adenauer's reëlection. Thus the Social Democrats have been severely handicapped in all major elections—they have lost the battle for Washington's love, and they have failed to arouse the Communists' enmity. The FDP's neutralist and nationalist proposals, and the SPD's opposition to Adenauer's conduct of foreign policy, made it appear that both these parties, if they came to power, would desert the Western security program, depriving the Federal Republic of the protection of the Western powers. These were damaging charges. Most West Germans are convinced that the Federal Republic needs the protection of the Western powers, chiefly the United States. The Social Democratic proposals up to 1959, which would have made it im-

48. See *Die Zeit,* October 31, 1957.

possible for a reunited Germany to join in a military alliance with the United States, received no official support in the West, while causing many West Germans to fear that an SPD election victory would increase the chances of Communist domination or of a general war.

An overwhelming majority of West Germans, including the few who are concerned with foreign policy and the masses who are not, have a generally Western orientation. This orientation is not a product of the Cold War, although it has been reinforced by the division of Europe between East and West. It is, rather, an integral part of German history and tradition. Cultural ties are the most substantial and soundest factor in the country's orientation, and Germany's cultural heritage is essentially Western. The Germans have contributed to, and have shared in, the great creative impulses that produced Western civilization. Although these have been relegated to a place of diminished importance by the cynical materialism that has swept the Federal Republic, the legacies of Christian belief and of creative endeavor have survived. The new economic and political relationships with western Europe and the United States, and the increase in cultural exchanges with these nations since the war have multiplied and strengthened the ties binding the Federal Republic to the West. This is particularly noticeable among the younger West Germans who know little about eastern Europe, on the other side of the Iron Curtain.

The Germans' Western orientation is the product also of reaction against the East. Memories are still fresh of the bitter struggle against the "Russian hordes" during the last war, of the brutal rape of Germany by Soviet forces. Today the sufferings of East Germany under Communism serve as a constant reminder of the cruelty of Soviet tyranny. Other, chiefly negative, factors affecting the attitude of the West Germans toward the U.S.S.R. include the subtle but persistent attitude of superiority to the East generally, and particularly to Asia—to which, according to many Germans, Soviet Russia belongs. The Germans fear and respect Soviet Russia's industrial might, her scientific achievements, and, above all, her great military power. But their fear is mixed with disdain, and their respect is tempered with a strange condescension, even contempt, as if there were something unreal about the awesome Russian colossus. Their image of Soviet Russia is of a great, unpredictable giant, dangerous beyond compare, but not necessarily unapproachable or uncontrollable. In intellectual circles, especially, the belief is growing that the Soviet colossus can be dealt with, that it has its own problems and that these account for its menacing posture toward the rest of the world.

If increased self-confidence has led some Germans to minimize the dangers of Soviet aggression, for most of them the overwhelming power of the Soviet giant rules their attitude toward the East. The hazard of living within an arm's reach of this perilous power has forced them to recognize their dependence upon the United States for security and freedom.

Germany's geographical position in the middle of Europe sets limits to her Western orientation. As long as the country remains divided, reunification will continue to dominate political discussions, and these discussions inevitably will focus attention on the East. Reunification, the Germans know, cannot be achieved without the consent of the Russians. For this reason alone, the Federal Republic must maintain political contacts with the U.S.S.R. and with other eastern European peoples. The Germans regard East and West differently. They feel no threat of military action from the West and they believe they are equal to any economic or political challenge encountered there. More important, Germany and the West have a common history and mutual aspirations. An emotional attraction, transcending any formal arrangements for economic and political collaboration or mutual defense, binds the

Germans to the West. Their primary foreign policy goals lie in the East, but not their emotional or spiritual ties.

The preoccupation with domestic problems which is characteristic of the great majority of the West German people is not characteristic of that small but vocal minority of intellectuals, publicists, and journalists who are sometimes disparagingly referred to as "word merchants." In the Federal Republic this amorphous group is unique in its intense and sustained concern with foreign policy problems. Its members pose as implacable foes of materialism—although some of them make the most of it. These intellectuals could be classified as "outsiders," people who feel that they have been left out of the mainstream of the new society—more often than not it ignores them. They do not find the new German spirit congenial, or the prevalent style of life compatible with their conceptions of responsible living. In waging political battles, most of them suffer from the intellectual's typical political incompetence.

The outsiders comprise only a small number of persons, dissatisfied and unadjusted as intellectuals often are, yet their actual and potential influence in shaping West Germany's policies cannot be ignored. Their activities have been a painful thorn in Chancellor Adenauer's side, for although most probably have no party affiliation, they swell the chorus of SPD and FDP attacks on the Chancellor's leadership and on what they call the false idols of the society. They are less opposed to the new egalitarian ideal than to those individuals and groups whom the *Wirtschaftwunder* has brought to power: the Church hierarchy, the bankers, pollsters, industrial tycoons, and, above all, the Chancellor himself. The intellectuals realize that the people cannot be made to bite the hands that have been feeding them, and they have turned their own attention therefore almost exclusively to the country's external relations. Some display anti-American sentiments, holding the United States partly to blame for saddling the Federal Republic with its present leaders and idols. But most are genuinely concerned about the issues of peace and security, and many know more about foreign policy than the average Bundestag deputy.

The many differences of opinion among the outsiders make it difficult to generalize about their attitudes toward foreign countries. In the main, they are fascinated and preoccupied with the significance of Germany's middle position in Europe. Geography, they believe, imposes special responsibilities which the government in Bonn has failed to recognize. Characteristically, they decry what they call the "rigidity" of Western policies; they utter passionate pleas for a more dispassionate, objective conduct of foreign policy. They have repeatedly called for the development of an "Eastern policy." Many have steadfastly opposed West German rearmament in NATO, holding that the adoption of atomic arms by the Bundeswehr will increase the danger of war and reduce the chances of achieving reunification.

But the outsiders have not resigned themselves simply to criticizing the government's policies. Some of them, on occasion, have made positive proposals that deserve attention. They have called for "disengagement" of military forces in Europe, for the creation of a demilitarized zone in central Europe, and for making Germany's continued membership in NATO a matter to be considered in negotiations with the Russians on reunification. The outsiders have agitated also for setting up diplomatic relations with Poland and other East European countries. Most are prepared to declare themselves in favor of sacrificing Germany's claim to the Oder-Neisse territories. This prerequisite to the development of amicable Polish-German relations they believe would contribute to the lessening of tensions in all Europe.

The outsiders operate as individuals; they are not organized as a party or faction. None can claim to represent the opinions of all, and yet their views are reflected in several of the Federal Republic's most informative newspapers. The best known is Axel Springer's *Die Welt,* published daily in Hamburg, Essen, and Berlin, with a circulation of more than 200,000, and edited by Hans Zehrer, whose vitriolic attacks on the Federal government are reminiscent of his role in the destruction of the Weimar Republic when he was writing for *Die Tat*.[49] The staff of *Die Welt* has included several other brilliant journalists with unorthodox political views, men like Paul Sethe and Erich Kuby. The *Süddeutsche Zeitung*, a Munich daily paper, has become increasingly critical of Adenauer's leadership and must be counted as a leading exponent of the outsiders' views on foreign policy. Traces of a critical tendency are to be found also in the Stuttgart weekly *Christ und Welt* and now and then even in signed articles appearing in the usually pro-Adenauer *Frankfurter Allgemeine*. Among the magazines, Rudolf Augstein's widely read *Der Spiegel*, patterned on the American weekly *Time*, is as consistently hostile to Adenauer himself as it is to his foreign policy.

These newspapers and magazines are not representative of the Federal Republic's press. Their total circulation hovers around the one-million mark and they are likely to attract many more readers. Yet no other important German language newspapers (except the Swiss *Neue Zürcher Zeitung*, a staunch supporter of Adenauer's government) give broad coverage to foreign news and therefore *Die Welt*, the *Frankfurter Allgemeine*, and the *Süddeutsche Zeitung* are widely read by all leaders of public opinion in the Federal Republic. Some readers share the papers' editorial bias on foreign policy; the views of others, it may be assumed, are colored by the news items and editorials. Information and opinion slowly filter down to a much larger group of West Germans who are only beginning to stir from their political lethargy. As interest in matters of foreign policy spreads, the influence of these major newspapers can be expected to increase. The potential political power of Axel Springer, who owns by far the largest press concentration in West Germany, cannot be disregarded. In addition to *Die Welt*, Springer owns the tabloid *Bild-Zeitung*, with the largest circulation of any newspaper in western Europe, several weekly

49. *Neue Zürcher Zeitung*, February 9, 1958.

magazines, with a total circulation of over three million, the *Hamburger Abendblatt,* with approximately 300,000 readers, and an interest in the great Ullstein publishing house. Springer has never revealed what his political sympathies are, but he has at times let *Die Welt* follow a strong anti-Adenauer line, especially in foreign policy questions, and has permitted its passionate advocacy of greater efforts to achieve reunification. As a businessman, Springer may never allow his tabloid and popular journals to editorialize on political subjects. That would almost certainly "cut down" circulation and revenue. But if his politics should ever take precedence over his business interests, he could exercise considerable power throughout the Federal Republic by ordering all his publications to adopt a uniform editorial policy.[50]

The number of West Germans who are sufficiently well informed to participate constructively in deliberating Bonn's relations with the outside world appears to be on the increase. Teachers, government officials, publicists, and trade unionists are still quick to decry the lack of public interest in, and understanding of, foreign policy, but more and more often they couple criticism with an optimistic prognosis. They believe that spiritual and intellectual recovery from Nazism and from the last war, which has thus far lagged behind and been overshadowed by economic revival, will progress at a faster pace now that the people have achieved a new level of material security, and have put a distance of some years between themselves and "the catastrophe." Progress toward increased political awareness and a greater sense of communal responsibility is a step-by-step process. Many skeptical observers, both German and foreign, doubt that there is any real trend toward greater political maturity. Others are convinced that the trend is real but that it will not last because "of the two risks of petrification

50. There were indications that at least *Die Welt* would follow definite political lines from 1961. See "A Hamburg Publisher," *The Economist,* November 19, 1960.

of German politics and a break in the rhythm of economic expansion, the Germans prefer the first."[51]

Because they attack the staunchly pro-Western Chancellor, and criticize NATO's military strategy and the West's attitude toward negotiations with Moscow, the intellectual and journalist outsiders are frequently denounced by West German officials and in the foreign press as anti-Western, neutralists, and nationalists.[52] These charges, applied to a number of individuals, are just, but they are unjust to the great majority of those against whom they have been levelled. A few individuals, among them Hans Zehrer, can be accused on the basis of what they write, say, and do today, of wanting the Federal Republic "to cut her western ties" and to seek a "romantic 'Third' position between Bolshevism and Democracy."[53] These people are dangerous principally because they attack contemporary German society and Bonn's policies without having anything constructive to offer. In a crisis they could whip up hostility against the existing authorities, creating chaos in public opinion and a sense of futility, conditions which would make the country ripe for a revolution from above or below. Nihilists and Communist fellow-travelers are distinctly in the minority among them, though some, who are naïve, tend to believe that good will and summit conferences can settle all major East-West political problems. They are led by this illusion to play up Moscow's apparent willingness to compromise, and to discount Communist revolutionary aims. The majority are more realistic

51. Terrence Prittie in the *Manchester Guardian,* August 28, 1957. Cf. W. P. Davison, "Trends in West German Public Opinion, 1946-1956," *West German Leadership and Foreign Policy,* pp. 295-296, 304.

52. For example, see the *Neue Zürcher Zeitung,* February 9, 1958. Officials of the Federal Chancellory (*Bundeskanzleramt*) and a high-ranking American official in Bonn told the present writer that the intellectual outsiders are "weak toward Communism" and that they exert a "sinister influence."

53. *Ibid.*

and more responsible. They are in full accord with the basic aims of Bonn's policies; none of their criticisms can be accurately interpreted as a rejection of the Federal Republic's predominant Western orientation, or as a desire to repudiate its treaty obligations. They would not willingly sacrifice individual liberties or the nation's security to achieve reunification.

Despite the demands of the intellectuals, the outsiders, and the opposition parties that more and greater efforts be made to achieve unification, Bonn's foreign policy has consistently given priority to the strengthening of West German power, to the unification of western Europe, and to rearmament against the threat of Soviet aggression. The people's endorsement of Adenauer has had the effect of continuing these policies; this has been the primary significance in the CDU's election victories for contemporary West German relations with the U.S. and the West generally.

Interest in West Germany's foreign policy is interrelated with the intensity of the desire to achieve reunification, which, ostensibly at least, is the chief aim of Bonn's policies. The Adenauer government has repeatedly assured the people that German unity is its primary goal and that its activities are designed to solve the problem of partition without sacrificing the freedom and security of the Federal Republic. The opposition parties have gone even further, demanding that reunification must have priority at all times and that nothing be done that might make its achievement more difficult.

It is hardly surprising that all West German political forces focus attention on reunification. The Germans are not alone in seeking a solution, but the problem is, after all, first and foremost a German one. Public debates, newspaper articles, and political campaigns emphasize reunification, yet the depth and intensity of the West German people's interest in the matter is uncertain. Are they, perhaps, simply paying lip-service to an ideal? Is the government using the issue to exert pressure on the former Occupation powers for other objectives? Is reunification an urgent need, or could the

West Germans be reconciled to partition for a long time, perhaps indefinitely? Only when answers have been found to these questions can a sound judgment be made on a related question crucial for Western interests: What would West Germany be willing to do, and what would its people be willing to sacrifice for reunification?

No precise measurement is possible of the strength in West Germany of the desire for reunification. It varies from one section of the population to another and fluctuates from month to month. For most people partition is chiefly an emotional problem. It has uprooted many East Germans, dispossessed many more, and disrupted their family life. The plight of those who still suffer behind the Iron Curtain fills West Germans with a feeling of helpless anger. There are almost daily reports of outrages committed by the Ulbricht regime. The weekly influx of up to three thousand refugees dramatizes the situation. It is true that only a handful are, strictly speaking, political fugitives; some are criminals or otherwise undesirable, many come for personal reasons, but all, in some way or other, are victims of Communist rule and of the division of their country. Many West Germans who dislike their East German countrymen demand reunification in order to get the refugees out of the Federal Republic's towns and villages and back to their farms and cities beyond the Elbe. Others resent having to pay special taxes to resettle the refugees and wonder if they would have to pay more or less after reunification. The East German revolt of 1953 and the Hungarian action in 1956 confronted the West Germans with a dilemma. Some angrily demanded greater efforts to liberate the Eastern peoples; others became timid, fearing that the Federal Republic might become involved in a war.

Patriotism and selfish motives are combined in the complex of emotions that determine the attitudes of West Germans on reunification. They have been exposed to so many speeches on the subject that fresh efforts to arouse their interest, for example by the programs sponsored by *Unteilbares Deutschland* (Indivisible Germany), an organization partly financed by government, often fall on deaf ears. They find it difficult to keep their attention on a highly complex problem which, time and again, has defied solution. But it would be wrong to conclude that a significant number of West Germans have lost interest in restoring national unity. On the contrary, all are very much aware of the problem, believing that, sooner or later, action will have to be taken to solve it. Now that they have achieved a new level of personal welfare and a measure of self-confidence, we can expect that they will pay closer attention to their country's foreign relations and to proposals for unity. The propaganda of extremists could appeal only as long as the Germans were compensating for the lack of genuine national feeling by the deification of the tribe or race. What happens to be building up now is a genuine national feeling, a belief in the individual's right to freedom, including the right to live in peace in his homeland. Relapse into nationalist fanaticism would only be possible in the event of a collapse of the economy or some other grave misfortune.

With respect to reunification, the *Oberschicht*—the leaders in various sectors of West German life, commercial and cultural—are subject to the same cross-currents of emotion that affect the general public. Special interests cause some to favor steps to end partition. Foreign traders have not been strong proponents of German unity; the West German economy, without access to the markets of the Communist world, is dependent instead upon European, Asian, and American markets, and the prospects for trade with the Sino-Soviet bloc are not bright, though the desire to resume trade with these countries is growing.

Some commercial interests in the Federal Republic have been particularly hard hit by the division of the country. The port of Hamburg, because of the shipping business and allied activities concentrated there, has suffered severely. Cut off from traditional markets in eastern Europe, its merchants have found no substitutes. Conscious of the advantages of other ports more fortunately situated for trade with the West, and fearful that more of Hamburg's traditional trade will be lost to the new ports being built on the

Baltic, the city's traders and workers take a particularly strong interest in the early achievement of German unity.

For many intellectuals reunification is primarily a question of national responsibility in foreign affairs. Among them there is a strong current of opinion that Germany's middle position in Europe makes it incumbent upon her to build a bridge of understanding between East and West. They believe that Bonn has a special responsibility not only to reunify Germany but to aid the peaceful development of greater freedom in the East European countries. This belief may be illusory and dangerous. It certainly runs counter to current West German and NATO policies. But its motivation is neither wicked nor sinister. Those who espouse it are convinced that Germany's strategic central position in Europe gives her a unique opportunity to help in the restoration of peace in the world; some among them assert that Germany has a "moral debt" to mankind. The small circle of those who take this position includes, not surprisingly, some of the participants in the German resistance against Nazism and their descendants. They are conscience-stricken because they believe that the present tyranny in eastern Europe is a direct outcome of Hitler's aggression. If this accurate and honorable conception of special responsibility infects a larger segment of the population it may be transformed into an ambitious political drive for power under cover of a moral crusade. The danger of such a drive must be taken into account as long as Germany is divided, whether or not the lofty conception of special German responsibility for the peace of the world gains in popularity. In any event, there is a current of opinion in the Federal Republic which holds that Bonn can take steps to aid the peaceful liberation of East Germany and the rest of eastern Europe without jeopardizing the freedom and security of the West. Competent observers of the German scene disagree on nothing so much as on the chance that this opinion will become an effective political force.

Leading businessmen, West German members of the clergy, and

others—the kind of people who are most likely to have contacts with American, British, and other visitors—declare themselves in favor of reunification. Some of them, however, will confide even to foreigners that to achieve this goal they would not sacrifice the Federal Republic's relations with the West or even a measure of the security obtained from her ties with the United States. Their insistence that not only their own political leaders but also the Federal Republic's allies must continue to pay lip-service to the early achievement of reunification, one suspects, is due to the desire to impress the listener with their confidence in the trustworthiness of the Federal Republic. The Germans know their allies fear that resurgent German nationalism will take the form of a drive for reunification at the expense of Bonn's obligations to NATO and western Europe. They are anxious to be reassuring, caring less whether or not what they say really represents their thoughts. In many cases their statements are sincere.

Businessmen, bankers, and churchmen in close contact with the Bonn government are better informed than most of their countrymen about the Soviets' intractable attitude on reunification. They have come to the conclusion that nothing their government or its allies can do, without taking dangerous risks, will speed a solution of the problem. Furthermore, many bankers and industrialists in West Germany have no strong economic motives for restoring national unity. As long as East Germany remains comparatively poor, with an economy organized on Communist lines, reunification would impose greater hardships on West Germany and raise more difficulties than the satisfaction of achieving territorial unity would seem to warrant. If the East German economy is strengthened, becoming, on balance, a desirable component of an all-German economy, West Germany's powerful financial and commercial leaders may decide that, taking into account human and political as well as economic factors, unity is worth working and sacrificing for. In any event, it would be unwise to assume that, over a longer period, economic motives will determine political behavior to the exclusion of patriotic sentiments and other motives. And if a major economic setback in West Germany should occur it would, as we have suggested earlier, almost certainly intensify the demand for unification in all areas of West German life.

The Roman Catholic Church has often been designated by Germans and others as the opponent of German reunification. Many members of the hierarchy are indeed something less than enthusiastic about reincorporating the Protestant East into the German nation, but there is no evidence that they are actively opposed to reunification. A few Roman Catholics who draw inspiration from the weekly diatribes of the *Rheinischen Merkur,* cherish the fanciful notion of realizing Charlemagne's ideal and may fear that reunification will spoil their dream. Their belief that the "Christian West" has a divine mission is potentially a dangerous one. It has not been adopted by any significant political group, although Adenauer has upheld it on at least one public occasion, when in January 1960 he told Pope John XXIII, "I believe that God has given the German people a special task in these stormy times, to be the guardians of the West against the powerful influences which are pressing upon us from the East."[54] Adenauer may actually believe this or he may have thought it politically expedient to say so. But certainly the Roman Catholic Church does not oppose German unity or support a militant "liberation" policy. Its considerable political influence with Adenauer and with the country could not conceivably be aimed at a purpose contrary to that of the Vatican, which is dedicated to freeing all Roman Catholics from the yoke of Communism. Indeed, the Church seems more likely to lend itself to conciliatory efforts between Bonn and eastern Europe—Warsaw for example—than to the reprehensible purpose of widening the gulf that separates East and West.

In summary, significant forces in the Federal Republic are unenthusiastic about reunification. One finds conflicts of interest, especially in the commercial world, which dissipate the power behind reunification efforts. Such conflicts are not of lasting importance and in all sectors of society one finds a keen awareness of the

54. *Bulletin,* January 23, 1960.

partition problem which, as interest in foreign policy increases, will inevitably arouse a more widespread concern.

The general lassitude about reunification is a manifestation of frustration at repeated failures to make progress toward a solution through diplomatic means. Hopes for a settlement are intimately connected with the display of public interest. This, in turn, depends upon the people's understanding of Moscow's aims, policies, and actions, and their approval or disapproval of the military and political responses of the West. World events will help to determine the extent to which the West Germans will exercise patience with the impasse. But occasional signs of apathy and discouragement resulting from increased fears and diminished hopes should not obscure the firm resolve of the major political parties and all major West German social groups to focus attention on reunification. Most Germans in the West realize that there is no quick or easy way to reunite their divided country, but they are not resigned to the status quo as more than a temporary expedient. Nothing is more likely to cause them to take precipitous action to redress their grievance than evidence that their allies have lost interest in their plight.

Reunification, then, is the principal issue in Bonn's foreign policy. The problem requires constant attention. It cannot be ignored; sooner or later it will have to be solved. Partition is a source of potential peril to the stability of the Federal Republic. Outside influences or a major economic setback may, at the most unexpected time, give rise to demands for a drastic remedy.

There is no single answer to the question: How much would the West Germans sacrifice to achieve unity? What their government can do to bring about reunification depends largely on factors beyond its control—on world events and on the policies of other nations. But the government can depend at all times on widespread popular support for initiatives it might want to take in this direction.

four

■

WEST GERMANY, DE GAULLE, AND EUROPEAN UNITY

The Adenauer government experienced its blackest moments during the crisis of the Fourth Republic and the accession of De Gaulle in 1958. Since the war, German opinion has been divided about the relative merits of a strong or a weak French neighbor. There has been a fundamental disagreement on this point even among the many elements that support collaboration with France, including leading members of the major parties, the trade unions, and industrial interests. Some believed that the weaknesses of French governments under the Fourth Republic, and their preoccupation with the remnants of Empire in Asia and Africa and the dislocation of French economic life, constituted a blessing in disguise for West Germany during her political and economic rehabilitation. A France distracted from Europe and intent on domestic problems could not have the time or energy to hold back her aspiring neighbor to the east or compete effectively in new postwar markets. Thus it appeared to some Germans that the *rapprochement* with France advanced a pace with every new blow suffered by the Fourth Republic.

Other West Germans—among the leading public figures most prominently Walter Hallstein, Franz Etzel, and above all Adenauer himself—were of a contrary opinion. As the German architects of a united western Europe they feared that a weak France would not have the courage to enter into European economic and cultural coöperative schemes aimed at eventual political integration. As Christian Democrats, they aspired to the revitalization of a Christian Europe in which people could live without fear of the Soviet menace of revolution and military attack, and in which German aspirations for reunification could eventually be realized. Europe's rebirth would miscarry, they feared, if the economic, political, and military debilitation of France continued. Under the CDU's leadership Bonn's policies, especially since 1955, have therefore been aimed at helping France to become economically prosperous, politically stable, and militarily strong. Adenauer has taken every opportunity to support French governments and their policies, even backing them against Washington's occasional anticolonial sallies, although never to the extent of identifying Bonn with France's lost causes in Indo-China and North Africa.[1]

The Adenauer government had not, however, reckoned with the French crisis of 1958. For several years up to that time General De Gaulle's return to power had been considered in West German quarters as most unlikely. And the general opinion was that if De Gaulle succeeded in his ambition to regain power it would amount to a catastrophe second to none for West German policy. When the event took place, those Germans who had held that the *rapprochement* depended on a strong France feared the outbreak of a revolution that would destroy France's usefulness as a partner, while those who believed the partnership workable only if France were weak feared the accession of rightist-nationalist forces in Paris headed by De Gaulle, who himself had never been counted among Germany's friends. In 1945 he had advocated the dissolution of the vanquished German state on the ground that "the nature

1. For example, Adenauer backed Paris in the dispute over Anglo-American arms shipments to Tunisia in November 1957; *New York Times,* November 17, 1957. Also, Bonn's payments of support costs for French forces in West Germany in excess of the amount required to support the French troops actually stationed there constitutes a subsidy of French forces fighting in Algeria.

of the Germans inclines them to vast ambitions."[2] De Gaulle had all along been a consistently outspoken opponent of all forms of European integration. De Gaulle's assumption of power in 1958 was therefore bound to be regarded by Adenauer as a major threat to the policies which Bonn, with American support, had been following.

Some of the wildest German fears of De Gaulle were quickly laid to rest. He did not reverse what must surely be counted as a major accomplishment of the postwar period, the burial of the historic feud between France and Germany which had torn Europe asunder in two world wars. Indeed, in a limited sense De Gaulle has made the alliance with Bonn one of the pivots of the Fifth Republic's policies.

The future of the Bonn-Paris relationship will be shaped, above all, by the coincidence of German and French interests in Europe. Hardly less important will be the development of the French political system under De Gaulle and afterwards. Democracy in France has been stifled since the crisis of 1958. The "ambiguous and badly conceived Constitution [of the Fifth Republic] does not inspire confidence in anybody and does not seem destined to last."[3] The Constitution is, in fact, simply a vehicle for De Gaulle who, alone, inspires confidence in France today. Whether he will outlive the Constitution, or France's need of him, are uncertainties beyond fruitful speculation. France's allies, like the majority of Frenchmen themselves, have had to resign themselves to an indefinite period of autocratic rule, hoping for effective yet accountable government, and preparing for the worst to happen when the indispensable man no longer stands between France and disaster.

France's allies have been quick to learn that although De Gaulle's rule is leading to completely unpredictable ends, for as

2. Quoted by G. P. Gooch, "Franco-German Coexistence at Last?" *Foreign Affairs*, XXXVII (April 1959), 438.

3. Jean-Marie Domenach, "Democratic Paralysis in France," *Foreign Affairs*, XXXVII (October 1958), 43.

long as it lasts France's behavior is more readily predictable than it was under the Fourth Republic. For the first time since 1946, France is being given strong, active leadership. De Gaulle's massive ambition, the resurrection of France as a great power, and his conceit in the grandeur of France, have had their positive counterpart in the rebirth of self-confidence and the shrewd representation of French interests by his government.

De Gaulle's supreme confidence in France's innate greatness and in himself as the agent of its transformation, have made it possible for him to act decisively where the harassed leaders of the Fourth Republic feared to act at all. France had for years hesitated to commit herself firmly to the Common Market partnership with Germany without the involvement of Britain in the new association. The British, assuming France's dependency on their participation in the scheme, played on French fears of being left alone with the Germans. De Gaulle's France, however, could not be intimidated. Thus when the showdown over the Free Trade area came in the autumn and winter of 1958, De Gaulle, far from frightened by the prospect of a European market and protective wall in league with West Germany, boldly seized the initiative and insisted on implementing the Common Market treaty on schedule without acceding to the compromises that might have permitted Britain and other Free Trade countries to participate. This was a decisive step for France, away from protectionism within Europe and toward currency convertibility. De Gaulle could afford to take these risks, chiefly that France might become more dependent upon Ruhr heavy industry, because he was assured that Adenauer's Germany was prepared to aid France with loans if need be and because Germany's wealth could be used to develop France's African possessions.[4] West Germany's reserves have become, in effect, French assets.

4. According to C. L. Sulzberger, Adenauer believes that Europe must be "tightly linked" with Africa because "otherwise . . . Africa will go Communist"; *New York Times,* June 8, 1959; June 11, 1960.

De Gaulle, then, has been willing to gamble on France's future competition with German industry in order to have its support now, so that France may become independent of all foreign economic support, including American military aid, on which she has had to depend since 1948, and therefore also more independent of British and American foreign policy. So far the gamble has paid off.

French industry has taken to the Common Market as a duck to water. The fear that French prices would be too high and French methods too outdated to meet German competition has proved to be exaggerated. It is the Germans who have begun to wonder whether they will be the ones to run the show.[5]

In the course of the 1958 negotiations to expand the Common Market to provide for a Free Trade area, De Gaulle forced Adenauer to make a choice between, on the one hand, Britain and German economic interests in independent free trade, and on the other hand, collaboration with France and support of those German economic interests best served by the establishment of the Common Market. Up to this point Adenauer, with the urging of Minister of Economics Erhard, had tried to act as a mediator between London and Paris—between the Free Trade and Common Market proponents. But when De Gaulle forced Bonn to make a clear choice, there was absolutely no doubt which way Adenauer would go. He had, after all, never left any doubt that he attached overriding importance to Franco-German collaboration. Economic interests and Ludwig Erhard did not stand in the Chancellor's way (they never have) when he saw an opportunity to achieve his grand political design, the rebirth of the Empire of Charlemagne in modern times. If it was clear to Adenauer in November 1958 that by supporting France's obdurate stand against the Free Trade zone he risked a deterioration in the climate of relations between Bonn

5. "France and the Common Market," *Manchester Guardian Weekly,* April 28, 1960.

and London, this did not deter him.[6] In the event, the crisis in the Free Trade area negotiations coincided with the first fissure in the Western alliance over the response to Khrushchev's offensive against Berlin and Western policy towards Moscow generally. Bonn and Paris, for different reasons, feared that the Macmillan government would influence the Eisenhower administration to agree to compromise over Berlin to the extent of supporting some form of "disengagement" proposal in central Europe. The Adenauer-De Gaulle meeting at Bad Kreuznach took place under the shadow of this threat, and there are strong indications that the two leaders sealed a bargain which assured France of West German backing in support of the Common Market and against the Free Trade area proposal, while De Gaulle promised Adenauer support in resisting any Western tendency to compromise on Berlin.[7] Thus, instead of renouncing the links that had been forged between Paris and Bonn, as the Germans had feared, De Gaulle has in fact acted to strengthen the relationship.

But there is no Bonn-Paris axis. Very real ties have indeed grown up between Adenauer and De Gaulle personally; they are two of a kind. Even the personal relationship, although it is cordial, is not based on affection, and there is no identity of purpose between the two countries. It is a *mariage de convenance* rather than of love, and its purposes are conceived of differently by the two

6. The Free Trade area negotiations were broken off on November 16 following M. Soustelle's categorical rejection of the British idea. Ten days later, Adenauer met De Gaulle at Bad Kreuznach to discuss the relationship between the Six and the other OEEC members, and also the new Soviet threat to Berlin. The communique issued after these talks did not mention the Free Trade area. On December 10 Bonn announced that Adenauer could not visit London as planned because he had contracted flu "coupled with a light fever." The report went on to say that "no new date for the trip has been agreed upon"; *Informationsfunk der Bundesregierung,* December 10, 1958. In London Adenauer's cancellation of the visit was interpreted as an "abrupt about-face" indicating full German support of the French position; *New York Times,* February 24, 1959.

7. See, for example, the report in the *New York Times* cited in n. 6.

partners. De Gaulle is dedicated to France; he does not believe in a new Europe. His antagonism to integration and all forms of supranationalism is undiminished since his fight against the EDC and the Coal and Steel Community. "I have not changed my fundamental views," he said in the spring of 1959, "the only change, you might say, is that I have become more indulgent of others."[8] De Gaulle's indulgence toward those dedicated to integration goes just so far as it suits the interests of France, as he understands them. He does not share Adenauer's ideal of a European political community, but does not object if that is the Chancellor's over-all goal in collaborating with the French government.

Despite French hostility to his aims, Adenauer remains optimistic that an integrated political community will gradually emerge from the collaboration of the Six. The chief problem that seems to concern him in achieving political integration is continuity of leadership in the Six, especially in Germany and France. The Franco-German partnership today is widely regarded as dependent on the continued leadership of De Gaulle and Adenauer. Adenauer has at times made it appear that he believes himself indispensable to the continuance of the alliance and the achievement of political integration. He cited Secretary Dulles' death and the worsening international situation as the reasons for his disavowal of the CDU's nomination for the presidency of the Federal Republic in June 1959, yet there is very little doubt that the chief cause of Adenauer's *volte-face* was the fear of what would become of the alliance with Paris if the CDU named Erhard to succeed him as Chancellor instead of his hand-picked choice, Franz Etzel, who could have been expected to carry on Adenauer's foreign policy. It was generally believed that Erhard, unlike Etzel, could not have been dominated by his predecessor in the Chancellor's office,

8. D. Schoenbrun, "Measuring the Mystique of De Gaulle," *Saturday Review*, May 16, 1959. Cf. C. L. Sulzberger, "Paris Winner: II—Help To Europe's Unity," *New York Times,* June 11, 1960.

and that Erhard would have attempted to liberalize the terms of the Common Market to prevent the split into the Sixes and Sevens, even at the expense of straining the bonds of alliance with Paris. Adenauer's suspicions of Erhard, well founded or not, were at the root of his decision to remain as Chancellor after all. Although Adenauer pointed to Geneva and Washington to explain his decision, the real explanation was to be found in Paris. His disappointment with Etzel and the CDU has made Adenauer consider himself all the more indispensable now in the creation of a European political community.

In June 1959 Adenauer declared that he would not retire until after the 1961 elections. In the same interview he said that the Six "would have to work faster" towards economic and political unity than was agreed in the Rome treaty. The unification schedule had to be accelerated if Adenauer was to be sure that the Franco-German relationship could survive his retirement and the continuation of De Gaulle's rule and unpredictable indulgence.[9]

In the winter of 1959-1960 Walter Hallstein, President of the European Economic Community Commission, advocated precisely the kind of speed-up Adenauer had in mind. Hallstein proposed a twenty per cent tariff cut within the community and a thirty per cent adjustment of external duties toward an eventual single Common Market tariff against nonmember countries. The Hallstein Plan, which also envisioned a one-fifth reduction in the future common external tariff, was to go into effect July 1, 1960, eighteen months ahead of the timetable established in the Rome treaty of 1957. This plan was bitterly attacked by Britain and the other Outer Seven nations on two grounds. In the short run the acceleration would require a sharp increase in Dutch, Belgian, and especially in West German tariffs against outsiders. The West German increases would be the most damaging, since the Federal Republic lowered some tariffs by twenty-five per cent in 1957 and would now

9. *New York Times,* June 18, 1959.

be required to raise them above the 1957 levels. West Germany, moreover, is much the biggest market among the Six for members of the Seven.[10] The Seven opposed the Hallstein plan also on the grounds that if it had been put into effect on July 1, 1960 it would have prevented fresh attempts at negotiation to overcome the division of Western Europe into two trading and political entities. Despite the opposition of Britain and her Free Trade Area associates, the U.S. government strongly supported the acceleration proposal.[11]

In May 1960 Ludwig Erhard, West German Minister of Economics, gained Adenauer's acceptance of a compromise plan to postpone the starting date of the Hallstein Plan to January 1, 1961.

10. The effect of the Hallstein Plan on West German tariffs can be seen in the following table:

	PRESENT GERMAN TARIFF (*In per cents*)	FUTURE COMMON EEC TARIFF (*In per cents; excluding proposed 20-per-cent reduction*)
Automobiles	13-16	27-29
Motorcycles	11-14	24-26
Bicycles	9	21
Cameras	4	18
Watches	4-11	11-13
Radio & TV sets	11	22
Electrical household appliances	7	20
Machinery	0-9	4-17
Cutlery	4	17-18
Shoes & clothing	8-13	20-22
Artificial fibers	4-11	12-15
Linoleum	4	20
Carpets & rugs	14-16	22-40

Source: *International Financial News Survey* (International Fund) May 6, 1960.

11. *New York Times,* March 20 and May 1, 1960; *Bulletin Der Presse-Und Informationsamtes Der Bundesregierung,* March 19, 1960; and see below, pp. 134-135, 264-265.

Later in the same month representatives of the Six meeting in Luxembourg approved the Hallstein Plan in principle but also agreed to the postponement of the starting date. The delay appears to have been dictated more by necessity than by any general agreement with Erhard's desire to reopen negotiations with Britain and the other Free Trade Area nations. "Both the Italian and German representatives said in the [Luxembourg] meeting that it would take six months for their parliaments to approve necessary changes in tariff laws."[12] It is also widely believed that Adenauer's agreement to the postponement of the speed-up was dictated by a desire to assure that Erhard, a crucial vote-getting asset for the CDU, would again take second place on the party ticket in 1961.

The British government responded to the postponement of the Hallstein Plan by declaring its conditional preparedness to participate in the European Coal and Steel Community and Euratom. However, London was anxious not to give the impression that its more positive position toward Europe would lead to its joining the Common Market.[13]

For Adenauer the postponement of the Hallstein Plan was a necessary evil. From his standpoint the partnership with France has a transcendent value, going beyond immediate interests, and certainly beyond economic interests. Adenauer mistrusts his countrymen if they are left entirely to their own devices, and fears a revival of nationalism in France unless she is bound up with her continental neighbors in a working association, but he envisages a bright new future for a western European community which harnesses French intellectual qualities and German organizing genius. These hopes and fears have led Adenauer to tolerate, though grudgingly, occasional French nationalistic outbursts, and have made him willing to make economic sacrifices, or what some commercial interests in West Germany regard as economic sacrifices,

12. *New York Times,* May 11, 1960.
13. *Ibid.,* June 8, 1960; *British Record,* No. 10, June 27, 1960.

in order to maintain and strengthen the ties with Paris.[14] For the same reasons, Adenauer accepted with apparent calm De Gaulle's pronouncements favoring the Oder-Neisse line as Germany's final eastern boundary;[15] and when De Gaulle made a bid to gain special NATO status for France, on a par with Britain and the United States and above Bonn, the West German government did not make a public issue of the problem. By these means the German Chancellor has sought to increase the French political stake in collaboration with the Federal Republic, which, he knows, in the final analysis, will count more heavily than economic benefits. It is, in fact, a calculated play to De Gaulle's vanity. For, having turned his back on the entente with Britain, resentful of U.S. tutelage and determined to diminish it, preoccupied with the Algerian war abroad and the difficulties of establishing a stable government under a new constitution at home, De Gaulle has no alternative—in Bonn's view—but to rely for support on France's major continental neighbor. Adenauer seeks to transform this dependency into an indispensable alliance. The only alternative for De Gaulle is a theoretical one: a bilateral *modus vivendi* with Moscow. But Adenauer has reasoned that conditions have changed since De Gaulle made a bid for coöperation with Soviet Russia in 1944, which was unsuccessful, and that France's increasing financial dependence on the Federal Republic will rule out another such attempt, even if De

14. For West Germany's compromises in deference to French interests in the negotiations leading to the signing of the Rome treaties, see the English-language supplement to *Wirtschaftsdienst* (Hamburg), No. 7, July 1957; and Articles 19 and 20 and Annex A of the Treaty Establishing the European Economic Community (Rome treaties); *European Yearbook* (The Hague, 1958), IV, 425, 427, 539–545. The Federal Republic also contributed $200,000,000 to a common investment fund for the economic development of the overseas territories of the Six, although she herself has no overseas territories; *Bulletin from the European Community for Coal and Steel*, No. 22 (February-March 1957), p. 4.

15. De Gaulle's news conference statement of March 25, 1959, *New York Times*, March 26, 1959. An exceptionally mild West German retort was published the following day; *ibid.*, March 27, 1959.

Gaulle should remain in power long enough to have a realistic hope of accomplishing something by it.[16]

On both sides, then, the Franco-German collaboration is built, not on sentiment or—except for Adenauer personally—on a European consciousness, but rather on shrewd analysis of self-interest. The motives that have led France and the Federal Republic into their *mariage de convenance* are not only dissimilar but appear to be unreconcilable. It is, nevertheless, a working relationship because it benefits both parties, and each is willing to gamble that its interests are being served by the indefinite postponement of a showdown over the issue of political integration, and that its interests would be served by such a showdown if it ever takes place.

This realistic basis of contemporary Franco-German relations is to be welcomed, but the relationship at present gives no sign of leading toward a "United States of Europe" as some excessively credulous partisans of Franco-German unity believe. A cynic might say that a compromise has been reached between the Germans who want a united Europe without appearing to do so, and the French who do not mind giving the appearance of working toward unity as long as it is not achieved. In any event, Dr. Adenauer's blunt assurance "that we shall soon have a European Political Union," with which he has regaled audiences for more than ten years, remains more of an article of faith than a prediction of imminent accomplishment.[17]

American policy-makers who, under both administrations since 1945, have consistently urged military, economic, and political

16. In an obvious bid to undermine Franco-German confidence, the Moscow publication *International Life* published in May 1959 the Soviet stenographic report of De Gaulle's conversations with Stalin in December 1944. Excerpts from these accounts, which revealed De Gaulle's determination to emasculate the German nation and his acceptance of the Oder-Neisse boundary between Germany and Poland and of the Curzon line between Poland and Soviet Russia, were reprinted in *Die Welt*, May 29 and June 2, 1959.

17. See, for example, Adenauer's address at the Waldorf-Astoria Hotel on April 16, 1953, before the American Committee on United Europe.

unity on the Western Europeans, are faced today with a complex picture which shows some progress toward the ideal, but also, in apparent contradiction, a resurgence of nationalist aspirations and cant, in Germany as well as in France.

The Coal and Steel Community, which came into existence in 1952, is the progenitor of the European Economic Community and of the European Atomic Energy Community, and the only one of the collaborative ventures so far with functioning supranational powers invested in its High Authority. The Coal and Steel Community was especially beneficial for West Germany because it replaced the Ruhr Statute under which the Germans were denied maximum use of the resources and industrial capacity of the Ruhr which was to be placed under international administration. Since 1952 the Community has functioned efficiently. Although coal production has lagged, steel production has increased sharply; intra-Community trade in iron and steel products increased seventeen per cent during the first five years. Mining and steel-making targets for the period ending in 1965 indicate extraordinary potential gains which should make this coöperative effort a permanent feature of the European scene, of equal interest to the Six participating nations. The limited power of which the High Authority actually disposes, despite its nominally supranational standing, was made clear in March 1959, when France and Germany vetoed the authority's edict to cut back coal production.[18] In the course of a debate over this issue in the Assembly of the Community, the French Minister of Industry and Commerce, Jean-Marcel Jeanneney, indicated that De Gaulle, who had opposed the Coal and Steel treaty when it was submitted in 1951,

18. Thirty-two million tons of coal and coke had piled up at the Community's pitheads at this time. See the reports on the crisis in the *New York Times,* March 3, 5-8 and April 22, 1959. Earlier in the year Bonn had brushed aside American protests and imposed a 10-per-cent tariff in order to curb coal imports from the United States; *ibid.,* January 24, 30, and 31, 1959.

now wanted it revised, presumably to revoke those clauses which gave the High Authority nominal supranational powers. In the same vein, high officials of the Bonn government, backed by powerful business interests, were incensed by the High Authority's proposal in February 1959 to install an inspector in the Ruhr to guard against cartel marketing practices in coal, of which the Germans had been accused.[19] Although these retreats from the supranational principle at the first sign of crisis have not dismayed the advocates of greater unity, skeptical observers have pointed to such incidents as proof that the foundation of a European political community does not yet exist.

The experience of coördinating Europe's economic recovery under the Marshall Plan and the auspicious start of the Coal and Steel Community gave a strong impetus to the negotiations for a European Economic Community, to weld the European Six into a single mass market which could be competitive with the economic power of the United States and the Soviet bloc. This proposal had strong German support right from the first for a variety of reasons. The Adenauer government, which has given it a solid backing, has valued it above all for its importance as a step in the direction of a European political federation, and this remains the Chancellor's principal interest in it. Speaking at Brussels in 1956, Adenauer gave his reasons for emphasizing political integration. "Russia," he said, "has shown a tendency to expand, that is, to be a threat to her neighbors." If Russia was not to consolidate and possibly expand her postwar frontiers, Europe had to unify her defense against aggression. The defense of Europe, Adenauer continued, could only be undertaken with American support; but although he acknowledged "in all gratitude and admiration" that the United States had fulfilled the responsibility which her concentration of the free world's power entailed, he warned that "in

19. *Ibid.*, February 20, 1959 and *Journal Officiel* of the European Communities, March 7, 1959.

the long run the European countries cannot fully develop their
entire strength for their own benefit and that of mankind if they
continue to find their salvation and their security exclusively
under the patronage of the United States." The dependency upon
the United States "must not become a permanent condition"
Adenauer said, because "it would cause the energies of Europe
to wither" and "because surely the United States will not be
inclined to give Europe an unreasonable amount of assistance
permanently." Adenauer concluded this series of remarks with a
pointed warning which, since he was speaking against the background of Washington's hostile reaction to the Anglo-French
action in Suez, took on special meaning for the European governments: "The vital necessities of European countries need not
always be identical with the vital necessities of the United States
and vice versa."[20]

In the same speech Adenauer said that the failure of the EDC
could be traced to the "exaggerated perfectionism in creating the
treaties," a fault which he has elsewhere identified as a peculiarly
European "disease."[21] The remark can be interpreted also as a
slap at the rigid insistence of the United States on a particular
formula for the European army and, over-all, at the initial stress
on European military integration in Europe in American policy
during 1950-1954, which prevented the nations from starting on
economic and political collaboration, where, many believe, just
as essential and more fruitful progress could have been made
earlier.

The 1954 defeat of the EDC was a sharp setback for the
European cause. It led also to the acceptance of the Federal
Republic into NATO as a virtual equal. This unforeseen develop-
ment, in turn, permitted the emancipation of West Germany from
Allied occupation, and since the attainment of this objective had
been a principal driving force behind the European movement in

20. *The Bulletin* (English-language edition), Bonn, October 4, 1956.
21. Speech at the Waldorf-Astoria Hotel, April 16, 1953.

Germany—on the assumption by Germans that they would be permitted to live more independently only in the context of an integrated Europe—it led quite naturally to a reduction of German interest in European unity. Emancipation from foreign control, the resurrection of a stable society, and a thriving economy were achieved without sacrificing national sovereignty. Indeed, in return for pledges to collaborate in good faith with NATO, West Germany regained her sovereignty.

Some of the Christian Democratic leadership, especially the Roman Catholics among them, and the intellectual segment of the CDU rank and file, have all along considered West European unity an ideological mission—"the preservation of Western culture and the guardianship of peace," as Adenauer expressed it in his book.[22] For Adenauer and some others the unification of western Europe is a mission rooted in religious conviction. Most Germans, however, considered the Common Market and Euratom schemes simply on their merits. That is, they weighed the advantages and disadvantages for West Germany and decided to support or oppose the proposals on the basis of their particular self-interest. On this basis, both proposals have gradually gained strong support from the West German public. This has been demonstrated by the stands the major parties have taken on the proposals, including the opposition Free Democrats and Social Democrats who, after initially opposing the measures, gave their "unanimous" support for "extensions in the powers of the Community . . . which were found to be the best way of furthering European integration."[23] Most of the nonsectarian support for the Common Market in the Federal Republic comes from German businessmen who believe they are in an especially favorable position to exploit the new

22. *World Indivisible* (London, 1956), p. 49.

23. SPD declaration at the Common Assembly of the Coal and Steel Community in May 1955, cited in *Euratom and the Common Market,* pamphlet published by the American Committee on United Europe, December 1956.

European market. A dominant element in the Federation of German Industries has backed the Common Market from the start. Moreover, there is in German business a tendency towards bigness as such which has been taking the form of both horizontal and vertical industrial combinations in the Federal Republic, and this tendency has found a new outlet in the formation of powerful industrial amalgamations across Europe. Above all, West Germany has the capital to assure her a favorable position in the European combines and alliances that have been mushrooming among the Six.

There is opposition, too, to the Common Market in West German commercial circles, from business interests led by Vice-Chancellor Ludwig Erhard; they fear the loss of markets outside the Community if France, as expected, insists on setting up a tariff wall. These circles are confident that Germany can "go it alone" more profitably and that economic interests should not be sacrificed to theoretical—and some insist, denominational—political principles. Some businessmen are worried about the increased burden in social security payments when these are standardized among the Six; and there are industrial and, even more prominent, agricultural interests, which oppose the Common Market because they fear the loss of tariff protection within the Community. So far Chancellor Adenauer has exerted his influence to suppress this opposition, but under other, weaker leadership—and certainly if Ludwig Erhard should succeed to the Chancellor's post—elements favoring a slowdown in the creation of an economic community, those who desire a less stringent Free Trade area instead, and those who oppose, in principle, the imposition of supranational restrictions on their economic freedom will gain a stronger and possibly a dominant voice in Bonn.

The Euratom agreement also has opponents in Germany. Even after the Suez crisis demonstrated Europe's vulnerability as long as it is dependent on Middle Eastern oil, the Germans, geared to coal, were less anxious than their neighbors to develop atomic energy fuel alternatives. Some qualified technical and industrial circles in the Federal Republic are convinced that they could develop atomic energy for peaceful purposes themselves, provided that an established nuclear power were willing to make available to them on a bilateral basis a fraction of the financial and technical assistance the U.S. has promised to Euratom. These arguments, despite support in Adenauer's cabinet, have been overruled by the Chancellor himself. The opposition has not been suppressed permanently and will be heard from again now that the speed and programming of Euratom are clearly failing to meet the expectations of those interested in utilizing nuclear energy for peaceful purposes.

The division in the Federal Republic over the Common Market and Euratom emphasizes the primacy of political motives on the part of the chief forces supporting these measures and the economic motives of the opposition, yet the opposition also has strong political motives of growing importance, bound up with the prospects of German reunification and the development of a German Eastern policy.[24]

At the same time that the Schuman Plan, Common Market, and Euratom institutions were being created, some important though less spectacular coöperative developments of a more informal character were taking hold in Europe. Writers, government servants, school children, teachers, lawyers, and doctors from the European Six have exchanged visits with increased frequency. European conferences of all kinds have been held to increase understanding and to undertake common projects. A twelve-nation TV link (EUROVISION) now subjects a potential audience larger than an American nation-wide hook-up to its weekly blandishments; four European airlines have prepared to integrate their schedules, sales, and maintenance operations (EUROP-

24. See below, pp. 124-126, 131.

AIR); and under the label EUROP, the European railways have pooled their freight cars for maximum efficiency.

The effects of this quiet revolution are already being felt. Europeans have become better acquainted and are overcoming, though more slowly than many Americans imagine, the bitter hostility of two world wars and the nationalistic propaganda taught under the guise of history to generations of school children. Discontent with the divisions that led to the catastrophes of the past has led to the recognition that interdependence is not only a slogan, but an irrevocable fact of life. Discontent—"the first step in the progress of a man or a nation"—and fear of Soviet encroachments and of American abandonment, are enforcing the realization that the nations of Europe must coöperate or risk the loss of their national identity. Americans do not have a monopoly on togetherness; a sense of belonging together is evident among the Europeans too. But while the necessity and advantages of working together are clear, the form interdependence is to take remains in doubt and dispute.

The Council of Europe has been the most useful institution for formal and informal discussions of these coöperative enterprises. At its founding in 1949, the Council of Europe was hailed as "the first Parliament of Europe," a notion with as little validity today as ten years ago. The Committee of Ministers does indeed serve as a convenient framework for agreements among the West European governments, but these could just as well be reached in another setting. The annual meetings of the Consultative Assembly, which is to represent the peoples of the member states and discuss questions of common concern, echo with the platitudes of parliamentary representatives making a name for themselves. The Assembly has no real authority and no immediate prospect of gaining any. The debates under the Council's auspices have a useful purpose, nonetheless, for in the exchanges, often cutting across national allegiances and party loyalties, differences of opinion about the future of the European movement have been brought out into the open. The broad division has been between those favoring integration for particular purposes under supranational authorities with the aim of creating an integrated political community, and those who favor coöperative unity—the development of common policies in negotiations among sovereign governments.

Several subordinate themes have also been in the focus of attention: what countries are to be united? Is it Western Europe, and does that denote the Six—or are the Six only a nucleus to attract the Scandinavian countries, Switzerland, Austria, and Britain? What if the other OEEC members are not attracted to the Common Market? Will the Six compromise, or will they ignore the rest of Europe? And then a question that is asked with increased frequency: can the union of the Six endure as long as the Continent remains divided? And can the Common Market survive a reunification of Europe? Finally, and of chief importance here, how dependable a member is the Federal Republic, considering the changing balance of power between East and West and the approaching end of Adenauer's reign, and in the light of the persisting and, indeed, growing pressures for German reunification?

These are problems of more than academic and passing importance, and they must be answered not only by Bonn's European allies but also by the United States, whose economic, military, and political interests are certain to be profoundly affected by the manner in which they are resolved.

Nationalism was not a potent force on the surface of European politics in the early postwar period, and there were strong hopes that the growth of economic collaboration would keep nationalism dormant. Since 1958, experienced observers have been pointing to a "zealous nationalist tide" rising on the Continent.[25] At the closing session of the Atlantic Congress in June 1959, which

25. C. L. Sulzberger, "Europe's New Nationalist Generation," *New York Times,* January 14, 1959.

dutifully and solemnly passed resolutions calling for greater collaboration in all fields among NATO members, the most pertinent—and most vigorously applauded—remarks were made by Lewis W. Douglas. He said that "the greatest disease from which we now suffer" is "the increasing manifestations in every nation of excessive nationalism."[26] These manifestations are particularly evident in the middle-aged generation which will take power in France, Germany, and Italy from the senior statesmen who have controlled the European governments since 1945. It is an odd coincidence that Erhard and Strauss in the Federal Republic, Enrico Mattei in Italy, and Debré and Soustelle in France are on the verge of inheriting the apparatus of power just at the moment when distinct progress towards European integration is being made.

The unmistakable signs of resurgent nationalism, highlighted by De Gaulle but by no means restricted to France, would have come as less of a shock if analyses of European affairs, particularly in the United States, had not for so long focused attention on the left-wing opposition forces as the principal danger to European unity and collective defense. With respect to Germany in particular, U.S. policy-makers have been inclined to view the SPD, not Adenauer's rightist supporters, as the source of nationalist danger. Socialist opposition to European integration and to coördinated defense efforts with the United States was interpreted as a neutralist form of nationalism. Such tendencies do indeed exist in the radical wing of the SPD; but the prejudice against the opposition to Adenauer, which has been encouraged by former American Occupation officials who naturally have a stake in the government they helped to create, has resulted in exaggeration of the importance of the extremist wing and in simplifications of the role of the SPD as a whole in the postwar period. The party, starting under Kurt Schumacher's leadership, has been intent on not again becoming the scapegoat for the failures of the nation

26. *New York Times,* June 11, 1959.

and its political system, as it was in the Weimar Republic. This led it to concentrate on the issue of German unity and to oppose policies which the leadership considered inimicable to its achievement. Some SPD leaders are prepared to admit today that the stands they adopted on the Schuman Plan in 1953 and on re-armament in 1953 and 1957 were miscalculated, both as election tactics and from the point of view of German security interests. But they vigorously deny that the party has ever been guilty of neutralist-nationalist policies, of which they have been accused; indeed, there is no reason to doubt the SPD's honesty in professing loyalty to the West any more than its honesty in admitting to tactical mistakes.

American preoccupation with the supposed menace of Socialist policies in West Germany has obscured from view the long-run interests of the German right, the real source of a nationalist danger in West Germany. It may be that Moscow's analysis of West German political forces has all along been more astute than the interpretations that have dominated the thinking in Washington. From the Communist standpoint, Ludwig Erhard's "social market economy" consists of a series of ephemeral measures which will not survive the first "capitalist crisis." Social democracy, on the other hand, in Germany as in Britain, offers a genuine methodological alternative to achieve what the Communists claim can only come about through economic and social revolution. For the Communists, therefore, a strong social democratic regime in Bonn would offer a stronger challenge than the admixture of conservative and reactionary forces which have aligned themselves under Dr. Adenauer's rule.

Whatever validity this comparison may have, it is basically academic and unreal. The Soviet leadership knows that in present circumstances, and in all probability in the circumstances in which the next West German national elections will be held in 1961, the SPD cannot gain sufficient popular support to form a strong government. A weak SPD government, or a coalition led by the

SPD, would present an entirely different picture from a strong SPD government. Such a government in Bonn would probably offer less of a challenge and more of an opportunity to the Soviet government. The reasons for this are not to be found in the SPD, but rather outside the party, in powerful right-wing circles in the society. These have so far been contained in the CDU/CSU coalition and in a wing of the FDP, and have supported the existing political establishment (*Verfassung*) because of Adenauer's success in operating the machinery of government. However, if the CDU were to be defeated at the polls, if the SPD were to gain a share of political control on the national level, the CDU might disintegrate. At least some factions would form and these would tend to construct abortive political alliances; and it is by no means certain that these right-wing and also conservative dissidents would continue to support the *Verfassung* if it was no longer headed by a strong anti-leftist leader. From Moscow's point of view, in other words, a weak SPD regime or government coalition would open up possibilities of exploiting fissures in the social and economic structure of the Federal Republic, and make it more susceptible to the alternating Soviet policies of intimidation and seduction.

It may be, therefore, that Moscow's and Pankow's propaganda support of the SPD in West German elections has been aimed at alienating German rightists from the Bonn *Verfassung* in the event of a Social Democratic victory, rather than at bringing the SPD into power with a solid majority. The Communists, in other words, would rather deal with German industrialists than with trade unionists, with rightists rather than leftists; but before they can do this effectively the conservative-reactionary coalition which Adenauer has so far held together must be broken up.

What are the chances that the German right-wing, above all the representatives of heavy industry, will be prepared to deal with Moscow in present circumstances or in the event that the CDU loses control of the national government? Soviet Russia's strength today in comparison to West Germany's rules out the kind of cynical arrangement German business could afford to make with Moscow during the 1920's. National Bolshevism, although it still has adherents in the Ruhr and among rightist intellectuals, is not an important force. Marxism has been discredited in western Europe to the point where it cannot attract significant support even in a national disguise. The lure of Eastern markets, by itself, is not strong enough to make the Germans forego vital defensive alliances in the West. We must assume that the Communists know all this, and yet they appear to believe that, in time, the German industrialists will deal with them. They know that this is impossible as long as Adenauer dominates the government, since he represents the interests of the rightists and they admire his strong paternalistic rule. The respect West Germany has gained from the West, especially from the United States, and the economic benefits that have followed, are largely due to the Chancellor's stature and prestige. And as long as Adenauer is in power the trade union movement will remain weak and the SPD in opposition.

But when Adenauer is no longer in power all this will be subject to change. The ultimate aims of the Rhineland industrialists are masked. Though they have found Adenauer's rule useful, their ultimate aims may be incompatible with the goals of his policies. Many of those on the right are dissatisfied with the one-sidedness of Adenauer's policies, with his stress on the relationship with Paris to the virtual exclusion of other powers; they are worried about being bound up in a tight European economic and political structure which will lose them potential advantages in trade not only elsewhere in the West, but also in the Communist East. They see no reason why the continued reliance on the West for German security need exclude a more active foreign political and economic policy toward the East. Among the owners and managers of heavy industry, in particular, there is a general awakening to the possibilities of using the fruits of Adenauer's policies, the growing industrial and military capacities of the Federal Republic, as a bargaining power to sway the Continent's diplomatic balance between the two superpowers; and there are some who see this as the only way for the German people to be reunified without paying an exorbitant price in national security and without risking a world catastrophe.

The potentialities of a new nationalism in Germany have worried policy-makers in both the Truman and Eisenhower administrations. U.S. encouragement of European integration has sprung more from a conscious desire to ward off incipient nationalism than from the ideal of Americanizing the Continent or from the wish to unburden American taxpayers of a dependent European economy, to limit and direct West Germany's prodigious energies and ambitions toward creating a healthy economy and a sound military posture in western Europe, so that the Soviet menace could be contained and a new German menace prevented. Bureaucrats, industrialists, and politicians in West Germany are well aware of these motives in U.S. policy.[27] Many Germans resent American suspicions of Bonn's ambitions, but there have been few public protests. The reasons for this are first, that Adenauer himself is known to share the distrust of his countrymen if they are left wholly independent, and second, the general understanding by the German people that collaboration with the West is the price the Federal Republic must pay to be treated as an equal by her major allies. Many Germans may not like the motivation behind the drive to incorporate the Federal Republic into a Western and continental entity, but they still believe that their security and status depend upon continued collaboration.

27. Commenting on Secretary Dulles' testimony in June 1958 on the desirability of integrating the Federal Republic into western Europe, the Washington correspondent of *Die Welt* concluded: "In other words, in American eyes there is not only the Russian-Communist danger; there is also a German danger"; July 8, 1958. For Dulles' testimony, see below, pp. 126-127.

There is nevertheless a growing fear in Bonn, especially among government bureaucrats, that West European integration would cut the Federal Republic off from eastern Europe and curb her freedom of action to achieve German unity. The Federal Republic's strong economic position, her increasing military power and political stability, could be marshaled, they believe, to serve German interests, above all for the achievement of reunification. These fears and convictions are leading more and more Germans to look askance at the Chancellor's hectic efforts to create a European political community. These West German fears were heightened by the statements of two former secretaries of state, John Foster Dulles and Dean Acheson. Dulles, when asked by Senator Aiken if a united Germany would not represent a "threat to the peace of Europe and possibly the whole world," gave an unequivocal answer:

I think it is very important, Senator, that a reunited Germany should be integrated into the West through its association with NATO, through its participation in the Brussels Treaty of the Western European Union, through participation in the Coal and Steel Community, Euratom, the common market, and things of that sort.

I believe that a Germany which was left in a position of neutrality, or some people call it disengagement, in the center of Europe, would be under an almost irresistible temptation to play one side or the other, and that that would be a very dangerous situation, dangerous for the West, dangerous for the Soviet Union and dangerous for the Germans, themselves.

And I believe that that is recognized by Chancellor Adenauer, and that he has advocated this strong policy of the tying together of Germany with other countries of the West—France, Italy, the Benelux countries—because he sees that in that way the temptation to the Germans to try to go off on adventures of their own would be automatically changed, and they would have a future for that dynamic country in cooperation with the West rather than in possible antagonism with the West.

So the answer to your question is this: I would not think it was wise or prudent to try to buy reunification of Germany at the price of having Germany an independent country unrelated to the West. I have expressed that view to the Soviets many times, pointing out to them that from their own standpoint they ought to want to have Germany reunited and closely tied together, as Chancellor Adenauer wants them to be, with the other countries of the West, so that there would almost certainly be a harmonizing of German policies with those of other western countries, and that Germany would feel that its great destiny could be achieved by methods which would automatically be composed with the other countries of the West.[28]

Dulles' view is essentially the same one Premier Guy Mollet put forward more concisely in July 1956: "It is necessary to weave between the countries of Western Europe the bonds that will prevent Germany from turning to the East."[29]

The Germans can understand why the French and the people of the smaller European powers are something less than enthusiastic about reuniting Germany, but they cannot justify the United States' withholding of its support. It did not occur to the Germans who read Dulles' statement that he might be advocating West German integration in Western Europe without recognizing that the Soviet Union would not permit reunification to take place once this happened. They assumed that he knew this. Therefore, Dulles' protest that the Soviets "ought to want . . . Germany reunited and closely tied together with the West" was thought to be disingenuous, and aroused the suspicion that the United States regarded European integration as a means of curbing Bonn's ability to represent German interests, so that the unification of Germany which integration was ostensibly aimed at making possible could not, in fact, be negotiated.

Dean Acheson's blunt support of Dulles' policy increased these fears in Germany, because it indicated that neither party in the United States was concerned to leave a way open to negotiate a

28. Hearings, Committee on Foreign Relations, United States Senate, 85th Congress, 2d session, "Review of Foreign Policy, 1958" (Washington, 1958), Pt. 4, pp. 804-805.

29. Quoted by H. Lutz, *German-French Unity: Basis for European Peace* (Chicago, 1957), p. xi.

settlement of the partition problem on a basis acceptable to the Soviet government. Acheson stated his views on the matter, similar to Dulles' in all essentials, in the April 1958 issue of *Foreign Affairs,* where he derided proposals for enforcing military limitations on a reunited Germany by arguing that such a Germany, situated between two power systems and having "ambitions and purposes of its own," could not be restricted. He endorsed West European integration as a means of controlling the Federal Republic. In Acheson's view, the Federal Republic could be controlled; a reunited Germany could not be. Acheson warned that the grand nightmare of Western diplomacy, "a sort of new Ribbentrop-Molotov agreement," would become a reality if a reunified Germany were not integrated with the West and safeguarded by the presence of American troops.[30]

The real dangers inherent in the Acheson-Dulles rationale supporting West European integration are not to be found in German resentments, but in the premises which underlie this policy, which may turn out to be illusions. The premises are, that the success of West European integration is assured,[31] that integration will indubitably restrict West Germany's freedom of action, and that "a good many desirable consequences" that "both strengthen Western Europe and diminish the fears of Eastern Europe and of the Soviet Union" will follow.[32] The Acheson-Dulles policies were based on public assurances that "the pull of a vigorous free system" and the simultaneous decline in the attractions of the Communist one, which Acheson said he could already detect, would lead to progress in Europe. With robust confidence in his

30. Dean Acheson, "The Illusion of Disengagement," *Foreign Affairs,* XXXVI (April 1958), 377.

31. In the article cited above Acheson wrote: "The success of the movement toward unity in the west of Europe is no longer in doubt. Only the rate of progress is undecided. . . . A common currency and political community are on the way."

32. See Acheson's speech of April 15, 1958, published in *U.S. News and World Report,* April 25, 1958.

own judgment and imperious disdain for those who disagreed with
him, Acheson declared:

If one considers the changes which have already occurred within the
Soviet Union, one can see the time approaching when adjustments in
Eastern Europe are possible, when military forces can be reduced, and
when the menace of nuclear destruction will be greatly diminished, if
not removed.[33]

German readers were dismayed not to find reunification on Acheson's list of promised achievements,[34] and could not reconcile
Acheson's confidence that the end of the Cold War in Europe
was just around the corner with the appearances of increased
power and self-confidence in Soviet post-Sputnik policy. They
also found it difficult to understand Acheson's contention that
"a thriving Europe would continue its irresistible pull upon East
Germany and Eastern Europe." Whatever attractions the Common
Market may hold for the East Europeans (and one is bound to
be skeptical of these as long as Norway, Sweden, Denmark,
Austria, Switzerland, and Great Britain have not been pulled into
its ranks), it is the presence of Soviet troops and Moscow's firm
intention to dispose of eastern Europe on its own conditions which
are the solemn facts facing the West in making progress toward
its political objectives on the Continent. There is no evident reason
why improvements in the Russian standard of living should diminish the "Russian need for the forced communization and iron
control of Eastern Europe," which Acheson predicted;[35] and the
"trend in the Soviet Union to somewhat greater personal freedom,
somewhat greater freedom of expression, somewhat greater enjoy-
ment by people of the fruits of their labor," which Dulles hailed

33. Acheson, "The Illusion of Disengagement," p. 382.
34. However in a subsequent article Acheson pleased many Germans by
dispelling "the myth" that the West Germans do not really want the reunification of Germany. He wrote that "the sincerity and depth of their
desire for the reunification of Germany could not be doubted—at least, by
me." *New York Times,* February 29, 1960.
35. Acheson, "The Illusion of Disengagement," pp. 379-380.

in July 1957, does not vindicate Dulles' "working hypothesis, that free governments in the long run are going to prevail and despotic governments in the long run are going to go under. . . ."[36]

Evolutionary changes in the Soviet Union toward improved living standards and greater personal freedom, should these trends continue, may make Soviet foreign policy not less but more challenging. Its successes within the bloc are less likely to diminish the Soviet government's ambitions than to cause it to push ahead vigorously toward new successes abroad. It is indeed difficult to understand why the strengthening of Soviet Russia through evolutionary change in its social and economic structure should cause a change in Russian interests in dominating Europe, or reduce Soviet power in that area. Changes, many of them undoubtedly unexpected, will surely continue to take place within the Soviet Union and its orbit, but these will not necessarily benefit the West, integrated or not. Change is inevitable, but progress is not.

Dulles, according to his own testimony, told the Soviet leaders "many times" that a unified Germany closely tied together with the other Western nations would serve Russian interests. The Soviet leaders have clearly rejected Dulles' conception of Russian interests and continue to insist on other formulas for German reunification. Repeated Soviet rebuffs of his policy faced Dulles with a predicament. He insisted that the West would not change its policies in order to reach an acceptable agreement on Germany with Moscow, and since this was tantamount to an admission that German reunification would not proceed from Western political action, all that Secretary Dulles could hold out to the Germans was that reunification might take place by "surprise." The precedent Dulles cited for this slim hope was the Soviet agreement on an Austrian peace treaty:

36. News Conference of July 2, 1957, in *Department of State Bulletin,* Vol. XXXVII, No. 943, July 22, 1957.

. . . in 1955 the Soviet Union suddenly decided to liberate Austria. That decision came as a surprise, and in reversal of the adamant position which the Soviet Government had held for nearly a decade. It shows that we need not despair for Germany and for Berlin. The day will come when, probably unexpectedly and without predictability, the Geneva promises of 1955 will be fulfilled and Germany will again be reunited in freedom.[37]

This was really an admission that, since U.S. diplomacy will not lead to a realization of Western political objectives in Europe, the Germans must wait upon Soviet benignity to reach their goals. It was bound to dishearten the Germans, and especially the Berliners. They see no signs of Soviet benevolence. On the contrary, there is every evidence that Moscow has begun a resolute drive to integrate the satellite states, including the D.D.R. and all of Berlin, into a solid bloc of nations which, day by day, is growing apart from Western Europe.

Contrary to the expectation of many, the West Germans have not reacted to the political ineptitude of the United States and the signs of growing Soviet power with increased pessimism about the chances of reunification. Although more and more Germans realize that reunification is not just around the corner, there is a growing sentiment favoring more determined action than Chancellor Adenauer has taken so far. There is a new cautious attitude against making any commitments which might impair Bonn's freedom to negotiate a settlement of the German problem. This change of mood, this veiled, mostly hidden, resolve not to be diverted from Germany's national problem is likely to be a growing force in the Federal Republic. It is one of the essential components of the revival of national feeling which Adenauer has tried to suppress and which he has successfully expunged from most public government pronouncements and discussions. The sentiment is already strong enough today to forestall any move toward subordinating the

37. Text of Dulles' speech in Berlin on May 9, 1958, in *Department of State Bulletin*, Vol. XXXVIII, No. 987, May 26, 1958.

Federal Republic to a European political community in which Bonn does not have a decisive or at least a commanding voice.

For the present, most West German industrialists and intellectuals see no contradiction between supporting the Coal and Steel Community, Euratom, and the Common Market, and action to achieve national unity. It is not that they envisage a weakening of Moscow's rule in eastern Europe as a result of West European collaboration; rather they believe that the Federal Republic will be able to utilize the power of a united Europe in support of efforts, led by Bonn, to bargain for German reunification or, better still, European unification.

It is a mistake to visualize the resurgence of nationalist feeling in Germany as animated by hostility toward the West. There is neither *revanchisme* nor chauvinism in this philosophy which places special emphasis on the interests arising from Germany's middle position in Europe. On the other hand, in their efforts to elicit Western support for a policy toward the East, these West Germans will not hesitate to use the Federal Republic's growing economic power and crucial military support of NATO as bargaining counters. In some circumstances, they might try or at least threaten to withhold a measure of the coöperation which Bonn has so far given unstintingly to her allies. Nor would such action be unprecedented in the NATO alliance, as De Gaulle's unilateral decisions affecting NATO's command structure and stationing of forces prove.

Although the Common Market may strengthen the Continent against Communist economic exploitation and political encroachment, in its present form it also risks creating new divisions instead of the unity it is intended to achieve. There is not only a growing split between the Little Europe and the nations of the limited Free Trade Area, but a cleavage between western and eastern Europe, where the Soviet Union is enforcing its own economic integration. And despite all assurances to the contrary, and undoubtedly sincere desires for freer trade, the Common Market may lead to friction with the dollar area if the members of the European community, probably on the insistence of the French, are forced to throw up a high protective wall around their domain.

The new political strength the European Economic Community will contribute to the West has probably been overdrawn even as the difficulties it will cause in the U.S. in future negotiations with the Soviet Union have been underrated, if not ignored. There is certainly nothing inherent in the new collaborative efforts which improves the chances of reaching satisfactory accommodations with the Soviet government in Europe. The West Germans are beginning to realize that the prospects for the reunification of their land have not gained from their preparedness to participate in various economic and military programs with the West; it would be dangerous if the American public were long left ignorant of the same facts.

The questions of German unity and of Germany's eastern frontiers have been prominent on the agendas of succeeding high level conferences, but these questions have, in reality, been shelved—and not without Adenauer's acquiescence—since the Berlin Conference of 1954, in view of Soviet Russia's repeated rejections of Western terms and pending the success of the West's concentrated effort to effect a military build-up and closer economic and political coöperation. The Adenauer thesis, which has dominated Western policy on Germany since before the Geneva Conference of 1956, is that German reunification can only be achieved after NATO forces have been brought to full strength and the *Bundeswehr* is equipped with nuclear weapons. When these conditions are satisfied, according to Adenauer, there would then be the requisite degree of military strength to support a diplomatic offensive.[38]

The Adenauer thesis will almost certainly not be tested because, among the Federal Republic's allies, only the United States still

38. Terrence Prittie, "Solution for Berlin: A Symposium on the Lippmann Proposals," *New Republic,* May 11, 1959.

appears to have faith in it. Preponderant Western military strength is not being created, and perhaps cannot be created.[39] Moreover, in the Federal Republic itself there is growing skepticism of Adenauer's idea. This is not new in the opposition parties, but it has now also invaded the ranks of the Christian Democratic Union and even extends into the Chancellor's cabinet. It is therefore predictable that the German questions will be taken off the shelf as the next generation of Christian Democratic leaders comes to power; they do not share the illusion that the balance of power will change decisively to the West's favor, but do believe that German power within the West's alliances has reached a new high, although not yet its optimum level.

If Britain and France, and above all the United States, persist in efforts to sublimate German interests and to restrict Bonn's freedom of action by bundling the Federal Republic into an integrated West European community, the West Germans would undoubtedly sacrifice their interest in the Common Market before turning their backs on their brethren in East Germany. There is a greater danger that European federation will succeed prematurely, only to be reversed with a risk of disrupting all the coöperation that has developed, than that western Europe will be torn by renewed strife along the old lines, especially between Germany and France, if further steps toward the creation of a political community follow rather than precede a *modus vivendi* with the Soviet government to reunite the Continent.

United States policy, therefore, would also profit from a new measure of realism and caution in regard to West European unity and the institutionalizing of international relationships, not only to protect the real gains that have been made, but also to prevent a widening of the rift between the Little Europe and the Free Trade Area, the Six and the Seven, and of the split between East and West Europe.

Americans are unfortunately prone to apply the lessons they

39. See below, pp. 270 ff.

have learned from their own national experience to the conditions of contemporary Europe. A misreading of American history seems to be as important here as accurate analysis. For example, the slogan "unite or perish" which has been hurled at the Europeans has no significance in American history—and hopefully not to future European history either.[40] The hallowed Founding Fathers set themselves the humble task of forming from competing states "a more perfect union"—not a perfect union. The unification of the American states, furthermore, was favored by the advantages of a common language and tradition. The Intra-European institutions are the result of negative forces: the Communist threat and the search for a framework to permit German rearmament without creating a new danger. There is nothing in western Europe today comparable to the public idealism which supported the unification of the American states. The European masses crave the achievement of national ambitions and the achievement of national security; they have no desire to explore new frontiers. "The European idea is empty; it has neither the transcendence of Messianic ideologies nor the imminence of concrete patriotism. It was created by intellectuals, and that fact accounts at once for its genuine appeal to the mind and its feeble echo in the heart."[41]

Some expectations of revolutionary changes in Europe are clearly unduly optimistic; but there is no reason for pessimism. A discerning American historian wrote in 1953, three years before the Saar was reincorporated in a sovereign Germany:

The Saar may prove to be the specific case that keeps Germany and France divided; or it may be the specific case on which hinges the whole process of reconciliation between these old enemies . . . if the Saar is, quite literally, German at heart, its economic interests as the world now is lie very clearly in free trade with France. Rarely are

40. An editorial in the *New York Times* of June 16, 1959, declared: "The United States has urged European unification ever since the Marshall Plan. We must hope, therefore, that Europe will find a way to reconcile its trade interests and its political necessities—for indeed, it must 'unite or perish.' "

41. R. Aron, *The Century of Total War* (New York, 1954), p. 313.

emotions and interests, heart and head, so neatly opposed in this world. We should at least learn something about the relative importance of these contrary pulls on a human group from what happens in the Saar in the near future. Much more hopeful we cannot be. Heaven on earth is not likely to start in the Saar.[42]

42. Crane Brinton, *The Temper of Western Europe* (Cambridge, 1953), pp. 83-84.

five

■

THE REARMAMENT OF GERMANY

Throughout its first decade the history of the Federal Republic has been shaped principally by outside forces. Soviet policy, in particular, has had a profound impact on the West German people, on the one hand impelling them into closer relationships with western Europe and the United States, and on the other focusing their attention, and the attention of the world, on the plight of their divided nation. Moscow's obstinate refusal to permit reunification on any terms other than its own, and the equally obstinate refusal of the Adenauer government to reduce its maximum demands for unity on terms that Bonn's allies also subscribe to, have created a stalemate over the issue which has left the West Germans no choice but to look exclusively to the West for reassurances of their security and prosperity.[1]

A more conciliatory, or even flexible, Soviet policy or approach to the reunification issue could have slowed or possibly even prevented the development of Bonn's ties to the West by strengthening West German tendencies to achieve its national aims through taking initiatives within and possibly even outside the Western alliance. Any discussion of the German problem must deal with the circumstances as they are, but it would be unwise to exclude from consideration the disturbing influence that Moscow could exert on

1. For Soviet Russia's terms on German unity and the Western stand on this issue see above, pp. 11-12; and below, Chap. 8.

German public opinion and governmental policy against the best interests of the Western allies. The fact that this influence has so far been all one way, virtually impelling the Federal Republic to seek the closest Western associations, should not blind us to the opportunities Moscow has had, and may utilize, to disrupt those ties.[2] The alternatives Moscow proposes, and the picture she presents to the Germans, as a violent aggressor or as a peaceful competitor, may be as much a factor in this matter as the effectiveness of Western security guarantees. A NATO "shield" or some other formula may not guarantee West Germany's reliability as an Allied partner. Nevertheless, the West's military posture and strategy have a profound impact on German thinking and must be examined.

A variety of basic questions arise: What are the present state and the future prospects of the West German rearmament program? What are the military aims of this program, and what are its implications for Bonn's political policies, for NATO, and quite specifically, for the United States? Are Bonn's arms efforts in harmony with NATO's current strategic aims? With alternative strategies that have been proposed for the NATO alliance? Are West Germany's contributions vital to the defense of Europe? Is NATO today and will it be in the future capable of defending West Germany and Europe against attack? Is the Federal Republic's military partnership with the United States compatible with the achievement of Western aims in Europe?

The North Korean attack on South Korea in June 1950 heightened the danger of war in central Europe, particularly after Gromyko spelled out the analogy between Korea and the divided Germany. The Truman administration met what appeared to be an increased danger by sending American troops to Europe and proposing a new defensive strategy. Hitherto the United States had pledged that it would retaliate with atomic weapons against a Soviet invasion and implied that it would once again seek to liberate

2. For additional discussion of this point see below, Chaps. 7 and 8.

the Continent. Now, Washington promised aid to its NATO allies to defend their territory against attack. To this end, the United States proposed forming "an integrated force under centralized command, which shall be adequate to deter aggression and insure the defense of Western Europe."[3] To raise a sufficiently large force and to give each western European nation a stake in the defense of the Continent, the United States insisted that the West Germans be rearmed and be given as nearly equal status in the new defense organization as the other member states would permit.

These proposals were dominated by military considerations. From the Pentagon's point of view, the most efficient and therefore desirable means of reëstablishing German armed forces was on a national basis.[4] The American military establishment's high respect for German fighting qualities and organizational ability was also primarily to account for the initial exaggeration of the speed with which it expected the Bonn government to create a large military force.

On the State Department side, Secretary Acheson's Soviet experts advised him "that the North Korean invasion was a local affair" and that the Soviet Union was not prepared to precipitate a general conflagration, which an attack in Europe would have signified.[5] For Acheson, nevertheless, it seemed an opportune moment to gain Allied agreement on German rearmament, which he appears to have regarded as necessary sooner or later. Either because he actually accepted the Pentagon's estimates, or because he sought to dangle the bait of having Germany bear a major share of the arms burden in front of his British and French colleagues meeting in New York in the autumn of 1950, Acheson said he was confident that Bonn could raise ten divisions to meet any immediate European

3. Ben T. Moore, *NATO and the Future of Europe* (New York, 1958), p. 36.

4. H. Speier, *German Rearmament and Atomic War*, p. 8.

5. See Glenn D. Paige, "The United States Decision to Repel Aggression in Korea," Foreign Policy Analysis Project (unpublished, Northwestern University, 1956), p. 66.

emergency.[6] The Bonn government contributed to these miscalculations by exaggerating the size of the forces it could produce quickly, presumably to raise its bargaining power with the Big Three in the negotiations to grant the Federal Republic sovereignty in exchange for an arms contribution.[7] The West Germans could not have created ten divisions in a year under any circumstances; and a rapid build-up of forces could only have been accomplished if mostly *Wehrmacht* veterans had been enlisted. For this and other reasons there was strong and partly effective resistance to a rapid build-up in Adenauer's planning agency for the new army, the *Amt Blank,* whose officials (who were all civilians; even the former soldiers among them were distinctly civilian-minded) wanted to have a minimum of three to five years for the mobilization.

The chief cause of the delay in German rearmament was not American or German miscalculation, but rather French procrastination. Pleven's European Army alternative to the U.S. proposal of an integrated force of national armies was eventually defeated by the French National Assembly. Before its defeat, the EDC scheme was supported more vigorously by the Eisenhower administration than by its European sponsors, to the point where American diplomats in Europe were forbidden to discuss any alternative to it while Secretary Dulles threatened an "agonizing reappraisal" of U.S. policy if it should be rejected.

After the defeat of EDC something like the initial American proposal for German rearmament was revived.[8] But by that time (1954) Bonn had clearly reconsidered the scale and timing of its arms contribution. When the NATO commander suggested in September 1954 that it would take the Federal Republic two years to organize twelve divisions, he was disputed by West German

6. Richard P. Stebbins, *The U.S. in World Affairs, 1950,* p. 269.

7. Herbert Blankenhorn, "the Chancellor's alter ego," is reported to have told an American official in September 1950 regarding Adenauer's offer to recruit 12 German divisions: "We'll have the divisions ready in six months." Charles W. Thayer, *The Unquiet Germans* (New York, 1957), p. 224.

8. For the London and Paris Agreements of 1954 see above, p. 11.

spokesmen who talked of five years as the minimum period for such a force. Even this prognosis was unduly optimistic. West Germany will not complete its force of twelve divisions until 1962 at the earliest.

According to Bonn, the principal reasons for this long delay are that the *Bundeswehr,* and also the *Luftwaffe* and *Marine,* lack the proper facilities such as barracks, and also the necessary funds for a faster effort. Lack of requisite means has always been the least plausible explanation for the arms delay. The military budget has never been high compared to allocations for social services, which take the lion's share of the entire budget. Even so the military budget has been underspent year after year.[9] No more than eight million DM were spent on arms in 1958. The cabinet authorized eleven million DM for defense in 1959-1960, but the Minister of Finance, Franz Etzel, announced that in fact only nine million DM would be spent for armaments.[10] The 1960 budget provided for defense expenditures totalling ten million DM, an increase of one million DM over the planned 1959 total, but at the same time there was an increase of 1.8 million DM for social services in 1959 over the preceding year which, according to an official publication, was "necessitated by higher pensions for 'war victims,' that is, for disabled ex-soldiers and dependents of soldiers killed in action" and other pensioners.[11] Bonn's 1961 budget envisaged a twenty per cent increase in defense outlays.[12] Similarly, the lack of barrack space and other facilities for training is a lame excuse for the armaments slowdown. The authorities may have been understandably reluctant to construct the facilities which could be taken over from Occupation forces and refugee settlements in a few years, but doubtless this could have been done if they had willed it without so much as denting the boom in the building of private dwellings and

9. See "Germany's New Forces: The Slow Build-Up," *Manchester Guardian,* October 12, 1957.

10. *New York Times,* October 31, 1958.

11. *Bulletin* (English language edition), November 17, 1959.

12. *New York Times,* September 23, 1960.

churches. At least part of the need for training facilities, which in 1959 led Defense Minister Strauss into confidential discussions with the Franco government, only to be publicized half a year later to add grist to the Soviet propaganda mill, could have been met by timely construction and requisition measures by the West German government. Bonn's failure to take these measures does indeed lead to the suspicion that it sought an opportunity to establish a foothold on Spanish soil. The Germans do not, after all, succumb easily to material shortages. On the other hand, it is true that West German facilities for training pilots and for air maneuvers have been taken up by Allied forces, and until the spring of 1960 Bonn's neighbors proved reluctant to meet the *Luftwaffe*'s specifications for substitute training bases.[13]

Domestic political battles are certainly one of the chief causes of the slow West German arms build-up. In the national campaign of 1957 and still afterwards Adenauer was purported to see in the SPD's opposition to major tenets of his defense program real dangers of a CDU defeat at the polls. In addition to compromising on the prescribed length of military service, some of the Chancellor's collaborators say that he felt it necessary to safeguard his, and also his party's, chances in the national and succeeding *Länder* elections by mitigating the impact of the rearmament program, and that this was best accomplished by slowing it down. While

13. On the West German talks with the Franco government, see the *New York Times*, February 23, 26, 28 and March 1, 1960. Allied criticism of the German initiative virtually ceased following Secretary of State Herter's praise for the "democratic order" established in West Germany (*ibid.*, April 11, 1960) and Chancellor Adenauer's conversations with President Eisenhower in Washington early in April. In a Bundestag debate Foreign Minister Brentano nevertheless reiterated that Bonn might still sign an agreement with Madrid for supply and training facilities and put his government on record in favor of including Spain in the western European community (*ibid.*, April 7, 1960). By the winter of 1960, bases agreements between Bonn and France, Belgium, Britain, the Netherlands, and Norway were in varying degrees of completion and *Bundeswehr* trainees were actually stationed on French soil.

this may indeed have been Adenauer's reasoning, one cannot avoid noting that the Bonn government is and will be in a position to make a military and political virtue of what it has steadfastly claimed were material, financial, and domestic political necessities.

The immediate military advantages Bonn has been gaining from the slowdown of its rearmament program are to be found in the type of equipment with which the armed forces are being outfitted. These are, to an extraordinary extent, fully developed modern weapons of the newest types, nuclear and non-nuclear, including some that were originally proscribed in the Paris Agreements of 1954. By adopting only the best fully tested major weapons of the generation since the Korean War, the *Bundeswehr* has safeguarded itself against costly major replacements for years to come, while insuring that it will have the most modern force of any western European country. To be sure, all weapons without exception are outmoded sooner or later; but the Germans have shopped around very carefully, they have purchased weapons abroad, developed some themselves, and are manufacturing others on license. And by the time replacements have to be made of the major weapons—planes, tanks, troop carriers, missiles—the chances are that the German weapons-producing industry will have been revived to the point where these can be of German design and manufacture.

Further elaboration of this point in a meaningful way depends upon the drawing of a relationship between the pace of German rearmament, NATO strategy, and the future disposition of both tactical and strategic nuclear weapons. And it is to this we must now proceed.

Since 1950 NATO strategy has been predicated on a German defense contribution.[14] In September 1950, fully five and a half years before the first *Bundeswehr* soldier donned a uniform, Britain, France, and the United States agreed to "treat any attack on the Federal Republic or Berlin as an attack upon themselves."

14. See above, pp. 10-11, and Chap. 6.

This was tantamount to admitting West Germany to the benefits of the NATO shield without imposing any corresponding obligations. The guarantee had to be given in the interest of the Big Three powers who then found themselves in the depths of the Korean crisis. Moreover, the guarantee was given by the powers in the belief that they could "deal with the German Government on the [rearmament] issue, not as supplicants," as Secretary Acheson put it at the time, "but merely as agreeing to proposals already made by Adenauer to contribute units to European forces and force him to accept conditions to our acceptance of his proposal."[15] As we have already noted, it was not as simple as all that. After his proposals were accepted, Adenauer seemed to be less anxious to discharge the attending obligations rapidly. And although Bonn's rearmament lagged it was not forced to accept any new conditions. Its allies were left anxiously waiting on the doorstep, if not as supplicants, then as petitioners not quite certain that they would be granted an audience.

The delay of the German defense contribution lasted just long enough to make a real issue of whether or not the *Bundeswehr* would be equipped with what are referred to in West Germany euphemistically as "the most modern weapons," meaning nuclear weapons. Of course West Germany's leaders have denied this connection—and also their desire for nuclear weapons—repeatedly in public statements. In a comparatively mild statement on this issue in 1957, Defense Minister Strauss said that "it is perfectly possible to have no atomic weapons in German hands and in a collective defense system have atomic weapons."[16] In an interview a year later Strauss was emphatic:

I tell you, we Germans are much more prepared than either the Americans or the British governments to see nuclear weapons abolished altogether. It is the Americans who are afraid of nuclear disarmament,

15. Acheson's report to the President of September 15, 1950; Harry S Truman, *Years of Trial and Hope 1946-1952* (New York, 1956), p. 255.
16. *Manchester Guardian*, October 11, 1957.

because they rely on nuclear weapons to increase their fire-power and make up for our manpower shortage.[17]

In other words, West Germany would forego acquiring nuclear weapons if the existing nuclear powers would agree to abolish those weapons. But if the United States, Britain, and the Soviet Union did not abolish nuclear weapons—what would the Federal Republic do then? The fact of the matter is that by the time Strauss had made his statement, the Federal Republic was making strenuous efforts to gain access to a nuclear capability and had been doing so ever since its decision in 1957, two years before, to reduce the period of conscription and the over-all size of the projected army—even after the government's maximum demands on these issues had been legislated by the Bundestag. Thus, in retrospect, Strauss's statement to Crossman and others can only be interpreted as a maneuver to blame the opposition parties (who called for a reduced term of conscription and a smaller army) for measures that were not popular with Bonn's allies and to blame Bonn's nuclear allies for measures that were unpopular with the German electorate. For had it wanted to, the government could certainly have held out for a full eighteen months of conscription, instead of the twelve to which it was reduced, and Strauss could have raised a conventional force of 500,000 men even though the five to six U.S. divisions in Europe were being equipped with tactical atomic weapons.

Instead, Adenauer decided to give way to opposition demands for a smaller, short-term conscript army, and Strauss bargained (probably with Adenauer as well as with his Western opposites) for the creation of a West German quality army equipped with "the most modern weapons." Probably the key argument he used was that if the American divisions were acquiring tactical nuclear weapons there was no hope of restricting a conflict involving the Red Army to conventional weapons; that Germany was in other words bound to become an atomic battlefield and the *Bundeswehr*

17. R. H. S. Crossman, "A Talk with Franz Josef Strauss."

should be equipped with the requisite weapons to fight such a conflict.

Not only domestic political considerations and the reëquipping of American forces, but also simulated war conditions, as in NATO's exercise CARTE BLANCHE (June 1955) played an important role in spurring Bonn's bid for nuclear arms. The results of the exercise led the SPD to label the use of atomic weapons on the Continent sheer suicide. In public political debates government spokesmen tried to minimize the importance of the new weapons, but before long the Adenauer government had resolved to acquire them for the *Bundeswehr* and charted negotiations to that end in NATO and with Washington.[18]

This ambiguity can be demonstrated. For example, the account of CARTE BLANCHE in the organ of the semi-official *Gesell-schaft für Wehrkunde* concluded that West German ground forces would still be useful but that it was necessary "to give new thought to their organization, armament, training and use on the battle-field."[19] A reëvaluation of this kind was under way in Bonn by the beginning of 1956, but the government gave no public inkling of it. So far as the general public was concerned, Adenauer had given his last word in February 1955 when he made the extraordinary statement that "so long as we do not belong to NATO, we are the European battlefield in case of a hot war between Soviet Russia and the United States, and if we are in NATO then we will no longer be that battlefield."[20] Only after certain drastic changes in defense policy took place in the autumn of 1956 did the West German public become privy to the new thinking about nuclear weapons in the government. Even before Adenauer made almost overt efforts to obtain nuclear weapons for the *Bundeswehr,* the

18. See Speier, *German Rearmament and Atomic War,* pp. 145-150, 182-193, especially p. 187.
19. "Luftmanöver 'Carte Blanche' in Kommandobereich Mitteleuropa," *Wehrkunde,* August 1955, p. 352.
20. *Verhandlungen des Deutschen Bundestags,* February 25, 1955.

German public knew something was up. The mild-mannered Theodor Blank was replaced as chief of the Defense Ministry by his chief critic, the dynamic Franz Josef Strauss; and Strauss promptly reduced the force goals for 1957. At the same time, the government cut the period of conscription from eighteen to twelve months, signifying a reduction in Bonn's total force goal from 500,000 to 325,000, a reversal of the ratio of volunteers to conscripts from 40:60 to 60:40, and a lowering of the barriers against former SS officers.

These drastic changes had to be accounted for, and Adenauer found a convenient *Prügeljunge*. He blamed all the changes on the United States, citing the discussions of reductions in U.S. troop strength under the heading of the "Radford Plan."[21] But if it is really true that the publication of Admiral Radford's proposals caused Adenauer grave worries, and if Secretary Dulles' repeated assurances that U.S. troops would remain in Europe did not reduce them, if, in other words, Adenauer was really expecting an imminent cut-back in U.S. troop commitments, it was certainly strange that he should react by approving a general slowdown of German rearmament, including a reduction of conscript service and in the total force goals. Were these moves intended to force the United States to maintain its divisions on the Continent? Such policy changes could hardly have been calculated to increase European security in any event, and certainly not if U.S. forces were about to withdraw.

Whether or not the Federal Republic's armaments cut-backs

21. The so-called Radford Plan gained public notice from an article in the *New York Times* of July 17, 1956 entitled, "Radford Backs Reduction of 800,000 by 1960." For Bonn's reaction and U.S. disavowals of the plan see *ibid.*, July 21, 24, 26, and 27. Adenauer was particularly embarrassed by the "Radford Plan" because nothing had been said to him about it when he visited Washington a few weeks before, in the spring of 1956, and also because public discussion of the plan coincided with Moscow-Pankow negotiations which seemed to deepen the split between the two Germanies. See the article entitled, "Moscow Gives Up Hope of a Deal with Bonn," *ibid.*, July 22, 1956.

were responsible (U.S. sources deny that they were), U.S. troops were not withdrawn from the Continent, and the net effect of "streamlining" the forces into Pentomic divisions was to strengthen their fighting capacity.

Adenauer's words and deeds regarding the *Bundeswehr*'s acquisition of atomic weapons are as difficult to reconcile as his stated fear of American troop cuts with his reductions of *Bundeswehr* force goals. As late as August 21, 1956 the Chancellor declared that he regarded "shifting the principal emphasis to atomic weapons at the present time as a mistake" and that it was "of special importance to localize small conflicts that might occur" by maintaining divisions with conventional weapons. A month later Adenauer requested nuclear weapons for the *Bundeswehr*.[22] To explain this sudden reversal, Adenauer blamed not only the "Radford Plan," but also the transfer of French troops to Algeria, Belgium's reduction of the conscription period, Britain's decision to rely on nuclear weapons for her defense and her subsequent cut in the forces on the Rhine—all of which, the Chancellor insisted, precluded a non-nuclear response to a Soviet attack and therefore a limited conflict in Europe. There was bound to be a revamping of the Federal Republic's defensive preparations in the train of these changes, the Chancellor asserted. While this appears to be a rational argument it was really no more than a rationalization.

The British, French, and Belgian decisions were announced prior to Adenauer's declaration of August 21. The "Radford Plan" never did become official U.S. policy, as Dulles had insisted right along. And most important, the decision to equip some American forces in Europe with nuclear weapons would not have precluded a limited conflict in Europe provided that the Federal Republic had fulfilled its obligation to establish a conventional force of half a million men. It was, in fact, Bonn's decision to equip half or

22. *Bulletin,* August 21, 1956; Speier, *German Rearmament and Atomic War,* pp. 217-219.

more of its divisions with nuclear weapons that enforced a change
in NATO strategy—which Adenauer claimed to dislike—virtually
barring the limitation of any conflict with Soviet forces in central
Europe.

The military decisions of Bonn's allies were more a trigger than
a cause of Adenauer's *volte-face* on nuclear arms. The reversal
and its timing were certainly produced by a combination of fears
and aspirations in which the Allies did not figure as prominently
as has been thought. Adenauer was certainly being persuaded by
the summer of 1956, and convinced before the NATO Council
meeting of December 1956, that a limited war in central Europe
was impossible. If Soviet forces attacked they would advance on a
broad front; and since the NATO powers would not indulge in a
levée en masse, or at least in a comparable build-up, to match
Russia's huge conventional force, they would have to react
atomically. Furthermore, Adenauer and his government have been
extremely sensitive to any form of discrimination against them in
the alliance. Since conventional forces appeared to be outmoded,
and since Britain had made public her plans to expand her nuclear
arsenal, and with France and possibly other members of WEU
planning to create nuclear arsenals, the Chancellor felt the need
to demand West German parity immediately, fearing that a postponement of the request until 1957 might exclude the Federal
Republic from the ranks of the nuclear powers indefinitely and
perhaps permanently.

It must be noted that Adenauer also feared that if West Germany, alone among the major Western powers, was without
nuclear weapons, neutralist forces in the Federal Republic might
be encouraged, and public opinion in the United States (which
Adenauer has never trusted) might actively support a plan for
neutralizing Germany between East and West. The Chancellor undoubtedly overestimated the potency of American public opinion,
but the trend in West Germany justified some apprehension. The
government had succeeded in pushing the eighteen months con-

scription law through the Bundestag, as was previously noted, but this was done over the vehement objections of the SPD which had made inroads in the German populace. Anti-NATO sentiment was growing throughout 1956 even among members of the government coalition. Behind this sentiment was the notion that if West Germany could withdraw from NATO or demonstrate a special position in it there might be better chances of negotiating reunification with Moscow. In pressing for the adoption of nuclear weapons by the *Bundeswehr* Adenauer saw an opportunity to cut the ground from under the neutralists whom he believed to be misguided or worse. In his demand for nuclear weapons, which had multifarious causes as we have seen, Adenauer had the complete support of members of the CDU coalition, including cabinet members, who agreed that Bonn could not negotiate with Moscow from a weak position and looked forward to the day when the Federal Republic will have the strength to pursue such negotiations with a chance of success. They regarded the acquisition of nuclear weapons as a major step in that direction and have been willing to accept the Federal Republic's new dependency on the United States, which retains the nuclear warheads in its possession, as a temporary but necessary expedient.

In December 1956, therefore, Defense Minister Strauss was able to link his announcement of the reduction of the *Bundeswehr* target figure for 1957 from 270,000 to 120,000 with a declaration that the Federal Republic would seek to develop a smaller "quality army" to replace the larger, chiefly conscript, force which his predecessor Theodor Blank had promised but not produced.[23] Three months later on the eve of the Anglo-American Bermuda parley, where Britain was promised delivery of American intermediate range missiles, Adenauer publicly insisted on West German parity in all weapons with her WEU partners. He told a press conference that atomic armaments were in flood tide and "Germans must adapt themselves to new circumstances." He minimized

23. Speier, *German Rearmament and Atomic War*, pp. 212, 222.

the importance of the new weapons as merely a further development of modern artillery and assured the Germans that acquisition of them would not invite Soviet hostilities because "a Soviet attack against us would be automatically followed by a United States counterblow."[24] At about the same time Strauss announced that 165,000 men would be in uniform by April 1958 but that the creation of additional units was "still an open question" pending the "reorientation" in weapons then in process.[25] It was clear that for Herr Strauss the best chances of progress lay in delay.

Following the announcement from Washington of April 12, 1957 that it would make dual-purpose missiles available to certain NATO allies, Strauss negotiated the purchase of several squadrons of Matadors, a surface-to-surface weapon whose inaccuracy is said to make it useful only when equipped with a nuclear warhead. Subsequently the Federal Republic arranged for the purchase of batteries of conventional Nikes, Nikes of the nuclear Hercules type, nine batteries of Honest John atomic artillery, and laid plans for joint construction of missile systems with France, Italy, and the U.K. under the WEU scheme to encourage coöperation in weapon research and production. In November 1957 Strauss revealed his list of missile priorities which he seems to have followed scrupulously. At the top of the list are antitank rockets, of which one type is being acquired from France and another from Israel; second, surface-to-surface tactical missiles (Matadors, Corporals, Maces, Honest John artillery); third, anti-aircraft rockets (Nike, Nike-Hercules, Hawk), to be produced by a French, West German, Belgian, Italian, Dutch consortium, and also air-to-air Sidewinders to be produced by a consortium consisting of West Germany, Greece, Turkey, the Netherlands, Norway, and Denmark; and fourth, missiles to replace long-range artillery (Honest John) and fighter-bombers (the Lockheed F-104), meaning

24. *New York Times,* March 23, April 6, 1957.
25. *Ibid.,* March 22, 1957.

IRBMs. At the heads-of-government meeting sponsored by NATO in Paris in December 1957 following Soviet Russia's successful Sputnik launching, Chancellor Adenauer committed the Federal Republic to accepting IRBM sites on its soil if this were required by the NATO commander. In subsequent negotiations it was decided not to station IRBMs in West Germany because they would be vulnerable to attack and easily overrun in the event of a full-scale Soviet invasion. This reasoning was accepted in Bonn, but already in the late winter of 1958 a highly placed Foreign Ministry official confided that a request for IRBMs would be made as soon as these could be fired from mobile launching sites, when they would no longer be sitting ducks. The second generation IRBMs now being developed will use solid fuel and can be moved and fired quickly. Railroad spurs for flat cars serving as mobile missile launching sites are already being constructed in West Germany. The Defense Ministry has contracted to buy from the United States $120 million dollars' worth of Mace guided missiles, ground-to-ground weapons classifiable as IRBMs since they have a nuclear capability and a maximum range of about a thousand miles.

The Federal Republic is prohibited from manufacturing missiles exceeding thirty-two kilometers in range by the amendments to the Paris Agreements of 1954, and unless and until this restriction is lifted the Germans will have to pursue their missile experimentation outside their country; they must depend upon their allies for any IRBMs they may obtain. In June 1959 Strauss declared that in the third phase of the *Luftwaffe*'s development in the early 1960s it would seek agreements with its allies for joint production of intermediate range missiles.[26] The announcement in December 1959 of Anglo-West German coöperation on the now defunct Blue Streak would seem to indicate that this schedule had been accelerated. There is, therefore, every indication that the present

26. Speech before the *Bundesverband der Deutschen Luftfahrtindustrie,* *Die Welt,* June 24, 1959.

government in Bonn plans to complete Strauss's list of missile priorities within the next two or three years.

The Federal Republic will have the weapons, though not necessarily the warheads, for a nuclear capability—ranging from low-yield tactical shells and grenades to strategic-deterrent missiles and bombs—even before it acquires IRBMs. It will have a potent delivery system for nuclear weapons when the *Luftwaffe* acquires during the current second phase of its development 660 of the Lockheed F-104 fighter-bomber Starfighters, which can deliver atomic bombs.[27] The West German military establishment is an atomic force in being; it is acquiring delivery systems and the weapons themselves except for the warheads, for which it depends on U.S. or other foreign stockpiles. At the same time, teams of *Bundeswehr* soldiers are receiving functional training from U.S. experts in the use of the nuclear weapons. This training does not include instruction in the theory of operation of these weapons which the Germans would have to know in order to manufacture them on their own. The Atomic Energy Act of 1954 imposes certain restrictions in this regard which have not been exceeded, at least not overtly. On the other hand, qualified experts are of the opinion that the West Germans have the theoretical basis to develop a nuclear weapons capacity of their own whenever they choose to do so, provided they are willing to appropriate sufficient funds for this purpose and can gain the assent of, or somehow circumvent, WEU—which is charged with the responsibility of administering the ban on West German manufacture of the so-called ABC (Atomic, Biological, Chemical) weapons.[28]

The Bonn government has not so far made a formal request to be exempted from the proscriptions in regard to atomic weapons in the Paris Agreements. On the contrary, Bonn has turned down

27. See below, pp. 164-165.
28. WEU has already permitted Bonn to manufacture certain weapons that had been proscribed in the Paris Agreements of 1954; see below, p. 157, n. 34.

feelers from Paris to have Germans participate and presumably share in France's efforts to become a member of the nuclear club. There is very little public knowledge about this, but it appears that France offered a limited partnership to the Germans for the principal purposes of using West German financial resources and technical talent in the Sahara experiments. Apparently the Germans felt that they could make use of these resources for developing the Federal Republic's own nuclear capacity one day, and the French were probably not willing either to share the bombs produced or to let the Germans in on any of their closely guarded secrets. Moreover, a German request for dispensation from the nuclear weapons restrictions in the Paris Agreements would have been premature in 1958, when the French first suggested such coöperation. The technical groundwork had not been laid in the Federal Republic, and the government feared that the WEU members would rebuff its petition if it came too quickly after the lifting of the first restrictions, which did not pertain to the ABC weapons.[29] Bonn is extremely sensitive to rebuffs from its allies, just as it is determined to achieve complete equality with its partners in all military and political matters. Therefore, when Strauss was asked by a foreigner if the Federal Republic intended to manufacture atomic weapons, he replied, "we will not give those who are not yet our friends any reason to fear us";[30] and when some Germans expressed anxiety about the *Bundeswehr*'s dependence on its allies for atomic warheads, pointing to the political limitations which flowed from this, Strauss, like Adenauer, replied by counselling patience, the watchword of Bonn's policies at home and abroad. On occasion the Defense Minister has been candid, virtually admitting that when France achieves membership in the nuclear club West Germany's demand for parity will be heard again. In March 1958 he said that if France continued her

29. See below, p. 157, n. 34.
30. *Manchester Guardian*, October 11, 1957.

development of an H-bomb, he could not guarantee that the Federal Republic would not be "sucked in (*hineingesaugt*)."[31]

Those who ask us—quite rightly—to accept Soviet power as a reality, should after all not deny their own people the right and opportunity to become likewise a reality. In all negotiations about reunification, risks and chances must be weighed against each other. The risks will diminish, the chances will improve, the more Germany herself has to throw into the scales. . . . A policy of strength in the age of the hydrogen bomb means in no case that one wants to use military pressure, with the risk of a third World War, in order to bring about some territorial changes. . . . A policy of strength means rather that one's own freedom of decision cannot be influenced by pressure from hostile or unfriendly quarters. . . . Germany . . . must become so indispensable to her Western friends, and so respectable for her potential adversary, that both will value her presence in the negotiations.[32]

On another occasion Strauss was quoted as saying that "without possessing potential power, Germany will never have a chance to be heard."[33] The implications of such remarks for Bonn's armament policies are perfectly clear.

There is no longer any doubt that the West German government is extremely anxious to gain possession of its own nuclear weapons and of a nuclear weapons producing capacity. It is going to be a

31. See R. H. S. Crossman's account of an interview with Strauss in the *Daily Mirror* (London), April 2, 1958. The Defense Ministry denied the accuracy of this quotation, but the present writer was given an almost identical answer in an interview with Strauss, also in March 1958. In this connection it is also of interest that in July 1957 the CDU—with Adenauer's express support—caused the defeat of its own amendment to the Basic Law which was intended to permit German "production and use of atomic energy." The Chancellor apparently feared that it might not be possible in the future to muster the two-thirds majority in the Bundestag to excise the clause "for peaceful purposes" which the SPD had tacked on to the amendment during committee consideration. See *Die Zeit,* July 4, 1957; and *The Economist,* July 6 and 13, 1957.

32. Franz Josef Strauss, "Sicherheit und Wiedervereinigung," *Aussenpolitik,* March 1957, pp. 140-147, quoted by Deutsch and Edinger, *Germany Rejoins the Powers,* p. 221.

33. *New York Times,* February 20, 1957, quoted by Deutsch and Edinger, *Germany Rejoins the Powers,* p. 221.

difficult task to exclude the Federal Republic from the nuclear club in the long run, perhaps an insuperable task if Bonn is to remain a coöperative partner in NATO. It is important, therefore, to consider not only whether Bonn should have a nuclear capacity, but in what form it should have it.

The Federal Republic's acquisition of delivery systems for nuclear weapons and her ambitions to gain possession of the warheads themselves, and possibly a capacity for producing nuclear weapons, cannot be ignored in discussing the present state of Bonn's forces and their future development. The military balance, and the political policies of the Western allies and the Communist bloc are bound to be affected by the kind of military establishment West Germany is building.

Of the revised target figure of 325,000 *Bundeswehr* men who are to become part of the NATO force by April 1962, 200,000 will be motorized ground troops organized in twelve divisions of five brigades each. The force will be highly mobile, concentrating on armor but also including airborne and Alpine units. The brigades, each numbering about 3500 men, were developed on the advice of former Field Marshal Erich von Manstein, the most eminent *Wehrmacht* commander to survive World War II with his honor intact. Manstein has exercised considerable influence on Strauss and high-ranking *Bundeswehr* officers in organizational matters and strategic doctrine. The brigades he proposed are versions of the pentomic operating groups first successfully experimented with by the 101st U.S. Airborne Division. They can be dispersed for effective use under nuclear war conditions or reassembled as a division without impairing their combat ability. For the *Bundeswehr,* in particular, the brigade units have the added advantage of effectiveness with or without tactical nuclear weapons. This is especially important for the *Bundeswehr* so long as it does not control the warheads for its stock of tactical nuclear and dual-purpose weapons; and it also insures that the *Bundes-*

wehr would not be emasculated if it were decided for any reason to maintain the army as a conventional force. The *Bundeswehr* is being protected against all threats, against nuclear warfare, and against nuclear disarmament.

The present *Luftwaffe* program calls for twenty-four squadrons by 1960 and sixty squadrons by 1963-1964, comprising 100,000 men and 2000 planes organized around the Mach 2 Lockheed F-104 Starfighter and the Fiat G-91 fighter-bombers. This program will probably be revised and augmented as the *Luftwaffe* takes possession of missiles for anti-aircraft purposes and also short- and possibly longer-range missiles for other missions.

A modern German navy is to emerge from the 150 vessels which are to be built over the next five or six years. Altogether the navy is expected to have 200 ships totalling 200,000 tons, manned by 25,000 men for patrolling German waters and the western Baltic Sea, the task assigned to it by NATO. Submarines and eight 4000-ton destroyers equipped for missile launching will form the core of the fleet, according to current plans.[34]

West Germany is creating two additional forces which are not scheduled to fall under the authority of NATO. These are the Territorial Defense and the Border Security Force, both of which have received surprisingly little attention abroad.

The Territorial Defense now comprises about half its planned peacetime maximum of 25,000 to 30,000 men. Designed as a cadre command and organized on the familiar lines of the *Wehrmacht*'s *Wehrkreis* commands, the Territorial Defense force can be expanded rapidly by calling up army reservists. It is, in

34. West Germany gained NATO assent and WEU permission to construct these destroyers, which exceed the 3,000-ton limit set in the Paris Agreements; *New York Times,* March 8, 1959. This is only one, and not the first, in a series of dispensations granted the Federal Republic by the WEU from the arms manufacture limitations in the Paris Agreements. See, for example, *ibid.,* November 7, 1958, for a report on WEU action permitting the Germans to produce an antitank weapon which German engineers had already tested in Switzerland.

other words, "similar to the Swiss system."[35] A total of 250,000 trained men will be held in readiness for any emergency. These men "are combatants in the full meaning of the word, with all rights and obligations of soldiers."[36] They are organized into army units, chiefly engineer and signal, and also air defense units (*Heimatluftverteidigung*), and their official missions are to maintain communications and protect bridges, railway installations, and other targets against espionage and airborne operations.

The Border Security Force evolved from the Border Police created by the Western Occupation powers. In 1956 the government authorized the 18,000 men in the force to apply for transfer to the *Bundeswehr,* but stated its intention of retaining the Security Force side by side with the army and to recruit to it a full complement of 20,000 men. This decision was explained by the Minister of Interior, Gerhard Schröder, at the time:

This specialized police force cannot be dispensed with because the Iron Curtain which constitutes West Germany's eastern border creates an unusual situation . . . the Iron Curtain cuts through the midst of Germany and . . . , therefore, the preservation of peace along the demarcation line is first of all a task for the police rather than the military. . . . The zonal border . . . is a demarcation line inside our country rather than an international frontier.[37]

Schröder's argument is not easily reconcilable with the official West German (and U.S.) position that the Soviet Union is the sovereign power in East Germany, for if this is the case then the Elbe line is an international frontier. Anyhow the former Western Occupation powers have never pretended that their actions were guided by legal niceties. They favored the maintenance of the Border Security Force on practical grounds, chiefly so that no

35. Interview with Defense Minister Strauss, *Der Spiegel,* January 2, 1957.
36. *Ibid.*
37. *Deutsche Korrespondentz,* December 1, 1956.

"small international incident might develop into a conflict involving NATO."[38]

The Territorial Defense and Border Security forces, then, are parts of what will be, if it is not already, the most powerful military force in Europe exclusive of the Soviet army, with a total manpower of 600,000 serving independently and in a NATO framework. The potential power of this force is causing a good deal of concern to the Federal Republic's neighbors, especially in eastern Europe. The possibility that Bonn may gain a nuclear capability naturally multiplies these fears. With the horrors of World War II still very lively in the minds of the Europeans, such fears are wholly understandable, though also unwarranted—even with strategic nuclear weapons, the *Bundeswehr* will not be capable of waging a successful offensive campaign against any great power, or against any state under the benign or solicitous protection of a great power. The fear that Mr. Khrushchev has voiced on several occasions, that Bonn may precipitate a *revanchiste* war against Soviet Russia which would embroil the United States and other NATO allies, has an understandable emotional basis but is hardly credible. Even if West Germany were inclined to unleash a global conflict, of which there is no indication under its present leadership and in the current temper of its people, it would be inhibited by the certain foreknowledge that in any such conflict the Federal Republic would immediately be turned into an atomized wasteland.

West Germany's rearmament has far greater implications for inter-Allied politics and Western policy toward Soviet Russia than as a military threat to the Federal Republic's neighbors, including Russia and the satellites. An American critic of Western strategy has claimed that there is a contradiction between the Federal Republic's quest for nuclear weapons and its natural interest in limiting conflicts that may arise in central Europe to short, localized conventional engagements. Bonn, he concludes, is "beset with the

38. Speier, *German Rearmament and Atomic War*, p. 196.

same ambivalence toward nuclear weapons which characterizes strategic thought in Britain and the United States"; it seeks "to be prepared for every contingency while evading the real issues of a nuclear strategy."[39] According to this line of criticism, the only "coherent strategy" for West Germany is one that provides a graduated defense, ranging from the strategic deterrent to large-scale conventional forces capable of resisting Soviet or satellite attacks aimed at limited objectives.

This prescription may have real merit; but the reasoning that leads up to it is more questionable. Although it is true of Kissinger's book to a lesser extent than of a number of others that have tried to deal with military strategy in the nuclear age, one can nevertheless detect even in this extremely competent strategist a propensity to make the military requirements of the Western alliance of foremost importance, not only subordinating political factors, but actually replacing the political approach to problems with a military one. This is now a common disease which afflicts the scholarly as well as the governmental community.

The seeming ambivalence of West Germany's military preparations makes more sense than the foregoing criticism suggests; and the prescription for a "coherent strategy," whatever its theoretical merits may be and regardless of the logical consequences if it is not heeded, may be detrimental to the German national interest *as the West Germans conceive it.* Rightly or wrongly, the Bonn government appears to have concluded that an attack by satellite forces is unlikely but possible, that an attack by the Russian Army is most unlikely but that if it should take place it would be virtually impossible to restrict the resulting engagement to a conventional or limited (geographically) struggle. The reasons qualified German sources give for these conclusions are the same ones that are given in other responsible Western quarters: (1) Russia's vast armed manpower superiority, which the NATO powers could

39. Henry A. Kissinger, *Nuclear Weapons and Foreign Policy* (New York, 1958), p. 294.

match to a significant extent, but will not because they are unwilling to pay the social and economic price, and because no political party in the United States or on the Continent will risk its future by advocating what will appear as a sustained *levée en masse;* (2) the introduction of tactical nuclear weapons in the twenty to twenty-two Red Army divisions stationed in East Germany, at least matching the fire-power of the American, West German, and associated European forces in the West; (3) the concentrations of population and the proximity of primarily military to civilian targets in central Europe; (4) the decisive importance of central Europe to both East and West, which makes a limited defeat there intolerable to either side and insures that what may conceivably begin as a conventional war will turn into a nuclear engagement. These are the most prominent reasons why Bonn rules out the chance of a limited conflict in central Europe involving Soviet troops, though it does not rule out a "probing action" or an "incident" provoked by a satellite, presumably by East Germany. Even this is considered unlikely. East German troops would not advance of their own volition, and Moscow would probably not order them to advance—its satellite forces have proven to be unreliable (Poland, Hungary) and there is a great risk that a limited action will get out of hand—and the East Germans cannot be expected to wage a vigorous campaign against their brethren in the West. The *Bundeswehr* (and the Border Security Force) are being readied nonetheless to counter any such action with conventional weapons.

It is the West German supposition that a major conflict would start with an all-out attack on the United States' retaliatory and productive capacities. If a Red Army invasion of western Europe materializes, simultaneously or subsequently, the *Bundeswehr* wants to be equipped to play a role in NATO's nuclear defense.

As a result of Europe's decline in relative political power following the two world wars, no German chancellor is in a position of ultimate responsibility. Responsibility rests where power rests, and the seat of ultimate power on the Western side is Washington. This fact determines a certain interrelationship among the NATO powers which cannot be reversed, but is susceptible to gradual change. Bonn finds itself in a pivotal position on the front line between East and West, and its location, wealth, vigor, and growing military prowess make the Federal Republic a crucial factor within the Western alliance. The West German government has not hesitated to make use of its position to reëstablish itself as the most powerful non-Communist European state. Although its present leaders have wisely abjured any pretense to the country's becoming a "great power," the Federal Republic can be expected to continue to maximize its power and make full use of its crucial position to achieve its primary national goals. Bonn may not be able to call the tune within the Western alliance; it will, however, insist on being heard more and more and will represent its interests vigorously. By the same token, the Federal Republic cannot force Moscow to permit German reunification, but it will certainly do what it can to make this palatable to the Russians on something short of their maximal terms.

West Germany is counting on the acquisition of a nuclear weapons capacity or—at worst—a decisive voice in controlling a European nuclear defense union to gain bargaining power within the Western alliance and greater freedom of action *vis-à-vis* Moscow. Bonn may be underestimating the difficulties of translating a military capacity into a productive foreign policy, but its leadership seems to be convinced that without this capacity it would be condemned to a permanent place on the second team among the Western allies, and would have no chance of bargaining with Moscow, with or without Western support, for the eventual unity of Germany.

Although much of the evidence is self-contradictory, West Germany appears to be taking steps toward a position of viable foreign policy action in non-nuclear weapons development and procurement. Initially, of course, the fledgling German army was almost completely dependent upon the United States for its supplies of weapons of all kinds. But over the years since 1950, and especially since 1954, this dependency was replaced by collaboration in arms development and manufacture with WEU powers, especially with France and Italy, but also with Britain, and since 1956 has turned more and more toward production in Germany itself. Approximately sixty per cent of Bonn's arms expenditures were made abroad and forty per cent at home in 1956; by 1959 these figures had been reversed: sixty per cent of the nine-million-DM defense budget for 1959 was earmarked for purchases in West Germany and only forty per cent for purchases abroad.[40]

The continuing trend toward self-sufficiency in arms production "involves a switch from purely economic to more political thinking."[41] Initially it produced major controversies in Bonn, especially between the Defense Ministry and the Economics Ministry, between Strauss and Erhard, who was backed by the Foreign and Finance Ministries. The gist of the disagreement, carried on in an exchange of letters between Strauss and Erhard, was this: Strauss maintained that it would be cheaper in the long run and would serve Germany's national defense interests better to invest in a new aircraft industry and in the development (in the Federal Republic) of tanks, and the production of weapons carriers and lighter weapons (40 mm. and under), than to purchase these abroad. The political aspect of his argument was that these investments would also enable West German industry to catch up with other advanced (Western) nations in modern technology, implying that these other nations could not, or at the very least should not, be depended upon. Erhard, on the other hand, insisted that the German aircraft companies (the center of the controversy in the early months of 1959) could not catch up with French, British, and American technology and that the investment of several million dol-

40. *Die Welt,* July 4, 1959.
41. *Christian Science Monitor,* October 14, 1959.

lars would be more profitably made in the development of civilian industry. Erhard warned that heavier domestic arms expenditures would give significant influence over the economy to "the generals," an argument undoubtedly brought to the Chancellor's attention. Strauss was the decisive victor when Erhard suddenly withdrew his objections in the spring of 1959 under the influence, it is believed, of a growing body of West German industrialists who, since 1955, had swung around from opposing heavy domestic arms expenditures to the support of Strauss's arguments.[42] As a result it was decided to order two hundred of the Lockheed Starfighters from German factories and the rest from the American company. By December 1959 the plans were changed once again when the Defense Ministry decided to order 564 of these planes from German factories and only ninety-six direct from the Lockheed Corporation.[43]

The pooling of weapons development and research with France, Italy, and Britain has been promoted by the Defense Ministry on the grounds of economy. This collaboration has been endorsed by Herr Strauss with a good deal of bravado and he has tried to use it as proof that he is not aiming toward self-sufficiency in armaments. As a matter of fact, the advantage of such collaboration for the Germans lies both in economy and in their need to gain insight into research and production methods in which they are far behind. It offers them presently the only chance of working with missiles beyond the thirty-two-kilometer range to which they were restricted by the Paris Agreements. The collaboration with other Western powers in arms production is therefore a means to an end. Once the more complex and expensive weapons, such as rockets, are developed by a pool of collaborators or through bilateral

42. In 1955 the Federation of German Industry went on record as opposing the creation of a West German armaments industry. In 1958 Fritz Berg, president of the federation, announced a reversal of this stand; *New York Times,* February 22 and March 1, 1959.

43. *New York Times,* December 11, 1959.

coöperation, Strauss can argue, as he did in the case of the Lockheed F-104's, that it would be more economical as well as beneficial to Germany's defense interests to produce these weapons in quantity in German factories.[44]

On several occasions Strauss has taken umbrage at the allegation that his procurement policies are aimed at achieving self-sufficiency in armaments and are forerunners of nationalist military and political policies. "There can be no autarchical armaments industry and logistical base for us," he said. "For the German armed forces they lie far outside German borders." And on another occasion he said: "The Federal Republic does not want any instrument for national power politics, rather only the necessary means for national independence."[45] But these statements do not carry conviction. Once the military instruments for national independence are available there is also an ability, in fact a requirement, to pursue "national power politics." There is no reason to believe that West Germany will fail to try to exploit the greater freedom of action her strategic location and weapons advances will confer on her; and, surely, one must assume that national interests, not sentiment or emotion, will inspire and be the basis of her policies. We have previously mentioned the greater leverage and viability of Bonn's foreign policy within the West should it obtain a nuclear capacity or something tantamount to self-sufficiency in other forms of armament including missiles.[46] The same holds true for Bonn's relations with the Communist East. The greater the Federal Republic's self-sufficiency in maintaining its diverse forces, the less theoretical and more practical are the possibilities for direct German dealings with Moscow over the problem of German reunifica-

44. In the winter of 1958-1959 Strauss argued that the cost of establishing repair facilities for the F-104s would not be substantially less than production lines for the planes.

45. *Die Welt,* June 24, 1959.

46. See above, pp. 159 ff.

tion.[47] To be sure, Strauss has explicitly denied that "a solo trip of German leaders to Moscow" could achieve anything. "We can solve the German problem only in community with the West," he wrote.[48] But it has surely not escaped his notice, or the attention of his compatriots, that the Soviet leaders have not ruled out a bilateral settlement of the German problem at some stage,[49] and the Germans certainly also realize, as must the Soviet government, that once the decision to give atomic weapons to the *Bundeswehr* has been taken, the opportunities for effecting a change in the status quo in central Europe through U.S. initiative is diminished, while West Germany's ability to negotiate is enhanced.

The issue here is not whether Bonn would "keep faith" with its NATO allies if it negotiated directly with Moscow, or whether such negotiations might not eventually bring about the best possible solution to the partition problem, which is certainly possible. The issue is whether Bonn's armaments policies, in particular its procurement policies and aspirations to become a viable nuclear power, are going to bring the Federal Republic into a position from which it can negotiate directly with Moscow with or without prior consultation in NATO, and with or without taking the interests of its Western allies into account. If current policies will make this possible then—whether or not Bonn would consult its allies—they are clearly detrimental to U.S. interests and need to be reconsidered. Once it attains such a viable position while the Western powers still rely upon it as part of their defensive alliance, the Germans no matter how often they profess "loyalty" to their allies, cannot, and cannot be expected to, subordinate their interests to those of others. They will not forego opportunities for achieving

47. On this point see the discussion in George F. Kennan, "Disengagement Revisited," *Foreign Affairs,* XXXVII (January 1959), especially 203-204.

48. "Soviet Aims and German Unity," *Foreign Affairs,* XXXVII (April 1959), 377.

49. For example, see Khrushchev's statements to Walter Lippmann, *The Communist World and Ours* (Boston, 1959), p. 18.

their national aims for the sake of emotional attachments, which is all that NATO may come to represent to them.

In the present configuration of the Western alliance, the only alternative to American leadership in negotiations with Moscow over European, and particularly German, problems, is Bonn itself. If and when West Germany's power increases, above all if the Federal Republic becomes a member of the nuclear club, it becomes a potent force with which the Soviet leaders must reckon. Moscow will not fail to recognize the opportunities offered by bilateral dealings with West Germany. From the Soviet standpoint, an arrangement with West Germany becomes more attractive as the potential shock value and predictable disruptive influence on the Western alliance resulting from a Russo-German deal over reunification increase. The Federal Republic's armament policies seem to lead in the direction of such a possibility:

A separate German-Soviet agreement, however innocuous or even constructive in its consequences, would set in motion trains of memory, suspicion and resentment of which only the Communists would be the beneficiaries . . . a Western community which had nailed its flag to the mast of an unconditional capitulation of the Soviet interest in Central and Eastern Europe could find itself only humiliated, deflated and injured in its unity and prestige by a German-Soviet compromise.[50]

This warning has been sounded; there is no sign that it is being heeded.

50. Kennan, "Disengagement Revisited," p. 205.

Six

■

BONN AND NATO: NEUTRAL OR ALLY?

The North Atlantic Treaty Organization was born out of fear of Communist aggression, and frustration over the failure of the United Nations to function effectively as a universal security system. Its principal purpose was military and defensive, to improve the security of the United States and Canada and to assure the western European nations that the United States and Canada would —as Ernest Bevin put it—"back" them against the threat of aggression, which up to 1949 had impeded Europe's recovery from the effects of World War II. In order to prevent further Soviet conquests in Europe, the NATO member nations pledged themselves "to safeguard the freedom, common heritage and civilization of their peoples" through collaborative action.[1]

During the more than ten years of its existence, NATO has undergone changes in membership and organization; the member states have considered (and for the most part rejected) a variety of proposals to evolve or transform the organization into a European or Atlantic, political or economic, unity.[2] But throughout this period the basic purpose of NATO, "to create a shield against aggression and the fear of aggression," has remained unchanged.[3]

1. *The Signing of the North Atlantic Treaty* (Washington, 1949), p. 50.
2. See M. M. Ball, *N.A.T.O. and the European Union Movement* (London, 1959), pp. 31 ff.
3. President Harry S Truman, in *The Signing of the North Atlantic Treaty*, p. 35.

In accepting the invitation to join NATO (and the Brussels Treaty), the West German government explicitly recognized "the strictly defensive character of the two treaties."[4] At the same time, the British, French, and American governments declared that "the achievement through peaceful means of a fully free and unified Germany remains a fundamental goal of their policy,"[5] in this way relating as closely as possible the responsibilities following from their role as Occupation powers and Bonn's principal political interests in joining NATO.

The link between NATO and what constitute not only West German but also over-all Western political aims in Europe, does not rest upon a tenuous juridical point. It follows, rather, from the widely held belief that Soviet Russia's exercise of exclusive influence over the territory extending from Russia's western boundaries to the Elbe is unacceptable, both because it constitutes a continuing danger to peace on the Continent and because it imposes the unnatural condition of partition on Germany and on Europe as a whole. If not NATO itself, then the foremost members of it are bound to view the defensive alliance as a means of cultivating the West's strength in order to place it "in a position where it would some day be able to negotiate the liquidation of the . . . division of the continent."[6] The construction of a military barrier against overt Communist aggression was certainly the basic and immediate task of the NATO allies in 1948-1949; but the containment of the Red Army was not viewed—at least not by all the architects of that policy—as an end in itself, but rather as a precondition for negotiating acceptable agreements of issues, among which the future of Germany was and remains paramount. NATO is more

4. "Declaration by the Federal Government of Germany," Pt. V, *Final Act of the Nine-Power Conference held in London September 28-October 3, 1954,* and incorporated as Annex A in the Documents agreed on by the Conference of Ministers in Paris October 20-23, 1954.

5. "Joint Declaration by the Governments of France, the United Kingdom and United States of America," in *ibid.*

6. Kennan, "Disengagement Revisited," p. 206.

than a military alliance; it is a framework for Allied diplomacy. Regarded primarily as a defensive military alliance, NATO has certainly been successful. If one presumes that Stalin would have driven the Red Army across the Elbe in the anticipation of negligible resistance, or that the Communists in Italy and France would have been able to seize power had these countries not been able to reconstruct an orderly social and economic life behind a military shield supported by the United States and Canada, then certainly NATO deserves a share of the credit for preventing Communist advances in Europe after 1949. Ironically, today, when there are signs that the threat of armed Communist aggression in Europe is diminishing, at least temporarily, NATO, which "must be judged strong or impotent by the extent to which it gives assurance of advancing the security of its members," seems to be losing rather than gaining effectiveness.[7] There are two reasons for this. First, the so-called nuclear dilemma—the crisis over the role of nuclear weapons in Western strategy and over how and by whom they will be produced, possessed, and controlled. And second, the failure of NATO as a framework for inter-Allied, and as a center for coalition, diplomacy, as a consequence of the unresolved "nuclear dilemma," and of NATO's failure to serve the particular foreign policy interests of several of its members, most prominently France and the Federal Republic.

In 1950 NATO adopted the so-called "forward strategy," a defense plan to hold "the potential enemy as far to the east in Europe as possible,"[8] implying that Germany would be defended at the Elbe rather than the Rhine. At the Lisbon Conference in 1952 it was decided that NATO would have to have ninety-six divisions in order to defend against the kind of attack the Soviet bloc forces

---

7. R. E. Osgood, "NATO: Problems of Security and Collaboration," *American Political Science Review*, LIV (March 1960), 106.

8. Lord Ismay, *NATO: The First Five Years 1949-1954* (New York, n.d.), pp. 101, 102.

were capable of mounting. For a variety of reasons, among which the very slow pace of German rearmament was not prominent, the Lisbon force goal and the conventional strategy on which it was based were soon superseded by Secretary Dulles' doctrine of "massive retaliation" and a decision to substitute nuclear firepower for manpower.[9] In December 1954 the NATO Council reaffirmed the "forward strategy" and decided to effect it by adopting tactical atomic weapons on the shield. Explaining this decision General Gruenther said: "Even with the German contribution we are not going to be able to match the Soviet in the field of conventional troops and conventional armament." Marshal Montgomery added in positive terms: "We could not match the strength that could be brought against us unless we used nuclear weapons."[10] The failure to mobilize a sufficient number of conventionally armed divisions required the adoption of tactical nuclear weapons in order to maintain the "forward strategy." And this strategy could have been revised only at the cost of the Federal Republic's membership in NATO, since any other strategy implied that the territory between the Elbe and the Rhine was expendable, and that in the event of a Soviet invasion West German troops would be sacrificed as a screen for NATO forces to the west. This prospect could obviously not appeal to the Germans, whether or not it were coupled with a vague hope of eventual liberation from Soviet occupation. "The Germans are not interested in winning the last battle," a German officer remarked in 1955. "They want to be defended, not liberated."[11]

The reformulation of the defensive line on the Elbe, by equipping NATO's divisions with tactical atomic weapons, failed to provide for an adequate defensive strategy and raised new prob-

9. For a brief discussion of the changes in the strategic situation after 1952 see R. Hilsman, "On NATO Strategy," in A. Wolfers, ed., *Alliance Policy in the Cold War* (Baltimore, 1959), p. 150.

10. Richard P. Stebbins, *The U.S. in World Affairs, 1954*, pp. 176-177.

11. Geye von Schweppenburg in the *Süddeutsche Zeitung*, October 22, 1955, quoted by Kissinger, *Nuclear Weapons and Foreign Policy*, p. 288.

lems for East-West relations and for the Federal Republic's relations with her NATO allies. For one thing, the prospect of atomic devastation through a "suicidal" response to a Red Army attack could be no more comforting to the Germans than the prospect of an indefinite Soviet occupation, and possibly less so. And other problems were raised: Which of the NATO forces were to be equipped with atomic weapons? Only the American divisions, or other Western ground forces, too? Who was to control the weapons? When France joined the nuclear club, would Bonn have to be admitted too?

After the 1954 decisions certain stop-gap measures were taken to enable NATO to avoid having to answer these perplexing questions categorically. The stop-gap measures consisted of equipping the five or six U.S. divisions with a variety of tactical atomic weapons and handing over a number of atomic weapons and delivery systems, with everything except the actual warheads, which are stockpiled nearby under American control, to five or six NATO countries including the Federal Republic. But neither these actions nor the decision taken in December 1957 to station IRBMs and their warheads in Europe have developed a convincing NATO strategy for defending its members against limited or major aggression. On the contrary, the Allies have grown more dissatisfied under these arrangements which make them more vulnerable to attack while the United States and Britain retain control of the nuclear warheads and stockpiles. There are still only approximately sixteen "combat ready" NATO divisions, just about half the number General Norstad considers the minimum required to contend with the forward line of Soviet and satellite forces. And since the Red Army is now equipped with tactical atomic weapons, the NATO forces are not only outnumbered but also have less firing power than the twenty-two Russian divisions in East Germany. The tactical nuclear weapons on the shield have, in addition, failed to give the expected economies in manpower and expenditure. The net effect of the 1954 and 1957 NATO decisions has been to reduce the security of the United States and its NATO allies against a limited attack while Soviet progress in developing and stockpiling the strategic deterrent has reduced the doctrine of "massive retaliation" to the suicidal ridiculous. And at the same time, dangerous and possibly irrevocable steps have been taken in the direction of nuclear diffusion within the alliance.

France, West Germany, and other European countries justify their drive for acquiring nuclear weapons and nuclear-weapons-producing capacities by the assertion that Russia's missile capacity renders America's support of her continental allies in the event of a Soviet attack undependable. These countries hope to enhance their security through independent efforts rather than by strategic collaboration in NATO. The arguments of the Allies in this connection are fraught with ambiguity. On the one hand they insist that the five or six U.S. divisions remain in Europe as hostages, to guarantee the implementation of the American deterrent in the event of a Soviet attack; at the same time they insist on developing an independent nuclear capacity, asserting that they cannot depend upon the American deterrent. The Allies also insist that the U.S. divisions are needed to defend against a Soviet attack short of an all-out attack, and yet they refuse to create the conventionally equipped forces of their own to meet this contingency. And third, while they claim they do not have the money to raise sufficient forces to replace the American divisions, the Allies are prepared to expend enormous sums to construct independent nuclear capacities and delivery systems.

Washington's surprisingly tractable response to the Allies' contradictory arguments is apparently based on the belief that if the United States does not facilitate the process of nuclear diffusion it will drive the Allies toward neutralism. It has been argued that "sharing the control of nuclear weapons among allies may preserve the cohesion of NATO and even promote it by giving allies a greater sense of security, participation, and responsibility."[12]

There is, however, every reason to believe that the diffusion of nuclear weapons will erode the very basis of Allied interdependence:

The corrosive impact of nuclear diffusion upon the interdependence of the United States and her European allies could be especially serious. The diffusion of nuclear capabilities will increase American suspicion, if not the actual likelihood, of some ally committing, or threatening to commit, the United States to nuclear war under circumstances in which the United States would not be willing to bear the costs and risks of nuclear war. Indeed, considering the limited nuclear capabilities that allies are likely to achieve in the next decade or so, the ability to commit American nuclear power may appear to be the chief utility of independent nuclear capabilities. This situation would induce the United States to do exactly what her allies have always feared: to qualify or repudiate her obligation to come to the defense of Europe.[13]

The danger the continental allies claim to perceive today and the one which they use as justification for their drive to control atomic weapons and nuclear capacities, namely, that the United States cannot be relied upon to commit herself to the defense of the Continent, would in fact be created, or if the danger exists, heightened, by the diffusion of nuclear weapons and capabilities in NATO. This price would be worth paying, perhaps, if France or West Germany could defend themselves against either a limited or a major Soviet assault by relying entirely on their own atomic weapons. But this is extremely doubtful. Bonn, for example, even if it controlled tactical and strategic nuclear weapons, would still be dependent upon its allies for defense against any kind of an attack save an invasion by a conventionally equipped satellite force.[14]

12. R. E. Osgood, in a paper prepared for delivery at the Annual Meeting of the American Political Science Association, Washington, September 1959. The paper was later revised for publication, as cited in n. 7 above.
13. *Ibid.*
14. See the discussion in Hilsman, "On NATO Strategy," pp. 162-163.

What do France and West Germany expect to gain from acquiring these weapons?

At least in part, the Federal Republic's drive for these weapons follows France's insistence on joining the nuclear club. And De Gaulle has indicated that he expects to capitalize on France's standing as an independent nuclear power to achieve certain political aims. Since the autumn of 1958, and even more explicitly since the summer of 1959, he has demanded that France be permitted to join Britain and the United States in a "directorate" of the NATO alliance, and that Paris be consulted by Washington and London, "if only by telephone," about where and when the strategic deterrent would be used.[15]

Adenauer has only lagged a step behind De Gaulle in this matter since the General returned to power. As recently as the spring of 1957 Adenauer seemed to have complete confidence in the Anglo-American deterrent. "A Soviet attack against us," he said, "would be automatically followed by a United States counterblow." When Russia sent aloft her first Sputnik and unleashed a rocket psychosis in the West in which the vulnerability of the United States to Soviet missiles became a cardinal political fact, and also—and perhaps most important—after De Gaulle first proposed that France be granted superior standing in the alliance, in the autumn of 1958, the Chancellor seemed to become worried about West Germany's dependence on foreign weapons stationed on foreign territory under foreign control. He told an interviewer in the summer of 1959:

The two Anglo-Saxon countries are alone in a place where eventually the decision on war or peace may be made. If one considers the whole matter objectively, that is not a very pleasant situation.[16]

The Chancellor's misgivings, his doubts about the firmness of the American resolve to act, especially since the death of Secretary Dulles, the weaknesses of NATO, the antics of De Gaulle, and

15. *New York Times,* February 2, March 21, April 22, July 6, December 15, 1959.
16. *Ibid.,* June 18, 1959.

not forgetting the ambition of many Germans (one suspects including many in high positions) to gain the status and prestige of a nuclear power, all combine to construct a situation in which Bonn can argue effectively for control of nuclear warheads and for the acquisition of a variety of nuclear weapons. Now that France has joined the nuclear club, one may be sure that the German demand for parity will be heard again.

To become a nuclear power also opens the way, some West Germans believe, to a more viable and effective foreign policy. The Federal Republic, according to some Germans, has a "special position in NATO."[17] This phrase is interchangeable with another, "NATO is no dogma," which many West Germans, including defense and foreign affairs specialists in Bonn, are prone to use.[18] Although these phrases are used loosely and rarely defined, they stand for the additional responsibility the Germans feel for reuniting their country, over and above the responsibility the Occupation powers assumed at Potsdam and reiterated in the London and Paris Agreements, to which Bonn has relentlessly bound them ever since.

West Germany's NATO allies grant her special position only in so far as the reunification formulas that have been proposed by them give a future all-German government the choice whether or not to belong to NATO. In contrast, the view that many Germans have of their special position in NATO is that Bonn must be free to withdraw from NATO in order to achieve reunification on terms that West Germany finds acceptable. This special position, as many Germans conceive of it, seems to be reflected in and supported by the ambivalent rearmament efforts being made outside as well as within NATO, which provide for the possibility of "police actions"

17. For example, see the editorial entitled "Die deutsche Sonderstellung" in *Der Tagesspiegel*, December 15, 1957.

18. For example, see the statement of the former Bundestag deputy Kurt Georg Kiesinger (CDU), then chairman of the Foreign Relations Committee, in *Verhandlungen des Deutschen Bundestags*, January 23, 1958, p. 330.

West Germany could conduct on her own, and give her *Bundeswehr* divisions which could be effective with or without tactical atomic weapons.[19]

It is clearly to Bonn's interests to be in a position in which it can decide to remain in NATO or withdraw from it, depending upon its political interests. As the Federal Republic's military establishment becomes even stronger the Germans may find themselves in a position where their NATO membership is more of a hindrance than a help in achieving reunification. This is not an imminent danger but it can become one if West Germany controls nuclear weapons, and perhaps a nuclear productive capacity, especially if there is some reduction in the threat of Communist attack. In considering any West German request for atomic explosives, even if Bonn should suggest that this is its price for continued loyal membership in NATO, the West must realize that once the *Bundeswehr* controls the warheads, Bonn may regard the presence of U.S. divisions and the Federal Republic's membership in NATO differently from the way it does today. In theory at least, decisions could thereafter be made in Moscow and Bonn that until then could practically only be made in Moscow and Washington.

It is clear that the current period is an anxious one for the Bonn government. Defense Minister Strauss's awareness of this, but perhaps also his great expectations of where the current arms program is leading, may account for his evasive reply when he was asked what the impact would be on the *Bundeswehr* if the Federal Republic withdrew from NATO. Strauss gave his answer in the form of an anecdote. During maneuvers, Strauss said, he had asked a colonel how things were going. The colonel's reply was direct and equivocal: "*Jawohl*" (yes, Sir).

The diffusion of nuclear weapons will not strengthen NATO militarily and may have untoward political consequences for the alliance, but Britain and the United States may not have the power

19. See above, pp. 157-159.

to stop the spread of nuclear weapons to their allies. Indeed, France's entry into the nuclear club and the expected development of nuclear weapons by Sweden and Switzerland make the attempt to restrict the manufacture of these weapons in the West appear to be doomed to failure. To prevent the alarming development of competing nuclear systems within the NATO alliance, proposals have been made for an Atlantic Defense Union, in which the United States and United Kingdom would relinquish their ultimate power of decision over the strategic deterrent to the NATO command, giving each member nation a voice, and a veto, over its implementation, and, alternatively, for a European Nuclear Defense Union, a kind of EDC for atomic weapons.[20]

The strongest appeal of these schemes is that they provide safeguards for the continental allies against the failure of the United States and the United Kingdom to use the strategic deterrent in the event of a Soviet attack directed against western Europe only—a fear which, it is said, chiefly accounts for the drive toward acquiring nuclear weapons and toward autarky in armament generally by France and West Germany.

If the Atlantic Defense Union were formed it would have the effect of curbing the national freedom of action of its member states in exchange for the dubious advantages—dubious at least for the United States—of an integrated military and a united political front capable of formulating a coherent strategic doctrine. It would submit the U.S. power to act, presumably not only in Europe but also elsewhere in the world, to controls exercised by a majority of nations in the Union, and in some circumstances possibly to a veto power by even the smallest of the member nations. In the same way, Britain's responsibility in the Commonwealth,

20. For the Atlantic Defense Union, see Moore, *NATO*, pp. 200 ff. For the European Nuclear Defense Union, see the Introduction by John J. McCloy to Henry L. Roberts, *Russia and America: Dangers and Prospects* (New York, 1956), p. xvi. Also Moore, *NATO*, pp. 233 ff.; and Kissinger, *Nuclear Weapons and Foreign Policy*, p. 551.

still one of the fundamental pillars of world stability, would be hobbled.

In the view of some, including the present writer, the Atlantic Defense Union proposal is therefore the reverse of what is called for in the current political stalemate between East and West in Europe. For the best chance of ending the stalemate before the continuing weapons race results in catastrophe would seem to follow from a situation in which the United States and Soviet Union have the maximum freedom to maneuver and utilize their full political potential to negotiate agreements which provide for step-by-step solutions of the major problems that divide Europe. Such agreements, if they were to be reached, would of course have to safeguard the interests and aspirations of America's allies. But there cannot be equal responsibility in negotiating with Moscow—Mr. Khrushchev has shown a strong preference for bilateral dealings with Washington, and Western coalition diplomacy has proven to be unsuccessful. The compromises that have had to be made in inter-Allied negotiations preceding negotiations with Moscow have imposed inflexible positions on the West which, at one and the same time, have prevented the West from marshaling its full strength and exploiting Soviet weaknesses, while offering the Soviet leaders every opportunity to exploit differences among the Allies. A genuine reduction of East-West tensions, which can only follow from hard-headed accommodations of the conflicting interests among the great powers, is not possible if the United States does not retain the freedom of action to lead a vigorous Western policy; for the United States, and perhaps Britain, are the only Western states with a significant influence on the Soviet government. Any political restrictions to which Britain and the United States submit in order possibly to lay the basis for a coherent NATO strategy will atrophy the power which alone in present circumstances stands a chance of bringing about peaceful settlements of specific disputes between East and West in Europe.

It would surely be the greatest folly, no less from the Franco-

German standpoint than from the Anglo-American, if in order to extract NATO from its nuclear dilemma the United States agreed to join an Atlantic Defense Union and thereby created an even more serious political dilemma.

A strong case has been made for the alternative to an Atlantic Defense Union, the European Nuclear Defense Union which, as proposed, would control "the entire range of modern military power including nuclear weapons" and be "strong enough to deter aggression by the Soviet Union and resist its pressure."[21] In view of western Europe's fears that the American deterrent would not be used when needed, and considering that France's development of nuclear weapons is well under way and that other European powers aspire to join the nuclear club too, this scheme has a practical side to it and obvious attractions for some continental powers. From an American point of view great risks outweigh its benefits for Western defense. Allies do not become more valuable to the United States because they possess an independent nuclear capability; in fact, as has been explained, they become a source of danger for the United States.[22] A European Nuclear Defense Union, even if it were formed within the broader NATO framework, would enable the participating countries to pursue jointly an independent policy; and if the struggle to dominate the community brought any one nation into ascendancy, that nation could pursue its interests with vastly greater strength than it could hope to gain by any other means. Jointly or independently, the member nations could negotiate directly with the Communist bloc "or even attempt to play off the Soviet Union and the United States against each other to make gains at the expense of both."[23] Europe's nuclear independence would increase the chances that atomic hostilities might break out. In other words, if a European Nuclear Defense Union were created, the United States would be confronted not only with a new

21. Moore, *NATO*, pp. 233-234.
22. See above, p. 175.
23. Moore, *NATO*, p. 234.

political force, but by a new nuclear dilemma which would be fraught with dangers that are just as great as the ones it is intended to dispel. And while the scheme would not guarantee Europe's support of the United States, the United States would still become involved in any nuclear conflict that started in Europe.

The scheme has drawbacks from the point of view of both the French and the West Germans. If the two nations were to form a nuclear force, there would be nothing to prevent either one from withdrawing after a time and relying on a national nuclear capability. Why, then, should the French—who have such a headstart in nuclear armament today—enable the West Germans to come into possession of a nuclear capability? And could the West Germans, in joining a nuclear union with France and four or more European powers, be any more certain that their partners would use the deterrent in the event of Soviet threats or attack than they are today that the United States will honor its obligation?

It has been argued that the formation of a European Nuclear Defense Union would convince the Soviet leadership that Europe cannot be neutralized and in this way "improve the prospects for an agreement on arms control."[24] This is very doubtful. In a period which has seen the Soviet Union achieve nuclear parity with the United States, why should the creation of a European deterrent convince the Soviet government to agree to arms control terms which it repeatedly rejected when the United States and Britain had a virtual monopoly on atomic arms? It would appear that, on the contrary, the adoption of the nuclear union scheme would be a blow at the chances of reaching East-West arms control agreements, since these are currently aimed at preventing test explosions and restricting nuclear weapons to the present members of the nuclear club.

It appears that, for the time being at least, the military and political risks for the United States if the western European allies obtain a viable strategic deterrent would be greater than the political

24. *Ibid.*

risks, for NATO and the United States, in maintaining an Anglo-American monopoly on these weapons for as long as possible. If the three power negotiations to restrict or to abolish the production of nuclear weapons break down or fail repeatedly to reach satisfactory agreements, then the day may come when the United States will have to reconcile itself to a European deterrent in some form. Meanwhile, as long as France's atomic weapons are not far beyond the prototype stage, there is no military reason and no compelling political reason to rush ahead with plans for adding members to the nuclear club. In particular, any application from Bonn to take possession of nuclear warheads, to control a deterrent power, or establish its own nuclear weapons industry, must be firmly rejected. Bonn deserves sympathetic understanding and every consideration for its sensitivity about an inferior or secondary standing within NATO; but this does not require the United States or its other partners to accede to every demand for parity in weapons. When granting such requests adds to the dangers of nuclear war and entails new political liabilities without there being any comparable military or political advantages for the alliance as a whole or the United States in particular, acquiescence would not only be unjustified but even irresponsible.

It cannot be the purpose here to define a new strategic doctrine for NATO. However, certain facts regarding the nuclear stalemate between East and West and the nuclear dilemma of the NATO alliance must be cited to lay a basis for a discussion of possible Western political initiatives aimed at ending the partition of Germany and Europe.

Strategic weapons emplaced anywhere in western Europe are now within easy range of Soviet missiles and are therefore virtually useless for either deterrent or retaliatory purposes. The development of solid propellants for missiles will not cause any essential change in this situation. The deterrent weapons can be effective in the European theater as a whole only if they are highly mobile or are emplaced on the periphery of the Continent, in Britain, in the Mediterranean area, and under water. Similarly, the greater fire-power of tactical atomic weapons on the shield is no substitute for manpower in deterring a Soviet attack or defending against it, be-cause the Red Army is now also equipped with these weapons. These weapons are now "as dubious an asset for an army to carry around as were Hannibal's elephants."[25] The single function of NATO's tactical atomic weapons is that of a deterrent against Soviet use of *their* tactical atomic weapons in the event of a conflict.

The real need on the NATO shield is for a greater number of divisions equipped with conventional weapons, divisions contrib-uted by the Europeans themselves. There is certainly no assurance that the British forces stationed in West Germany will remain there for a longer time, and there is also no reason to count on an in-creased commitment of American troops, except in the event of hostilities if the United States has by that time created highly mobile pentomic divisions which can be airlifted from the Western Hemisphere to any point in the world where they may be needed. The Western Europeans must put up the bulk of the twenty-five to thirty divisions and reserve forces needed on the shield by them-selves; and they can do this if the French divisions in Algeria are returned to the mainland and not disbanded, and if the Federal Republic readopts the force goals originally envisaged in the EDC proposal and reaffirmed in the London and Paris agreements of 1954.

The build-up of conventional forces by western Europe, sup-ported by U.S. and, for the time being, British troops in possession of armed tactical atomic weapons, and backed by a deterrent-retaliatory force on the periphery of the Continent, would not only establish a sound military and strategic structure in view of the various pressures the Communist bloc can bring to bear on west-ern Europe, but would leave open the possibility of advancing Western proposals for ending the stalemate that prevents the unifi-

25. "Tomorrow's Strategy," *The Economist,* August 8, 1959.

cation of Germany and Europe. A reciprocal withdrawal of non-European forces from central Europe and the creation of a non-nuclear zone which eventually may become the core of a united, armed, but militarily neutral Europe, is possible only so long as West Germany does not gain possession of nuclear warheads, not to speak of a nuclear weapons producing capacity. Once the Federal Republic gains possession of atomic weapons, she will be able more actively to pursue the objective of reunification within the limits of acceptable security risks, while, at the same time, United States, British, and French bargaining power with respect to a German settlement will rapidly diminish to legalisms.

The United States will not find it easy to resist the demands of its European allies for a share in the deterrent power. There will be more expressions of the fear that the United States may withdraw into a "fortress America" rather than risk self-destruction in defense of western Europe. It may prove to be difficult to allay these suspicions, but it is not an insuperable task. What it will take, above all, is vigorous American leadership of the alliance. America's faithful allegiance to the Western cause since 1948 should be ample evidence that it will not desert its friends in future times of stress. The reasons why this is so must become evident to the American people and to their allies. They must see that, in the final analysis, it is not emotional attachments to the Old World but the hard facts of national interest that determine United States policy. The security of the United States is interrelated with that of western Europe. Secretary of State Acheson declared in 1949: "The control of Europe by a single aggressive, unfriendly power would constitute an intolerable threat to the national security of the United States."[26] This statement holds true today. None of the great technological advances of the past ten years, and none that may conceivably occur over the next ten years, can reduce the United States' immediate interest in the security of the Continent.

26. *Department of State Bulletin,* XX (March 27, 1949), p. 385.

"The concept of 'fortress America' is wholly obsolete," Adlai Stevenson said in March 1959:

Though Korea is, in contrast, of marginal strategic importance, the American response was clear and immediate. Who can suppose it would be less so if the vital security of Europe were at stake? . . . I do not believe we Americans can ever again stand aside while aggression attempts to take history by force.[27]

The United States cannot simply dismiss a genuine sense of insecurity in Europe; patient explanations and reassurances must be given. But if the doubts of the U.S. resolution to defend its own and western Europe's interests persist, and especially, if these are contrived in order that certain countries may gain national advantages, they must be firmly rebuffed.

Explanations, firmness, and solemn promises that the United States will honor its obligations cannot by themselves prevent divisive forces from weakening the alliance. It will be necessary, above all, for the United States to give vigorous political leadership to the alliance by taking diplomatic initiatives aimed at resolving the major disputes with the Communist bloc without sacrificing the vital security interests or the legitimate aspirations of any NATO member. Such leadership would be the best possible demonstration of the community of interest linking the American and European peoples, and of America's determination to defend Western interests with force if need be.

The resolve to act militarily, the credibility of the deterrent power, is best proven by determined political leadership, firmness in the face of threats, as in Berlin, both in 1949 and since 1958, and imaginative proposals backed by a sustained diplomatic effort —and this has not been shown in the current Berlin crisis, just as it has not been characteristic of the over-all American response to the challenge of communism outside of Europe.

There is no ideal military posture which can give western Europe an ironclad guarantee of American support. Any attempt to

27. *New York Times,* March 6, 1959.

create new military organizations, to devise new treaties, or to transform NATO into a global alliance for this purpose would be fruitless. Moreover, "the ideal military posture is simply the enemy of every political *détente* or compromise."[28]

The modern nuclear dilemma calls not for better strategic doctrines but for men who can give leadership and who can devise arms control policies which must be made to serve, not determine, the interests of nations.

28. Kennan, "Disengagement Revisited," p. 199.

Seven

■

GERMANY, RUSSIA, AND EASTERN EUROPE

Soviet policies have been decisive in shaping postwar German history. The failure to establish a unified Occupation rule owing to Soviet intransigence and the breakdown of negotiations for an all-German peace treaty led to the creation of an independent West German state. The consolidation of Communist rule in East Germany and Soviet policies menacing the freedom of western Europe resulted in the hardening of the split. East and West German rearmament, the creation of NATO, and the Warsaw Pact widened the gulf between East and West in Europe.

Midway through the second decade of partition there is certainly no reduction in the intensity of the power struggle for Germany. For the present, the means the Soviet leaders are employing to detach West Germany from its Western alliances and bring it under Communist-bloc influence are predominantly nonmilitary, and therefore conducive to a "reduction of tensions" in a world which has, unfortunately and mistakenly, become used to analyzing the balance of power largely in military terms and to identifying threats of aggression as chiefly military in origin. The emphasis in Soviet foreign policy has indeed shifted to economic and political means of gaining supremacy, but there has not been any radical departure from the foreign policy aims pursued by Stalin. And although Stalin was more prepared to use overt threats of military action than his successors have been, even he seemed to regard military power as a secondary means of exploiting revolutionary situations in order to extend Russia's sphere of influence during the postwar period. Khrushchev has deëmphasized the role of the military but he has clearly not excluded the use of military power to achieve foreign policy aims. This was shown by his reactions to the Suez crisis, the crisis over the Turkish-Syrian border, the Hungarian revolt, and the declarations in support of the East German regime during the first months of the new "Berlin crisis."

Khrushchev has left no doubt in the minds of those who have been willing to listen what the goals of Soviet foreign policy are. A realist in analyzing specific power relationships, pragmatic and adroit in manipulating the machinery of government to suit immediate and emergent needs, Khrushchev is nevertheless not a cynic, but a sincere and orthodox Communist. More than a true believer in the eventual supremacy of Marxist-Leninism, he is a zealot of the early Bolshevik type, possessed of the boundless energy and revivalist fervor found only in those who believe they are rediscovering and serving the cause of History.

For Khrushchev, as for Lenin, the key to the advance of the Communist revolution throughout Europe is the capture of Germany, the geographical and industrial heart of the Continent. The advance of the revolution through the Middle East and Africa is not a diversion, but a policy complementary to the direct expansion of Communist influence in Europe. The foothold that Communism has gained in central Europe through its control of East Germany is today being consolidated; but this is not an end in itself, nor simply a bargaining counter to assure the security of Soviet Russia. It is, in Khrushchev's mind, a step along the road to the domination of all Europe; and there is no force in existence today which can jar the Soviet leadership from the conviction that, eventually, the "Socialist" economic and political system, and with it Russia, "The Motherland of the Revolution," will reign supreme in all of Europe.

While it is important to recognize the nature of Soviet ideology today—which liberals in the West often fail to do—it is just as important to recognize the limited role which ideology plays in the conduct of day-to-day Soviet foreign policy, which conservatives and reactionaries in the West habitually fail to do. Although Soviet foreign policy evolves in a certain ideological framework consisting of unchanged (and for all practical purposes unchangeable) goals and beliefs, specific actions and reactions of the Soviet government to existing situations and developments are realistic—that is, based on shrewd analyses of power relationships and the consequences of alternative policies. The Soviet leaders are prudent men; they have a faith and are faithful to it, but they are not fanatics. In Germany and wherever else the West comes into conflict with Soviet power, Western policy-makers must be aware of Communist aims, because it is only with this awareness that complete policies can be devised to meet the real challenges which are never theoretical or abstract, but always concrete and specific.

As long as Moscow persists in holding on to its wartime territorial gains as a buffer and potential base for further advances, Eastern Germany will be forced into a tight-knit relationship with the rest of the Communist bloc, and the Federal Republic will be impelled into close ties with the West. In the absence of agreements leading to German unity, the "provisional" institutions of the West German state will be accepted as permanent. The continuing military threat represented by the Red Army in the D.D.R., Poland, and Hungary is bound to lead to a greater arms build-up in Western Germany, possibly even exceeding the targets set for 1961-1962.

So far, the Soviet impact on Germany and western Europe has been all one way. Russian threats, bluster, and intransigence have supplied the mortar for the unification of the West in Europe and between the continental states and the Atlantic powers. These policies seem to result both from the fears of the Soviet leadership and from their ideological convictions. Fears of Western aggression and of disaffection among the satellites create a need for large contingents of forces in East Germany, the linchpin of Soviet Russia's control machinery in its own orbit. The unwavering belief in the inevitable advance of Communism beyond its present borders justifies the concentrations of Red Army troops in central Europe. Here they can be used to support the western European proletariat when it creates revolutionary situations.

In recent years the Iron Curtain across Europe has become as much a bar to the expansion of Soviet influence as it has been a means of consolidating Moscow's wartime gains. The realization of this, combined with a new self-assurance derived from the military and economic strengthening of the entire Communist bloc, has already led the Soviet government toward a far greater measure of flexibility in its European policies, with the hope of achieving by adroit political and economic tactics what calculated military threats failed to attain and cannot accomplish as long as the Western powers maintain an adequate defensive force. Throughout the postwar period, Soviet "peace offensives" and conciliatory gestures have had a divisive effect on the Western alliance. Just as Russian military threats have led toward greater unity in the West, the appearance of a compromising attitude in Moscow has tended to cause dissension among the Allies. There are good reasons for this. As long as the Soviet Union threatens the sovereignty of the Western nations they have an overwhelming interest in collective defense. When those threats are reduced, the particular interests and aspirations of each Western power assume a greater importance than the fears which lead them to coöperate. As the Soviet leaders become more self-assured, as Khrushchev gains more and more popular support from the Russian people and becomes more confident about the reliability of the satellite governments, Moscow will be in a better position to carry out more flexible policies toward the West—to brandish the carrot more often than the stick. Such tactics were foreshadowed by Khrushchev's proposal of a reciprocal withdrawal of foreign troops from central Europe. In the future, if the East German regime continues to gain in status and its institutions take on at least a semblance of permanence, the Soviet government may feel sufficiently confident not only to propose a military disengagement, but—if the West continues to refuse to discuss such proposals—may score a major political and propaganda victory by withdrawing unilaterally most of the Red Army divisions from the D.D.R., all of its troops from Hungary, and all but a skeleton force to maintain supply lines, from Poland.

Soviet offers of disengagement or possible unilateral withdrawals would have as their primary purpose luring the Federal Republic from her Western ties and persuading the West Germans to accept Communist terms for reunification. Because of their key position in central Europe and the continuing anguish of partition, the Germans are more susceptible to pressures of all kinds from Moscow, to both the hot and the cold in Soviet foreign policy, than other Western nations. This is readily acknowledged in Bonn, where it has long been axiomatic that no government could refuse to take the country out of NATO if the Russians were to make this the *sine qua non* of reunification "in freedom." Until now, however, the Soviet leaders have been unwilling to give assurances that a reunited, neutral Germany would be truly independent, and not just a vehicle for further Communist advances. As the D.D.R. becomes more firmly established, the West Germans are being forced to give up the illusion that unity could be achieved simply by incorporating the East German territories into the existing West German establishment, or by imposing other Western terms on the Communists. Whether it is to be called a confederation, federation, or something else, the process of German reunification, if it takes place at all, will be gradual; reunification cannot be accomplished by an *Anschluss,* not even if the Soviet Union were willing to "sacrifice" the Pankow regime as part of a Russian-West German bargain, of which there is only the remotest chance at the present time in any event. Most West German officials, probably including the Chancellor, realize that the West's formula for reunification, which never stood a chance of being adopted by the Russians voluntarily, cannot be imposed on the Communists either. The question that is therefore coming more and more to the fore in Bonn is, what will replace the old and now untenable reunification policy? If Bonn's allies are being forced to give at least *de facto* recognition to the existence of a second Germany, the Federal Republic cannot maintain the fiction that the D.D.R. does not exist; and however abominable the prospect may appear to the West Germans, they must then deal with the D.D.R. if they are to make any practical political moves to achieve unity. But where does this process of facing facts lead? How far will the West Germans go, not only in recognizing the Pankow regime but in accepting Soviet terms for unifying the two Germanies? What would be the impact on the Federal Republic's reunification policy of renewed Soviet proposals for a military disengagement? As the *Bundeswehr* is fully developed, possibly with a nuclear capability of its own, how would a West German government react to disengagement proposals? In the event of a unilateral withdrawal of Red Army contingents from the D.D.R., would Bonn press for the withdrawal of U.S. forces from its soil in order to gain concessions from the Soviet and Pankow governments in reunification negotiations?

All of these questions are of key significance for the future of U.S.-German relations and reveal the great impact future German policies will have on American security. There are no categorical answers to these questions; the answers will be found in Bonn's future East European policies.

The influence of Soviet policies on postwar Germany points up a basic truth which, though often obscured by the propaganda of the Cold War, remains a central and fixed fact of European geography: Germany faces east as well as west. The Federal Republic is today dependent upon its Western allies for its security; for the realization of its chief political aims it must turn east. Since neither an act of God nor Russian benevolence is likely to achieve these aims for them, the situation requires that the Germans adopt an Eastern policy that can influence the course of events in their favor. This is obvious and would not have to be pointed out were it not for the astounding fact that West Germany has not, so far, adopted a constructive policy toward eastern Europe, despite its strong and persistent interests there.

One of the characteristics of public foreign policy discussions in the Federal Republic since 1950 is a penchant for devising elaborate proposals and plans for resolving the dilemmas of partition. It is notable that this activity has been carried on almost exclusively by the opposition parties and private groups. With very few exceptions, members of the governing coalition have refrained from participating in the planning mania. Only during one short period in 1958, significantly while Adenauer was out of the country and left the direction of the government in the hands of the Vice-Chancellor, Ludwig Erhard, did members of the government make their own specific proposals for German reunification.

Although none of the plans for "disengagement," "atom free zones," and "neutrality" devised by the SPD and FDP parties have been adopted, and although it is doubtful that such preconceived and detailed plans will ever be adopted, the fact that members of the government coalition have simply rejected each one and not come up with specific alternatives of their own, which might at least have gained them an advantage in domestic political debates, is indicative of the paucity of thought given to the problems of Germany's East European policies in the higher echelon of CDU officialdom. Each one of the opposition plans has been based on an "activation" of West Germany's Eastern policy; the Adenauer government, on the other hand, has restricted its East European policy to condemnations of the Pankow regime and Soviet policy, rigidly subordinating all proposals for exercising a positive influence on the Soviet orbit to the tasks of achieving unity with the West. For Adenauer this imbalance seems to represent a deep-rooted conviction that there can be no compromise with the "atheist principles" of Communism, and that Germany's future lies exclusively with the West. Others in the Adenauer government are less dogmatic, but have lacked the courage to propose definite steps. One minister told an American visitor in 1958 that he has always kept in mind Stresemann's comment on his Locarno policies: "I never thought more about the East than during the time I was looking for an understanding in the West." And Franz Josef Strauss, perhaps the most independent-minded and dynamic member of Adenauer's cabinet, when asked if he thought there would ever be down-to-earth discussions between the West and the Soviet government, was anything but dogmatic:

In response to this question I want to make a fundamental point: Foreign policy does not have a programmatic, rather a pragmatic nature. It must have basic themes, but must be able to adjust itself to particular situations. . . . One will have to be prepared to carry on negotiations with the Soviets over a period of years, for which the American-Chinese talks in Warsaw can serve as a model of patience and tenacity.[1]

Strauss's reply would seem to indicate that not all of Adenauer's advisors are as "inflexible" as their critics contend; but in the first ten years of the Federal Republic's existence, Bonn's attitude toward the Communist states has nevertheless been legalistic rather than imaginative. Adenauer's policy toward eastern Europe has consisted of assertions that the Federal Republic alone can speak for all the German people, that the "so-called D.D.R." is simply the zone of Soviet occupation and its puppet regime an agency of Moscow domination, and that West Germany does not recognize the Pankow government and will not carry on diplomatic relations with any nation that does recognize it except the Soviet Union itself, which is considered to be in occupation of German territory. The West German government continues to follow these principles today, and as a result has had no diplomatic relations with any Communist states except Soviet Russia, and also Yugoslavia, with which relations were broken off when Belgrade recognized Pankow in 1957.

1. *Bulletin,* June 30, 1959.

The crisis in relations with Yugoslavia was the one occasion during the past decade when there was any real chance of Bonn's replacing the negative assertions with a positive policy. Before the crisis, which took place in October 1957, Bonn was seriously considering taking up diplomatic relations with Warsaw. Adenauer was being persuaded to make such a move with the argument that Poland, like Soviet Russia, could be recognized as an occupation power since it had taken possession of the "lost German provinces" —"the Third Germany," as many West Germans call the trans-Oder-Neisse territories. The Poles balked at this formulation, for they were even more anxious to obtain West German recognition of the Oder-Neisse line as Poland's final western frontier than they were to have German credits, expanded trade relations, and diplomatic exchange. However, Polish-West German talks were still in progress through a variety of channels to try to reach an acceptable formula for establishing diplomatic relations when Tito, apparently at Moscow's instigation, recognized the East German regime. The Yugoslavs clearly did not believe that Bonn would carry out its threat to break off relations, and Gomulka, too, may have miscalculated that Tito's move would force West Germany to take up relations with Poland on the basis of its sovereignty over the Oder-Neisse provinces. Whether the Soviet government also believed that Bonn would do this rather than break off relations with Tito, or was deliberately trying to prevent West German ties with Poland, is known only to Moscow. In any event, Bonn did choose to break off relations with Belgrade rather than drop its rigid adherence to the doctrine, enunciated by Herr von Brentano in 1956 (but known in Bonn as the Hallstein Doctrine, after the former State Secretary and close collaborator of Adenauer), that it would not have relations with any country that recognized the Pankow government. The reiteration of this doctrine in October 1957 also forced the project of relations with Warsaw to be dropped. No one doubted the logic of the doctrine's basic thesis—that general recognition of the Pankow regime would lead to the acceptance of Khrushchev's assertion that there are in fact "two Germanies," which, in turn, would harden the division of Germany. Indeed, the logical and legal bases of the West German claim to be the only spokesman for all Germans have been amplified in a seemingly endless stream of self-justifying documents sponsored by the Bonn government. But from the standpoint of political realities the nonrecognition doctrine weakens the Federal Republic and puts it at a severe disadvantage in relations with its East European neighbors, as the Yugoslav crisis of 1957 showed.

The reality of Soviet power behind the Ulbricht regime has transformed the Communist myth that a sovereign East German state actually exists into a significant political fact, while the comparable West German myth, that Bonn alone speaks for all Germans, has steadily lost rather than gained significance and support. Its only significance is that, still in the 1960's, Bonn is able to persuade its allies to pay lip-service to the myth. The longer Moscow is able to keep an East German government in existence, the more difficult it is for Bonn to make its claim convincing. And although Bonn is able to keep Washington, London, and Paris from dealing with the Russians on the basis of "two Germanies" as long as it insists on holding them to the letter of the Paris Agreements of 1954, this is poor compensation for the other consequence of the nonrecognition doctrine, which is that Bonn remains cut off from Poland, Czechoslovakia, and the Balkan states. This, precisely, was the point made by the Federal Republic's Ambassador to Belgrade, Kurt Georg Pfleiderer, during the crisis of October 1957. Pfleiderer had apparently succeeded in convincing both Adenauer and Heuss that the ties with Belgrade should be maintained and that diplomatic relations should be taken up with all the satellite governments except Hungary and Albania. Pfleiderer's argument that such moves would be the most effective challenge to Pankow's pretense that it represented any significant number of German people, also made a distinct impression on Foreign Minister von Brentano. But Pfleiderer's sudden death in the midst of the crisis permitted State

Secretary Hallstein and the then Director of the Foreign Ministry's Legal and Political Division, Wilhelm Grewe, to hold Brentano and, subsequently, Adenauer to the old negative doctrine. Hallstein and Grewe successfully raised the specter of a host of Asian and Middle Eastern states granting recognition to Pankow if Bonn failed to "punish" Belgrade for doing so.[2] The upshot of the decision to break off relations with Belgrade was to prevent, at least for a while longer, general recognition of the Pankow regime, but also to prolong West Germany's isolation from Eastern Europe.[3]

There was no doubt that Chancellor Adenauer remained dissatisfied with this situation. Throughout the election campaign of 1957 he gave every indication of wanting to "reactivate" an Eastern policy.[4] But the Chancellor was handicapped by a paucity of information and by often very one-sided advice on eastern Europe, especially after Pfleiderer's death.[5] Despite his misgivings, he accepted the cautionary legalistic counsel to terminate diplomatic (though not commercial) relations with Yugoslavia and call off the talks with Warsaw, thereby automatically prolonging the Federal Republic's negative policy and its isolation from eastern Europe.

◆

2. *New York Times,* October 20, 1957. The account of Pfleiderer's views given by *Der Spiegel* (January 1, 1958) has not been challenged by any official sources in Bonn.

3. *Süddeutsche Zeitung,* October 26, 1957.

4. *Frankfurter Allgemeine Zeitung,* September 21, 1957; *New York Times,* October 14, 1957.

5. Adenauer's information on eastern Europe has come chiefly from three sources: Bonn's representatives at the listening posts in Belgrade (until 1957) and the Vatican; General Gehlen's intelligence agency *(Bundesamt für Verfassungsschutz)* formerly part of the General Staff's intelligence service which was taken over by the United States' OSS and then CIA, and now Bonn's own intelligence agency, although it is still heavily dependent upon American sources of information; and, third, the *Neue Zürcher Zeitung.* The Chancellor has repeatedly cited the *NZZ* as a basic source of his information and opinions. See, for example, Norbert Muhlen, "An Encyclopedia with Three Deadlines a Day," *The Reporter,* July 23, 1959.

The doctrine of not recognizing Pankow or nations that recognize it is one of two guiding principles of West Germany's policy toward eastern Europe. The other is the Federal Republic's stand on the trans-Oder-Neisse territories, including East Prussia, over which Poland has claimed sovereignty. The D.D.R. and all other Communist states have recognized the Polish claim to these territories. However, the Federal Republic, with wavering support from its major allies, continues to insist that Polish rule over these areas is provisional pending a final, all-German, peace treaty settlement of all boundary questions as specified in the Potsdam Agreements. According to the Bonn government, only an all-German government has the right to dispose of these territories; therefore Pankow's recognition as Germany's final eastern boundary has no legal significance.

This doctrine, like that of nonrecognition, has merit in legal terms. Like the nonrecognition doctrine, it also has inescapable domestic and foreign political implications. The West German government's position has been that recognition of Polish title to the eastern lands is a major concession and part of Bonn's bargaining power in negotiating German unity, and should not, therefore, be made prematurely. All the major West German parties are keenly aware of the voting power of the refugees from the eastern territories and do not want to alienate their political support. On the other hand, Adenauer has repeatedly pledged that Germany will not resort to force to gain what it considers a just settlement of the border dispute, at the same time maintaining that all German expellees and refugees, not only from the trans-Oder-Neisse territories, but also from East Prussia and the Sudetenland, have a *Heimatrecht,* a right to return to their homelands.[6] The SPD and FPD generally support this position. Informed circles in Warsaw seem to believe in the sincerity of Adenauer's pledge against the

6. See Adenauer's speech of June 28, 1959, at the Silesian Convention in Cologne; *Bulletin,* June 30, 1959.

use of force, but they doubt that this pledge will necessarily be upheld by his successors. From Warsaw's point of view, a nonagression pledge is not a substitute for outright recognition of Poland's title to the Oder-Neisse territories. Moreover, the demand of *Heimatrecht* raises the specter of hordes of expatriates returning to claim properties which have been taken over by new owners and frightens the Poles and other East Europeans with the possibility that a large German minority may again agitate for autonomous rule or for an *Anschluss* with Germany. The Poles maintain their traditional hostility toward Soviet Russia, but this does not come close to matching their fear and hatred of all Germans, regardless of whether they are West Germans or East Germans. Since the Poles recognize that West Germany is much more powerful than the D.D.R., East Germany's recognition of the Oder-Neisse frontier does not give them any real security in the light of West Germany's refusal to do so. And while East Germany is controlled by the Russians, to whom the Poles owe their "liberation" from the Germans in 1945, and Soviet pressure on the internal policies of the Warsaw government has been relaxed since 1956, the build-up of West Germany's military forces, which is skillfully exploited by Communist propaganda to keep alive the memory of Nazi brutality, has kept the German peril uppermost in the Polish mind.[7] As a result, Stalin's brilliant stroke of diplomacy in gaining Allied agreement to compensate Poland with German territory for Russia's aggrandizement at Poland's expense, is still reaping dividends. For as long as the German peril is uppermost in their minds, the Poles are bound to regard the Soviet Union as the "protector of Polish reconquests." And because Red Army forces are in and around Poland, and Moscow can rely on Ulbricht's D.D.R. as an ally against any too-radical Polish devia-

7. For a discussion of the "balance" of Polish fears, as between Russia and Germany, see George Steiner, "Notes from Eastern Europe," *Harper's,* June 1959, especially p. 54.

tion from the Marxist-Leninist code of behavior, Poland cannot have an independent policy.[8]

Poland's absolute security dependence on Moscow cannot be broken until the West German government, or an all-German government, renounces all claims to the Oder-Neisse territories. However, even if Bonn were to make such a declaration now, Warsaw would continue to be at the mercy of the Soviet government as long as the Red Army holds Poland in an enormous pincer. When pressed, West German officials use this as the ultimate justification of their refusal to recognize the Oder-Neisse boundary. As long as Soviet troops remain in East Germany, they say, recognition would not result in Warsaw's supporting the cause of German reunification. What the Germans tend to ignore is that the Poles will not be enthusiastic about the prospect of German unity even in the best of circumstances, and that Bonn's only

8. The basic Oder-Neisse dispute has been obscured by masses of propaganda. At the Yalta Conference, the Allies agreed on the Curzon Line as the postwar Russian-Polish boundary and decided to compensate Poland for her losses by "substantial accessions of territory in the north and west." These agreements were reaffirmed at Potsdam where the trans-Oder-Neisse territories were put under Polish administration pending a final peace treaty with Germany, which has not been concluded. Warsaw, with the support of the Soviet Government, subsequently claimed sovereignty over the former German provinces, while Bonn, with unenthusiastic support from its major allies, disputes Poland's title to the territories. This is the basic dispute, but both sides have been maneuvering to support their claims to strengthen the positions they may be expected to take in future negotiations. Thus the Poles assert that the Oder-Neisse territories, even before the German exodus of 1945, were settled by more Slavs than Germans. The Bonn government asserts the opposite ("Die Bevölkerung der Oder-Neisse Gebiete," *Bulletin*, July 10, 1959), and refugee propagandists sponsored by a variety of West German "institutes" publish a seemingly endless stream of exhaustive legalistic tracts purporting to "prove" that the "lost provinces" belong to Germany. Some refugee revisionists attack the wartime agreements as "illegal"; see, for example, Kurt Rabl (*Die Gegenwärtige Völkerrechtliche Lage der Deutschen Ostgebiete,* Munich, 1958), who argues that the inviolability of Germany's sovereignty over the provinces is assured by the Atlantic Charter, and that the expulsion of Germans from the area was an act of "genocide" as defined by the UN.

chance of gaining Warsaw's indirect support for German unity would be to give the Polish government a stronger interest in the withdrawal of the Red Army from the D.D.R. The icy attitude of the East Europeans toward Germany as a whole will not begin to thaw until the Germans have renounced all claims and have at least made a start toward reacquainting themselves with eastern Europe—and the East Europeans with a new, peaceful Germany. Until this happens, the Poles, Czechs, and Balkan peoples—even those who fervently wish to throw off Soviet domination—will perforce choose Communist tyranny over a repetition of the nightmare of German tyranny and brutality.

The basic impediments to German unity are the presence of Soviet troops and Soviet political domination in Eastern Germany. Since Russia's political power depends upon the presence of Soviet military forces, and inasmuch as these cannot be dislodged from East Germany by force except at the risk of a general conflagration, the Germans must mount a political and diplomatic offensive which can be most effective only if it elicits support from the East European governments. The only other alternative for Bonn if it wants to achieve German unity, one which petrifies the East Europeans and tends to drive them still further into the arms of the Soviet government, is a deal between West Germany and Soviet Russia at the expense of the states lying in between. While it is difficult to see how such a deal would improve the position of the Soviet Union, and Bonn steadfastly disclaims any intention of negotiating one, such an accommodation is not beyond the realm of possibility and might become a more immediate concern in the future.[9]

Chancellor Adenauer's celebrated visit to Moscow in September 1955 was marked by an exchange of recriminations and a sharp Soviet rebuff to what the Chancellor's official biographer has called

9. See below, Chaps. 7 and 8.

the German's "ethico-political criteria" in the talks.[10] The Soviet leaders were shocked by Adenauer's apparent insensitivity to their pride; the Chancellor was shocked by the Russians' scornful rejection of his appeal for "humane" and "realistic" relations between Moscow and Bonn, based on the achievement of German unity in freedom, and Adenauer, in turn, shocked the Federal Republic's allies by yielding to the Soviet demand for diplomatic relations on the ambassadorial level—precisely what Adenauer had assured Washington, London, and Paris he would not do except in exchange for genuine concessions leading toward reunification. All that the Chancellor actually received by agreeing to diplomatic relations was a promise that the prisoners-of-war who were still detained by the Soviet Union nine years after the Unconditional Surrender would be repatriated. This enabled Adenauer to return with something to show for his venture to Russia.

The acrimonious exchanges in Moscow set the tone for relations between Bonn and Moscow for more than a year, and a hostile atmosphere has prevailed to the present time. But there have been interludes when relations seemed to be improving. In December 1956, for example, following the suppression of the Hungarian uprising, Bulganin declared that the Soviet government wanted good relations with the Federal Republic "since such relations . . . as the experiences of the past had shown, could be of great service to both sides." Over the following months Adenauer and Bulganin exchanged four letters and as many diplomatic notes in which the Germans charged that Moscow was going back on its commitment to reunify Germany and the Russians charged that Bonn was sabotaging East-West disarmament talks and was working to obtain atomic arms.[11] Despite the bitterness in these exchanges, there were hints that Soviet policy toward Germany might be given

10. Edgar Alexander, *Adenauer and the New Germany,* trans. T. E. Goldstein (New York, 1957), p. 217.

11. Extracts from these exchanges are discussed in *Ost Europa,* VII (July-August 1957), 517 ff.

new content if Bonn were willing to disentangle itself from the NATO alliance. Soviet periodicals pointedly recalled the Rapallo Treaty of 1922 which, the articles emphasized, was signed "at a time when Germany's foreign policy was directed by politicians with a 'Western' orientation. It was no coincidence [the articles asserted] that the German leaders signed such a treaty with Soviet Russia. They understood perfectly well that once Germany had been assured of Soviet Russia's friendly support, it could start talks as an equal with its western neighbors. The understanding between Germany and the East required the West to change its posture toward the German partner, treating him with greater respect."[12] Some West German officials have said that "there was nothing behind" this new Soviet line, meaning no concessions on reunification, while others in Bonn are sure that their government did not even investigate to find out if there was anything behind it because it feared repercussions in Allied capitals. In any event, Adenauer refused to engage in broad political talks with the Soviet government, but did agree to start trade and consular representation negotiations in July 1957. After months of negotiations marked by innumerable interruptions and much propaganda on both sides, chiefly over the issue of repatriating German civilians in the Soviet Union which Bonn made a condition of any treaty with Moscow, the agreements were finally concluded in early 1958. The fact that agreements were reached at all was of greater importance than the economic benefits either side gained from them. The political significance was deliberately underscored by the Soviet government in dispatching Deputy Premier Anastas Mikoyan to Bonn to sign the agreements instead of Foreign Minister Gromyko, whom the

12. *Die Sowjet Union Heute* (house organ of the Soviet Embassy in Bonn), April 10, 1957. The same general line on Rapallo also appeared in same, April 20, 1957; in *New Times,* No. 18, Moscow, 1957; *Dokumentation der Zeit,* Heft 142, East Berlin, May 20, 1957; and in *Izvestia,* April 16, 1957, in which a commentator, N. Polyanov, wrote: "The ideas . . . underlying the Rapallo Treaty are still valid today."

Germans would have preferred so as to minimize suspicions in Washington, London, and Paris.

During the course of the trade, consular, and repatriation negotiations in Moscow in 1957, both sides tacitly agreed that cultural exchange negotiations should be held "in reserve," possibly to serve as a vehicle for broader political discussions, but in any event to keep relations between the two countries "*im Gang*" (under way). A treaty providing for West German-Russian cultural and technical exchanges was subsequently negotiated and signed, but without effecting any noticeable change in relations between the two countries.[13]

Following an exchange of reasonably polite but inconsequential notes between Khrushchev and Adenauer in the autumn of 1959,[14] the Soviet government started its most virulent postwar campaign, villifying Adenauer personally and defaming the West German state in general. The campaign reached its zenith during Khrushchev's visit to France in March 1960 where the Soviet Premier made repeated anti-German speeches and remarks. These drew an angry protest from Bonn, accusing the Russians of "obvious untruthfulness"[15] and of spreading "distrust and enmity" on the eve of the then scheduled Paris summit conference.[16] After the U-2 spy-plane incident Soviet fire was drawn away from Adenauer and West Germany and directed against President Eisenhower and the United States; but it was evident that this episode in the spring of 1960 constituted only a lull in the Soviet campaign to defame the Federal Republic in order to alienate it from the NATO alliance.

13. The text of these agreements is in the *Bulletin,* June 2, 1959. The exchange programs were subsequently expanded; *ibid.,* March 12, 1960.
14. *Ibid.,* August 25 and September 1, 1959.
15. This charge referred to a report from the Soviet Embassy in Washington, published in *Izvestia,* that Chancellor Adenauer himself scrawled the swastika which appeared above his signature in the guest book at the National Gallery.
16. Text of the West German note in *New York Times,* April 7, 1960.

It appears that over the period since diplomatic relations were resumed in 1955, Bonn and Moscow have not had consistent direct discussions of the broad political problems between them, and no serious—that is, practical—proposals have been made by either side to solve these problems. Discussions of the reunification issue have either served propaganda purposes, especially on the part of the Russians, who have repeatedly tried to influence the course of West German politics, or confined themselves to wrangling within the framework of the incompatible positions developed on the one hand by the Western alliance, and on the other by Moscow in support of the Ulbricht regime. If any secret political talks have been held, these have obviously not met with more success. Only one such parley is known about. That was the discussions Adenauer's Minister of Finance (and later Minister of Justice) Fritz Schäffer held with Ambassador Pushkin and the D.D.R.'s Deputy Defense Minister in East Berlin during October 1956. When this venture was revealed in November 1958, Schäffer said that the purpose of his talks, about which he said Chancellor Adenauer had been informed in advance, was to sound out Soviet opinion with a view to furthering the Bonn government's "aspiration for peace and reunification."[17]

There are several good reasons for Adenauer's failure so far to sanction broad political discussions with representatives of the Soviet government regarding the German problems. The Chancellor is convinced that such talks would be useless. He assumes that the Russians would take the initiative through normal diplomatic channels if they were prepared to make new proposals which Bonn could accept as a basis for negotiations. Furthermore, the Chancellor is unwilling to take the chance that broad exploratory talks with Moscow might be misunderstood in Western capitals and cause friction in the alliance. The Chancellor is, in fact, extremely sensitive to what his chief assistant, Dr. Hans Globke,

17. *New York Times,* November 15, 1958; *Die Welt,* November 13, 14, and 15, 1958.

calls "volatile" American public opinion, which is regarded as highly suspicious of German motives and might even accuse Adenauer of "disloyalty" if he were to talk with the Russians about hypothetical solutions of the German problem that have not been strictly defined in prior inter-Allied negotiations.

The reaction to an interpolation in the Chancellor's speech at the Paris heads-of-government meeting on December 16, 1957, illustrates the causes of Bonn's fears of taking initiatives *vis-à-vis* Moscow. Adenauer was persuaded by Blankenhorn and von Eckhardt to say that the most recent letter from Bulganin had been unusually "temperate" and that it contained "suggestions" which he, the Chancellor, would like to have the Soviet government clarify through diplomatic channels.[18] According to one of the principals involved in this maneuver, the Chancellor was prepared to send von Eckhardt to Moscow immediately if the speech had been given a friendly reception by the Soviet government. The German delegation in Paris searched in vain through the Russian press and radio commentaries of the next days for any sign of understanding; but there was none. Adenauer not only had to suffer a rebuff from Moscow, but also severe Western criticism, especially from the press, for taking the initiative in the first place.[19] Commenting on the Chancellor's initiative a State Department official said that the Bulganin letter had not been temperate, that it contained no new suggestions, and that, in any event, Adenauer should not have acted independently at a meeting called to reassure the world that the Western powers remained firmly united despite the near panic reaction, especially in the United States, to Russia's surprise launching of the first Sputnik.

The net effect of this episode was to reinforce the Chancellor's

18. Text in *Informationsfunk der Bundesregierung*, December 17, 1957.

19. Adenauer was especially unhappy about the criticism of his speech in the *Neue Zürcher Zeitung* (December 18, 1957) and in a front-page editorial appearing in the Paris edition of the *New York Herald Tribune*, which some German delegates at the conference believed was inspired by Secretary Dulles.

cautionary attitude toward the taking of initiative in relations with Moscow. He not only dislikes the opprobrium attached to such acts, but, even more, is afraid that they may have dire consequences for the Federal Republic by giving its allies a reason or an excuse to renounce their responsibility for the achievement of German unity, in order to reach a *modus vivendi* with Moscow based on partition. Others in Bonn also fear that this may happen, but Adenauer is more suspicious than most West German officials.[20] His fear that the Big Three will be tempted to make such a deal has increased since the death of John Foster Dulles, whom Adenauer believed to have been "the only obstacle to appeasement of the Soviet Union."[21] British agitation within the coalition for discussions of military disengagement with the Soviet Union, at a time when the Soviet government was applying intense pressure on the Western powers to recognize the Pankow regime in exchange for a new guarantee of access to Berlin, finally drove the West German Foreign Ministry to issue a subtle warning that the Allies would "rob themselves of their right to influence" a German settlement if they submitted to Moscow's demands.[22] Whether or not this warning is turned into an active threat over the next years depends both on Bonn's readiness to follow a more independent line toward Moscow than it has to date and on the value the Soviet government places on the Pankow regime as it gains status. To insure the loyalty of its allies, the Federal Republic until now has been anxious to appear as the most fervent champion of the cause of "Western unity."

20. For example, in September 1957 Adenauer told James Reston that "President Eisenhower was engaged in a private correspondence with Soviet leaders against the wishes and without the knowledge of Mr. Dulles." (The quote is from Reston's account of an interview, *New York Times,* April 8, 1959.)

21. *Ibid.*

22. From a statement by the chief West German delegate participating in the Geneva Foreign Ministers' talks, May-August 1959, Ambassador Wilhelm Grewe; *Informationsfunk der Bundesregierung,* July 29, 1959.

This situation may not last if the West German people become impatient with fruitless East-West discussions of the German problem, and especially not if Washington, London, and Paris are driven to give some form of recognition to the Pankow regime. If that should happen, the Federal Republic's only alternative to either accepting the Communist confederation plan or holding futile reunification talks with an East German regime which cannot sanction free elections and remain in power, would be an independent approach to Moscow on some new basis. The success of such an effort, if it were made, as indeed the success of any negotiations regarding the German problem, depends upon the extent to which Russia's security interests balance against the achievement of Communist ideological goals in the thinking of the Soviet leadership.

It has been argued that in the period leading up to the Geneva Conferences of 1955, during the winter following the Polish and Hungarian uprisings of 1956, and again before the NATO decisions of December 1958 providing for the establishment of nuclear missile sites in western Europe, the major Western powers failed to explore possibilities and hesitated to make proposals which might have led to the withdrawal of the Red Army and to a solution of the German partition problem.[23] The merits of these arguments will have to be examined for their relevance to future policy;[24] but regardless of their validity, there can be no doubt that since 1955, and especially after 1956, the Soviet Union has made every effort to incorporate East Germany into the Communist orbit while at the same time flatly rejecting Western terms for German unity and giving no indication that these would become more acceptable if they were amended to guarantee that a freely united Germany would be excluded from NATO.

23. These arguments were most cogently stated by Kennan, *Russia, the Atom and the West,* especially Chaps. 3 and 6.
24. See below, Chap. 8.

The D.D.R. is playing a role of increased importance in the military strategy and economic plans of the Communist bloc. As a military base for twenty Soviet divisions, the D.D.R. poses a standing threat to western Europe, serves to protect the bloc against a Western attack, and is the guarantor of the loyalty of the satellite states, especially Poland. The Red Air Force has fighter bases in East Germany, and the Soviet Navy can make use of the fortified submarine station being rebuilt on the island of Rügen and of the harbor of Rostock, which "is being transformed into a first-rate naval port of a size which seems out of proportion to the potential strength of the D.D.R.'s navy."[25]

The D.D.R.'s economic importance to the Soviet Union is also great and potentially greater. Although its industrial plant was stripped and plundered by the Russians during Stalin's reign, the Soviet Union has more recently given credits and other forms of economic aid to reconstruct and develop the East German economy into the most efficient industrial producer among the satellites. Nationalized industry is becoming part of the Communist bloc's planning and production system (COMECON), signifying East Germany's integration into the Eurasian economic area, which is to be transformed into at least as tight an economic bloc as the West European Common Market Area.[26] By March 1959 East Germany and Soviet Russia had become each other's largest foreign trading customers, while the D.D.R's trade with the West (most of it through Berlin) was steadily reduced.[27] East Germany's industry has taken on a major role in fulfilling the ambitious targets of the Soviet Seven Year Plan, especially the chemical industry and certain other East German specialties, such as rolling mills, wire drawing machinery, and machine tools for

25. Dietrich Mende, "Soviet Policy and the German Problem," *The World Today*, XV (July 1959), 272.

26. *Ibid.*, p. 273. And see Khrushchev's speech at the 9th All-German Workers' Conference in Leipzig, March 7, 1959; *The Current Digest of the Soviet Press*, Vol. XI, No. 13, April 29, 1959.

27. *Wall Street Journal*, March 30, 1959.

the production of bearings. There is now every indication that the Soviet government will continue to support and give over-all direction to East Germany's industrial development and that this may soon be acclaimed as the second German economic "miracle."[28] In agriculture, too, the Communists have made headway. In mid-April 1960 East Germany's press hailed the success of a three-months collectivization drive which officially eliminated private land ownership.[29] Rationing of foodstuffs was finally ended in 1954, and although there are occasional and sometimes grave shortages (for example, East Berlin was without sufficient milk during the summer of 1959), food and diverse consumer goods are becoming available in greater quantity. Barring a recession in the Communist bloc, East Germany's per capita production will continue to rise and perhaps match that of the Federal Republic by the mid-1960's.[30] The greater availability of consumer goods and a general improvement in the standard of living should make the lot of the East German citizen an easier one, thereby reducing or even eliminating the economic motive for moving to West Germany, which has played such a prominent role in the flow of the young people, workers, and farmers to the West since 1945.

The decline in East Germany's population and the rapid advance in the mean age of the approximately seventeen million people who remain, due to the self-imposed exile of so many of its citizens, was a major factor in Ulbricht's successful appeal for Soviet economic aid and political support. As early as January

28. Soviet economic support to the D.D.R. was apparently an issue in Kremlin politics. Saburov's confession at the 21st Party Congress indicates that the opposition to giving aid had been defeated.

29. *Neues Deutschland,* April 15, 1960.

30. A Western expert on the East German economy recently stated that "a substantially improved performance of the planned East German economy is . . . possible and indeed likely. It is quite possible that in the future, growth rates in East and West Germany will be about the same." Wolfgang F. Stolper, "Germany Between East and West: An Economic Evaluation," *Looking Ahead* (National Planning Association), Washington, April 1960.

1957, Ulbricht seems to have confronted Khrushchev with the fact that, if he wanted the D.D.R. to keep in step with the economic and political integration of the bloc, if the Pankow regime was not to have to impose a "hard" Stalinist line on its people, and unless Soviet Russia was prepared to give East Germany more or less permanent financial subsidies, it would be necessary for Russia to help put East Germany on a sound economic footing and take the necessary steps to gain recognition for it and to cut off the flow of refugees to the West.[31] The Soviet leaders apparently recognized the force behind Ulbricht's arguments, for they themselves realized that, over the longer run, they could not maintain control over the D.D.R. without a repetition of the dangerous revolt that took place in June 1953, unless the people's needs were more adequately provided for, skilled workers and professional people remained to serve the regime, and the East German government received the benefit of more popular support which might come from the psychological boost of achieving general recognition. Ultimately these arguments motivated Khrushchev in provoking the "Berlin crisis" whose immediate aim appeared to be to gain Western recognition of the D.D.R. government, and in the long run, to force the West out of the city, thereby cutting off most of the refugee flow and giving East Germany an important new industrial center.[32]

The strategic value and economic importance of the D.D.R.

31. The Soviet Union pledged economic and political aid to the D.D.R. in the Moscow talks of January 1957. See the text of the communique issued following the meeting in the *New York Times,* January 8, 1957.

32. Theoretically, East Germany could stop the flow of refugees to West Berlin at any time by halting S-Bahn (elevated subway) traffic and cutting off other avenues of escape across the sector line. One can only conjecture as to the reasons why this has not been done: Presumably, many East Berliners would lose their jobs; East Berlin would be deprived of the labor of West Berliners who work in the Communist sector; the Communists could no longer send agents into West Germany posing as refugees; and West Berlin might retaliate by suspending trade relations which so far are still very valuable to East Germany.

are not the only advantages to the Soviet Union in keeping hold of the East German state. Ulbricht's strict adherence first to Stalin's and now to Khrushchev's policy line has been an invaluable asset to the Kremlin, especially during times of crisis within the bloc, such as the Polish and Hungarian revolts. Ulbricht's Marxist-Leninist orthodoxy has been second to none, and there have been times when it appeared that he would out-Herod Herod, as, for example, in his attacks on Yugoslav "revisionism." His only departures from the Kremlin line were his failure to echo vociferously the de-Stalinization anti-cult-of-personality chorus and occasional flirtation with Peiping's orthodoxy, but these do not appear to have jeopardized his standing with Moscow. Ulbricht's ideological loyalty has become a genuine asset to him in dealing with the Soviet leaders. They would be reluctant in any event to "sacrifice" the D.D.R. because of its strategic and economic importance; Ulbricht's ideological loyalty makes it doubly difficult to liquidate the D.D.R., for this "could not but result in a severe loss of prestige" for the Soviet Union which would "lower her standing in world Communism and enable that of China to rise. It might engender reactions in Eastern and South-Eastern Europe."[33] Above all, the Kremlin would lose an unwavering ally against Warsaw if the regime there should seek to stray too far from the right path. Indeed, Polish heretics would be emboldened by a Soviet withdrawal from East Germany.

Although the East German leaders do not wield as much power within the Communist bloc as Adenauer does in the West, Ulbricht, Grotewohl, and their colleagues are more than puppets; they have built up a certain bargaining power by making their leadership and East Germany's location and resources an important asset in Soviet policy. Khrushchev could "sacrifice" the East German leaders if he wanted to, and it is not beyond the realm of possibility that he might do so in the course of significant

33. Mende, "Soviet Policy and the German Problem," p. 273.

negotiations with the West as a whole or, more likely, with West Germany alone. Ulbricht is valuable to the Kremlin, but not invaluable. Part of his value is that he is despised so much, not only by the East Germans, but also by the West Germans, many of whom would be prepared to reconsider the Communist confederation scheme and the proposed all-German negotiations once Ulbricht was out of the way. No doubt the Soviet leaders are aware of this, and it may have been due to the influence of Russian protectors, not simply because of the new Communist practice of demoting rather than executing leaders who have been accused of "conspiracy" or "antiparty" behavior, that Oellsner, Wollweber, and Schirdewan—whom Ulbricht accused of deviation and disloyalty, charges which have resulted in the death sentence for other East Germans—are still in circulation. Oellsner (formerly a deputy premier), Schirdewan (formerly a member of the Central Committee who had been tipped as Ulbricht's successor), and Wollweber (formerly the Minister of State Security who was considered a fanatic Communist) were removed from their party and high government posts in February 1958 for criticizing Ulbricht's economic policies, the inflexibility of his foreign policy, and the harshness of his repressive measures against intellectual dissenters, particularly students. All three now have minor positions in the D.D.R., but there are many East and West Germans who believe they are being held back in the wings, ready to be sent out on stage whenever it pleases Moscow to replace Ulbricht with men who can make the old—or new versions of old—domestic and reunification policies more palatable to Germans on both sides of the line. Ulbricht has done his best to eliminate alternatives to his rule by surrounding himself with yes-men, but the Kremlin holds the power of decision as to who will succeed—or replace—him.

The power Moscow exercises over the D.D.R. was well illustrated during the "Berlin crisis." Khrushchev's charges and demands starting in November 1958 were exceeded by those

emanating from Pankow. Ulbricht was clearly attempting to hurry
Moscow toward a withdrawal of its authorities from East Berlin
and into a bilateral peace treaty with Pankow. Khrushchev was
much more cautious, especially on the issue of a peace treaty,
which is an important bargaining counter for the Soviet government, not only in relation to the West, but also in maintaining
control over the D.D.R. At every step of the way leading to the
high level talks of the summer and autumn of 1959 Ulbricht, who
was straining to rid himself of West Berlin, had to knuckle under
the tortuous twists and turns of Moscow's policy. At one point
this proved to be positively embarrassing for the East Germans.
Their bellicose insistence that Western troops had no right to be
in Berlin, which Khrushchev himself had initiated when he based
his demand for giving Berlin the status of a "free city" on the
supposed contraventions of the Potsdam Agreements by the
Western allies, had to be retracted after the Soviet leader suddenly
reversed himself and admitted that Western troops had a right to
be in Berlin as long as no German peace treaty was signed.

The future of the D.D.R., therefore, depends not only on its
usefulness in preserving the security of the U.S.S.R. and serving
Communist expansionist ambitions, but also on the extent to which
a process of reunification can serve these interests from the Soviet
point of view. Although the Soviet government's present support
of the Pankow government and of its interests is tantamount to a
position against German unity, this is not necessarily a permanent
policy. Changes in it depend upon revisions in the West's or in
West Germany's policy on reunification, and Moscow seems to be
convinced that the German demand for unity will grow and that
the price the Federal Republic will be willing to pay for reunification will rise. In this respect, the Russians may be wiser than those
in the West who imagine that partition can be maintained indefinitely and that any change in the so-called status quo is bound
to serve Western interests.

◆

The Geneva Conferences of 1955 succeeded in making more explicit the tacit agreement between East and West which had been in existence since the death of Stalin, to the effect that neither side considered a global conflict a worthwhile risk to take in solving either the ideological or the specific political conflicts between them. The net effect of this agreement was to downgrade the German problem, which was then and still is considered to be the chief political issue separating East and West. Both sides signified that they did not consider this issue worth fighting about, provided neither side actively challenged the control the other exercised over its half of the country. In retrospect, therefore, the West's success in getting Marshal Bulganin to sign his name to a directive instructing the foreign ministers to settle "the reunification of Germany by means of free elections" was no more than a propaganda victory, for the Soviet government almost immediately renounced the West's interpretation of this clause and continued to insist that a German solution could only be based on the equality of the D.D.R. with the Federal Republic and prior assurances that a reunited Germany would not be permittted to join NATO. The "free elections" formulation was adopted at Geneva, as Khrushchev later related, "only after heated debate, since we considered it more correct to solve the question of European security without tying it to the German question. . . . At the final [Geneva] session . . . we said that a settlement of the German question should be found through agreement between the two German states. . . ."[34] Khrushchev has repeatedly argued that the situation has changed since the victorious powers agreed at Potsdam to take responsibility for German unity. Two German states, he says, have been created since that time. Allied responsibility for German unity, therefore, is now restricted to encouraging negotiations between the two German states to achieve unity. Up to the Geneva conferences of 1955, the Soviet government rejected the

34. Khrushchev interview with *Il Tempo*, March 24, 1958; *Current Digest of the Soviet Press*, Vol. X, No. 13, May 7, 1959.

West's "free elections" formula on the basis that the NATO powers were unwilling to assure the military neutrality of a united German state. Most Western experts argued that the Russians would not have permitted genuine free elections even if the West had been willing to commit Germany to a neutral status, and that, in any event, a united neutral Germany would have succumbed to Soviet pressures. These Western arguments during the period up to the 1955 conferences are entirely conjectural inasmuch as the Soviet proposals for the creation of a neutral Germany by means of free elections were never fully explored. The Soviet government's statement of January 15, 1955, that "free elections" under "international supervision" could be held—which appeared to satisfy the West's major arguments against the Soviet position at the Berlin Conference of 1954—was denounced by Bonn, Washington, London, and Paris, even before the full text of the proposal was available, as simply a means of preventing the ratification of the Paris Agreements bringing the Federal Republic into NATO. Moscow certainly wanted to prevent the ratification of the Paris Agreements, but whether or not it was willing to make significant concessions in order to prevent German rearmament was never fully determined.[35]

The West German government was confident that Moscow would deal with Bonn even after it joined NATO.[36] This assumption was verified when Khrushchev told Adenauer during his visit to Moscow in September 1955: "We were not glad to see you join NATO; but the fact is that you have joined NATO and, as realists, we accept this as an accomplished fact."[37] But this says

35. However, some Western experts believe that if the Soviet government had had a new bargaining position to offer in January 1955 it would not have announced it through a press conference but via normal diplomatic channels.

36. *New York Times*, January 17, 1955.

37. Cited in Adenauer's letter to Bulganin of February 27, 1957; *Bulletin*, March 1, 1957.

nothing about the impact of German NATO membership on Moscow's willingness to permit the creation of a free but militarily neutral united Germany.

Whatever the merits of the argument that an agreement with Moscow could have been reached if the military alliance between Bonn and the West, especially with the United States, had been threatened but not formed in the period before the 1955 Geneva Conferences, since that time, and especially since the Polish and Hungarian revolts of 1956, the evidence is overwhelming that the Soviet government has been unwilling to accept any Western terms for German unity. The fomenting of the "Berlin crisis," aimed at achieving recognition of Pankow by the West and incorporating West Berlin in the D.D.R., is only the most recent example of Soviet support for the D.D.R. regime, which is the best indicator of Moscow's unwillingness to reunify Germany on terms that the West can agree to. In his first interview with representatives of the West German press, in January 1958, Khrushchev made it perfectly clear that "the key" to the solution of the German problems would not be found in Moscow, Washington, Paris, or London, "but must be sought in Bonn and Berlin [i.e., Pankow]."[38] In talks with Carlo Schmid and Fritz Erler of the SPD in March 1959, Khrushchev said boldly that "no one really wants Germany reunified"—meaning that neither the Western allies nor the Federal Republic on its own was willing to consider paying a price that Moscow would demand in effective negotiations.[39] He repeated this to a group of West German Socialist editors,[40] and in a conversation with Field Marshal Lord Montgomery (who agreed

38. Interview with Axel Springer and Hans Zehrer, January 29, 1958; *Die Welt*, February 7, 1958.

39. *New York Times*, March 19, 1959.

40. "Neither France, Great Britain nor the United States wants German reunification. They do not want it because they fear a reunited Germany . . . even Adenauer does not want reunification." *Current Digest of the Soviet Press*, Vol. XI, No. 19, June 10, 1959.

with Khrushchev),[41] and went one step further with Averell Harriman, to whom he said that Soviet Russia would not agree to any reunification scheme which did not provide for a "socialist system" in Germany.[42] But Khrushchev reserved the most blatant expression of the Soviet view on German unity for an East German audience:[43]

> . . . the German problem concerns chiefly Germany. Of course this is an acute and important problem. We stand for the unity of Germany and the German people want unity. But can the peoples of the world exist if the two German states are not unified? They can, and they can exist quite well. Can the Germans live without reunification? They can, and they can even live quite well. Although the problem is quite important, therefore, it is still not fundamental. . . . We do not favor reunification in just any form . . . the problem . . . should be approached primarily from class positions. . . . Why not reunify Germany by abolishing capitalism in West Germany and establishing a working class regime there? . . . This is unrealistic at the present time. But it is even more unrealistic to nuture illusions regarding the liquidation of socialist achievements in the G.D.R. . . .

In other sections of this revealing speech, Khrushchev declared that Germany would eventually be reunified. "It is merely a question of time," he insisted. In the meantime, there should be a peace treaty with "the two German states in actual existence," and "it would also be good" to form a confederation of the D.D.R. and the Federal Republic:

41. According to Montgomery's account of his conversation with Khrushchev in April 1959, the Soviet leader said: "Nobody wants to see the reunification of Germany at present, but few people have the courage to say so. Adenauer doesn't want it. The French don't want it, nor do the British. Russia certainly doesn't want it." The omission of the United States was undoubtedly a gambit to exploit Montgomery's occasional criticisms of American policy, and of President Eisenhower; *New York Times,* May 10, 1959.

42. *Life,* July 13, 1959.

43. The speech was given on March 7, 1959, but it was not published until the eve of the Geneva Foreign Ministers' Conference in May 1959.

I have repeated conversations with representatives of the Western powers, including . . . the Federal German Republic. I ask them: Why are you afraid of confederation? If you capitalists are strong spiritually and materially, as you say you are, you can obviously influence the socialist sector, "digest" it and have a reunified Germany on a capitalist basis. But the capitalists fear confederation. Apparently they don't trust their capitalist stomachs to "digest" the socialist achievements of the G.D.R. (Laughter in the Hall).[44]

In Poland some weeks later the Soviet leader amplified his earlier statements. The frontier between East and West Germany, he said, "divides the world of socialism and the world of capitalism and we will defend this frontier with all our strength."[45]

Some Western experts argue that, just as the Soviet government's obdurate stand on "free elections" after the conferences of 1955 resulted from the West's rearmament of the Federal Republic in NATO, the decision to incorporate the D.D.R. in the Communist bloc and to postpone indefinitely German reunification on any except confederational lines followed from the NATO decisions of December 1957 to establish nuclear missile retaliatory sites in western Europe. It would appear, however, that this is not the case. The Russian position in support of Pankow may have been reaffirmed as a result of the NATO decisions of 1958, but the fundamental Soviet policy on German unity which Khrushchev stated again and again during 1958 and 1959 had been outlined at least as early as 1956—fully a year and a half before the West's post-Sputnik reaction at Paris in December 1957.[46] The Russians naturally do not like the prospect of having the *Bundeswehr* armed

44. *Current Digest of the Soviet Press,* Vol. XI, No. 13, April 29, 1959.
45. *New York Times,* July 19, 1959.
46. Khrushchev told a French Socialist delegation in the spring of 1956: "Reunification depends on the Germans themselves. Sooner or later the West Germans will accept this position. . . . Peace could also be secured if there are two German states. . . . West Germany would remain in NATO; East Germany . . . a member of the Warsaw Pact." "Französische Sozialisten im Kreml," *Der Monat,* Heft 105 (June 1957), pp. 15 ff.

with nuclear weapons and would like to prevent this, but they scoff at the suggestion that they are afraid of West German military power. Khrushchev on several occasions has asserted that Soviet armed might could crush Germany—as it surely could—and that he is not "afraid" of German military power, but rather "apprehensive" that a *revanchiste* spirit dominating Bonn's policies could lead its NATO allies, particularly the United States, into a war against Soviet Russia. It would appear that a limitation on German arms would not be met with political concessions from the Soviet government, but since the Federal Republic's alliance with the United States, especially as West Germany becomes a more powerful partner through the acquisition of nuclear weapons—since this combination does worry the Soviet government—the dissolution of these ties, meaning the termination of Germany's membership in NATO, could perhaps lead to a change in Moscow's reunification policies. If Moscow's principal aim is to break up the Western alliance, then presumably it would be prepared to pay a price to achieve this.

Whether or not the West should contemplate bargaining with Moscow on this basis depends upon the basic interpretation of Soviet motives. If, as some believe, the principal Russian goal is to assure the security of the Soviet Union, then the exclusion of a united Germany from NATO would be a small price to pay for solving the partition problem. On the other hand, if the Soviet leaders are now convinced of their superior military strength and growing economic advantages, and believe that NATO's retaliatory bases in Europe can be neutralized, then a united but neutral Germany might become simply a stepping stone for Communist expansion across Europe.

Looked at from one point of view, these analyses of Khrushchev's motives are not necessarily contradictory. His position on German reunification, his support of the Pankow regime, the offensive against Berlin, are motivated by a combination of strengths and weaknesses, with Soviet Russia's military power chief among the former, and the fear of renewed outbreaks of antibloc hostility in the satellites prominent among the latter. The Western powers' steadfast refusal to discuss proposals for atom-free zones (Rapacki), reciprocal troop withdrawals (Gaitskell, Kennan), and German neutrality (Kennan) was not the reason for the Berlin crisis or Khrushchev's hardened position on the partition of Germany. The West's refusal to discuss these proposals played into the hands of those in the Kremlin who have been advocating the current rigid policy line all along against existing and potential sentiment in the satellites and in the Soviet hierarchy itself for a more conciliatory policy leading to political settlements. Only the British government seemed to be prepared to discuss disengagement proposals; Paris, Bonn, and Washington rejected them outright. This unyielding attitude is all the more disconcerting because the Western powers remain powerless to enforce their demands regarding Germany on Moscow, while the Soviet government loses nothing from holding on to the status quo which, with a sharp eye on the increased independence of West Germany, it confidently believes will continue to evolve in Russia's favor.

The weaknesses of the Western stand regarding German unity in the face of Soviet policies, which had long been identified by experts, were suddenly made evident to the general public when Khrushchev tightened the Communist noose around the necks of the West Berliners starting in November 1958. The British, French, and American governments protested that their legal occupation rights in Berlin cannot be voided by the Soviet Union because they exist "irrespective of any acts of the Soviets."[47] Khrushchev admitted that the Allies have "lawful rights for the deployment of troops in Berlin as occupiers," but said these rights would "automatically end" if Moscow signed a peace treaty with

47. *The Soviet Note of 27 November 1958 on Berlin: An Analysis,* Department of State, Washington, January 1959, p. 43.

Pankow, "because East Germany would be a sovereign state and West Berlin is inside its territory."[48]

Despite their legal rights in Berlin, the Western powers had to face the fact that, for all practical political purposes, two German states existed and would continue to exist as long as the Soviet government backed the D.D.R. Said Khrushchev:

> The post-war development of Germany has introduced . . . different problems from those that had faced the four powers in the first years after the destruction of Hitlerite Germany. It is now impossible to take even one step forward in the German problem if it is approached from the former point of view, without taking into account the existence of two different German states and the fundamental differences in the direction of their development. This situation will not be changed one iota by any number of notes or statements by the Western powers in order to refute facts created by life itself.[49]

Haltingly and grudgingly the major Western powers have been accommodating themselves to the existence of two German states, without, however, budging one inch regarding their rights in Berlin. Secretary Dulles persuaded a reluctant Adenauer that in order to maintain supply and communications lines in the event that Moscow handed over jurisdiction over the autobahns, canals, and rail lines to the city to the East Germans, Bonn's allies would have to deal with Pankow authorities as "agents" of the Soviet government. Adenauer's reluctance is easily understood. Although East Germans have been processing civilian traffic (which accounts for 97.5 per

48. *New York Times,* March 20, 1959. Wilhelm Grewe, West Germany's Ambassador to the United States, declared in April 1959 that " 'the right of conquest' is a bad expression" to justify the Allied position in West Berlin. "The presence of the Western forces is legally based on the right of belligerent occupation. . . . The right of conquest has been outruled [sic] by the common declaration of the victorious allies that they did not intend the annexation of Germany (Declaration regarding the defeat of Germany, June 5, 1945)." *News from the German Embassy,* Vol. CXI, No. 5, April 15, 1959.

49. From the Soviet note to Britain of March 2, 1959; *New York Times,* March 3, 1959.

cent of the total) from the West to Berlin since March 1954, if Allied military transport were to submit to the same authorities a major step will have been taken toward at least de facto recognition of the D.D.R. government. That even Dulles was willing to take this step underlined the weakness of the West's position regarding Germany and—without exaggeration—the bankruptcy of Bonn's entire policy *vis-à-vis* eastern Europe. The fact that the Soviet government precipitated the "Berlin crisis" by threatening the unilateral abrogation of rights which Bonn and its allies considered inviolable, does nothing to mitigate this disaster. The threat of a nuclear conflict, the West's only effective response to the Soviet political offensive, indicates that Western policy had been based on a combination of legal principles and threats of military action which, if carried out, would amount to suicide.

The Soviet offensive against Berlin was not only an important milestone in Moscow's support of the Ulbricht regime, but also marked the decisive—though undoubtedly not the final—defeat of Bonn's nonrecognition policy toward Pankow and eastern Europe. Instead of driving a wedge between Moscow and the Pankow government, Bonn's policies and those of the West as a whole have helped to make their policy interests coincide while failing to exploit differences between them. There is no doubt that such differences exist. Khrushchev wants to "relax tensions" between East and West, but this is inimical to Ulbricht's interests, at least until he has gained recognition from the Western powers. Similarly, the Soviet leader continues to advocate the confederation of the "two Germanies," while Ulbricht wants a separate peace treaty with the U.S.S.R. and is against reunification discussions of any kind until it has been signed, for he knows that the adoption of the confederation proposal could lead to a serious weakening of Communist authority in East Germany unless Moscow were to step in, as it did in 1953, and this would frustrate Ulbricht's drive toward equal standing for the D.D.R. in the Communist bloc. As long as the

Federal Republic does not have an active Eastern policy and the Western powers refuse to discuss Soviet proposals for "relaxing tensions," there is no chance that these tactical divergencies between Moscow and Pankow will be exploited or that they will lead the Soviet leadership to downgrade the value of their German ally.

East Germany's successful drive for status within the Communist bloc and toward recognition from the other powers has been a key factor in Bonn's search for a new Eastern policy. Since 1957 there has been a tendency in West German intellectual and opposition circles to flirt with the idea of taking up more technical and, eventually, political relations with Pankow authorities. This development has gone to the point where some have actually proposed that the Federal Republic recognize the East German regime and negotiate with it to achieve reunification.[50] Party discipline kept them from saying so publicly, yet a number of Christian Democrats, including Bundestag deputies, were also swinging around to the view that "talks should begin" between Bonn and Pankow. By midsummer of 1959, the political axiom that advocacy of recognizing Pankow was "political suicide" in the Federal Republic was no longer assured.[51] The Bonn government continues to have "technical" and "commercial" relations with the East German regime and has agreed to continue these, but it has not changed its stand on recognizing the D.D.R. regime. Adenauer has insisted that the technical dealings with East Germany do not imply recognition of any kind. Gradual changes in West German policy regarding Pankow are nevertheless discernible. Ernst Lemmer, the Minister of All-German Affairs, has, for example, been soft-pedalling the non-recognition line and anti-Pankow propaganda since early in 1958, stressing instead the Federal Republic's efforts to help improve the conditions of life in East Germany, encouraging travel across the frontier, all-German sports teams and events, meetings of East and

50. For example, Rudolf Augstein, publisher of *Der Spiegel*, in an editorial of February 1959. See the *New York Times*, February 24, 1959.
51. *New York Times*, February 24, 1959.

West professional societies, and the like. The general purpose of this campaign is twofold: to maintain a maximum of contact between the two halves of Germany, and to leave open the possibility of negotiating reunification through some confederation or federation scheme, provided that the proper conditions for such a union obtain in both parts of the country.[52] Just what these conditions must be is, of course, the crucial question. Until the autumn of 1958 genuine "free elections" in East Germany was certainly one of them, and the removal of Ulbricht, "with whom a confederation is impossible," another.[53] The demand for Ulbricht's removal remains and is certainly unchangeable; but the requirement of "free elections" is now of secondary importance. Starting at the end of 1957, there was a definite tendency within the West German government, in the bureaucracy and in all the parties, to downgrade "free elections" from the top priority to an indeterminate place on the reunification agenda. The Germans were caught more unaware than unprepared by Secretary Dulles' press conference remark in January 1959 that "free elections" were not "the only method by which reunification could be accomplished." Chancellor Adenauer was shocked that Dulles should appear to make a major concession to the Soviet government without a *quid pro quo* and without prior consultation with Bonn, but he was forced to accept the new position which Dulles subsequently justified by pointing out that he was under strong pressure from the British and members of Congress to adopt a more "flexible" negotiating position on the German problem.[54] Having been forced to make the tactical concessions which virtually eliminated "free elections" as an immediate

52. See Hellmuth Brennecke's article in *Die Welt*, May 15/16, 1958, subtitled "Neuer Inhalt der Wiedervereinigungs-Politik?"

53. *Frankfurter Allgemeine Zeitung*, March 1, 1958. Also see the interview with Ernst Lemmer in the *Süddeutsche Zeitung*, February 20, 1958.

54. Senator Mike Mansfield has been prominent among the Congressional critics of the West's German policies. He has on several occasions advocated reunification negotiations between Pankow and Bonn. See *Die Welt*, May 24, 1959; *New York Times*, February 13, 14, 19, and 27, 1959.

reunification issue and permitted the Western allies to treat East German authorities as "agents," Adenauer stubbornly held out against any further compromises in the course of inter-Allied negotiations to devise the "package plan" to be presented at the Geneva Foreign Ministers' Conference of May 1959. The Chancellor spared few adjectives in rejecting British proposals for putting a controlled zone of limited armaments in central Europe on the Foreign Ministers' agenda, and he also opposed an American plan which envisaged a federation of the East and West German *Länder*.[55] Adenauer had full support from the French in opposing both the British and American proposals. In keeping them off the Geneva agenda, Adenauer (and De Gaulle, who is certainly unenthusiastic about any plan for advancing the cause of German unity) in effect prevented the Western powers from adopting the principle of federation in solving the German partition problem. The East German delegation was seated on an equal basis with the Federal Republic at the Geneva Conferences during the summer of 1959, thereby gaining a form of recognition. Adenauer, however, managed to keep the Western powers from moving closer to the Communist confederation plan, though he agreed to have an equal representation of East and West German advisors sitting with representatives of the Big Four in any subsequent reunification talks.

Nevertheless, the federation proposals appear to have a future. There is hardly a chance that Adenauer or his successors, even with continued support from France, can continue to hold out against

55. The American plan was intended as a compromise between the Communist insistence on "parity" between the D.D.R. and Federal Republic in reunification negotiations (1:1 ratio) and Adenauer's insistence that representation in any all-German body be based on the population of the two Germanies (giving Bonn the advantage of a 3:1 ratio). The American plan was based on the prewar German states and would have given Bonn a 10:6 advantage. Adenauer opposed this on the grounds that some Socialists would be included among the West German *Länder* representatives and that these might vote with the Communists on some issues. *Die Welt*, March 19, 1959; *New York Times*, April 29, 1959.

Anglo-American compromise plans in regard to the ratio of representation between East and West Germans on an all-German commission. The fact that popular support in the Federal Republic for all-German talks of some kind is growing under the pressure of the existence of the D.D.R. and the increasing demand for greater efforts to achieve German unity, makes it almost inevitable that the Western negotiating position will be changed to include the principle of federation. In what may prove to have been a most perceptive paragraph, Walter Lippmann wrote:

What we are going to see, it seems to me, is—as unfortunately only the Russians have had the wit to suggest—negotiations between the two German governments. As a matter of fact there is already negotiation about the currency and about trade, all of it nominally at a technical rather than at a political level. These negotiations will almost certainly broaden greatly into some sort of political arrangement which might one day take the form of a dual state.[56]

By midsummer of 1959 it was clear to all observers that West Germany's position in regard to Pankow, the Soviet Union, and eastern Europe had become untenable. Officially, Chancellor Adenauer still clung to the conception of a "position of strength" as a basis for a diplomatic offensive to force Soviet Russia into withdrawing her forces, leaving East Germany to be annexed by the Federal Republic. This conception had little reality in view of the growing power and stability of the Communist bloc. Only France among the major powers still paid lip-service to it. Privately, Adenauer was said to rationalize his continued adherence to the old policy by arguing that Moscow would accept Western terms in Europe when its policies came into conflict with those of China in the Far East. Most of Bonn's officialdom is not satisfied to let the fate of central Europe be decided by events which may or may not take place in Asia decades hence. For several years there has been much speculation and discussion in official quarters about the

56. *New York Herald Tribune,* April 1, 1958.

policies Bonn could adopt toward eastern Europe in order to achieve German aims. One of the alternatives that has been proposed has not gained many adherents and deserves only a brief mention. It is the idea recently put forward by William Schlamm in his book *Germany and the East-West Crisis* of forming a bilateral U.S.-West German alliance, vastly increasing West German armaments, and then imposing ultimata on the Soviet Union. The Russians are to be threatened with a war unless the Red Army is withdrawn to within Soviet frontiers. Schlamm believes the Russians would retreat rather than fight, and there are some, but not many, West German fanatics who would gamble along with him. Presumably, they are prepared to suffer the *Götterdämmerung* that this proposal invites. Perhaps it was inevitable that such a blatant "liberation" policy would be proposed sooner or later to make sense out of the otherwise untenable conception of a "position of strength" as a means of achieving Western political aims. That is the only virtue of Schlamm's proposal. Overt threats of violence do not constitute a policy; they signify that policy has given way to naked brutality.

The other extreme, the idea that reunification could be achieved by a policy of self-abnegation, by unilateral disarmament, and withdrawal from the NATO alliance into a neutralized position, also has no important backing from any major party in Bonn. The belief that Moscow would react benevolently in response to an appeal from calculated weakness has no more to recommend it than the belief that the Soviet leaders can be bludgeoned into capitulation. The arguments of some SPD members that the Soviet Union has legitimate security interests in Europe (which no Western power denies) has been parlayed by Adenauer and by some of his American supporters into accusations that the SPD is "soft" on Communism and might sell out to Moscow if it came to power. This charge, which amounts to treason, has played a prominent role in West German domestic politics; it has no other significance. What many Social Democrats, independents, and a growing number of Christian Democrats are prepared to accept is the military neutrality of a reunited Germany, and some of them would be prepared to bind Germany to this in an all-German peace treaty, provided both East and West were to give the country adequate guarantees against aggression. But this is a far cry from a policy of "neutralization" which, unlike "neutrality," signifies submission to terms imposed by outside forces, and which, again unlike a status of armed neutrality, would leave Germany open to Soviet pressure while precluding reunification except on Communist terms.

The possibility of a militarily neutral status underlies both of the realistic alternatives to the "position of strength" conception; each has strong support in the government and among the *Oberschicht*—the leaders of West German public opinion. These two broad courses of action could be followed simultaneously for a certain time; but they are incompatible in certain significant respects, and ultimately a choice would have to be made between them.

One of these proposed policies toward eastern Europe would have the Federal Republic take up diplomatic relations, multiply mutually beneficial trade relationships, and generally "reacquaint" the East Europeans with (West) Germany. The aim would be to strengthen the satellite states to become more self-reliant, with the ultimate purpose of obtaining their support for German and Western policies which could lead to a withdrawal of the Red Army as part of a reciprocal withdrawal of forces from central Europe. The proponents of this general program include the foreign policy experts of the SPD and some in the FDP, officials of the *Auswärtiges Amt,* journalists, and influential people in the academic world, and—most important—a group in the CDU, especially the Protestant and "progressive" element which frequently looks to Bundestag President Eugen Gerstenmaier for leadership. While there appears to be agreement on the general lines of the East European policy among all these different groups, there is still disagreement about certain significant issues. For example, the CDU element is prepared to extend "technical" relations with the D.D.R., yet unwilling to go to the lengths of actually recognizing the Pankow government which individual members of the SPD left-wing and certain FDP deputies have privately admitted they would do. A still more important problem is whether the Federal Republic should be prepared to recognize the Oder-Neisse boundary and possibly discard its insistence on *Heimatrecht*. The opinions about this differ within each party, where domestic political repercussions certainly play a role, and also among Foreign Ministry officials. A dominant group in the government believes Bonn should restrict its overtures toward Warsaw and Prague to offering nonaggression pacts and resuming diplomatic relations. Indeed, there were indications during the summer of 1959 that the Cabinet would approve this suggestion, but Chancellor Adenauer vetoed it and rebuked the Foreign Ministry officials responsible for it.[57] Others were convinced that Bonn would also have to recognize the Oder-Neisse line, at least in principle, and renounce all claims to the Sudeten area if the initiatives were to have the desired effect of making the major satellite states less dependent for their security on Moscow. They argued that only by making the greater sacrifice could West Germany hope to elicit a measure of support from the East European states for a Soviet troop withdrawal from East Germany and a compromise solution of the partition problem. Despite De Gaulle's public suport of the Oder-Neisse lines as the final German-Polish boundary and strong indications that London and Washington would not support any German efforts for major revisions in the line, it seems most unlikely that Chancellor Adenauer will at any

57. The *New York Times* reported on May 21, 1959, that Bonn was prepared to sign nonaggression treaties with Poland and Czechoslovakia and to take up diplomatic relations with both states and also Bulgaria, Rumania, and Hungary. At the end of July the West German press reported that the Cabinet was studying the idea of taking these initiatives (*Die Welt,* July 27, 1959) but a government spokesman revealed that the offer of nonaggression pacts was "not imminent" (*Informationsfunk der Bundesregierung,* July 28, 1959).

point take the risk of losing political support from refugee and right-wing elements by recognizing Polish sovereignty over the "third Germany."

The second school of thought is also anxious to "reactivate" Germany's Eastern policy, but it differs sharply from the first in all other ways. It is composed chiefly of conservative and right-wing groups, the refugee associations, strong admirers of Franz Josef Strauss and of the tradition of *"realpolitik,"* and includes many industrialists, especially those who believe that there are still great markets for Germany in Soviet Russia and, via Moscow, in the rest of the Communist bloc. Emotional factors also play an important role in making up the general policy these people advocate. One finds among them strong nationalist feelings, especially in regard to the "lost provinces." Some are animated by an intense hatred of the Poles and Czechs, others are admirers of Soviet power, and although they claim to be "democrats" and anti-Communist, they are typically even more militantly anti-Social Democratic. One also finds a good deal of animosity toward the West in these circles. The Western powers are blamed at least as much as Soviet Russia for the partition of Germany, and the United States is held in contempt for "its lack of culture" and its "inability to make effective use of its military power." But the dominant note is nationalism: "What God, geography and we Germans have created cannot be rent asunder by fumbling politicians."[58]

The Eastern policy advocated by these people differs basically from the first program discussed above in that they are skeptical of the aid the satellite states may be able or willing to give to the cause of German unity, whether or not Bonn takes up diplomatic relations with them. They argue that Bonn should not give the East European states any commercial or political support which might antagonize the Soviet leaders who alone can make German reunifi-

58. The former Ambassador to Indonesia, von Hentig, quoted by Terrence Prittie, "The Germans in Search of Reunification," *The Listener,* February 24, 1955.

cation possible. They see no real purpose in recognizing the satellite governments and are vehemently opposed to admitting Polish sovereignty over the "lost provinces." What they propose instead is that Bonn deal directly with Moscow, with Western support if possible, without it if not, to reach a *modus vivendi* providing for German unity and German recognition of Soviet Russia's sphere of influence in the territory up to Poland's prewar western frontier. They believe that Moscow would agree to such an arrangement to replace the uncertainties attending the present divided Germany and the West's refusal to recognize the status quo in eastern Europe. As an important first step in the direction of such a deal, the advocates of this policy insist that West Germany must become a major nuclear power, including possession of a deterrent capability. They believe that the Adenauer-Strauss rearmament policies will eventually gain them this military standing, although they are impatient with the rate of progress. They realize that Chancellor Adenauer can probably not be won for such an Eastern policy; therefore they are concentrating on preventing any moves—such as recognition of the Oder-Neisse line and the adoption of an East-West German federation plan—which might preclude its being adopted by a new Chancellor, perhaps by Strauss. Stated in the boldest terms, what is proposed here is that Germany purchase unity from the Russians at the expense of the nations in between.

There are, of course, strong arguments against the practicality of such a policy. Unless the major Western powers support it, which is most doubtful, the negotiations between Bonn and Moscow could not be carried on in the open; and yet the issues are much too complex for them to be settled in a few brief talks, as was the case in the Rapallo treaty. Once the Germans embark on secret negotiations with Moscow they would be at the mercy of the Soviet leaders, who could at any time threaten to reveal Germany's intentions to the Western powers in order to create discord between the Federal Republic and her allies. If this threat were carried out, Germany would remain divided and the Western alliance would be decidedly weakened. Probably the most effective criticism of the proposed policy is that Moscow in present circumstances has no more reason to reunify Germany on revised German terms than on Western terms, or to accept a more restricted sphere of power in eastern Europe than it has at the present time. Even if the Soviet government felt its hold on the satellites slipping, or if frictions in the Far East made it expedient for the Russians to give up some of their obligations in central Europe, a *modus vivendi* with West Germany might be impractical, for it would shatter whatever genuine support Moscow had gained from the East European peoples and leave its European frontier more rather than less exposed. Soviet interests in a bilateral agreement with West Germany in any foreseeable circumstances are difficult to envisage. Yet one cannot rule out the possibility that such an arrangement will be tried. Political events are not readily predictable over the longer run. The fact remains that the Germans want unity which only Moscow can offer; a major aim of the Soviet leaders is to emasculate the Western alliance by driving American military power from the Continent. A real hope of achieving this through bilateral dealings with the Germans may suffice to tip the scales in Moscow in favor of a radical departure from Russia's postwar European policy.

Within West Germany the pressure for trying this avenue of achieving unity will almost certainly grow as the *Bundeswehr* becomes stronger and as the people regain self-confidence. There are industrialists and others in the business world who would consider even the acceptance of "Socialist advances" in part of the reunified country a small price to pay for access to the new markets of eastern Europe and Communist Asia on favorable terms, which they think might be obtained as part of a working relationship with the Soviet government. Perhaps the most powerful incentive for a new approach to Moscow will be the growing futility—a combination of anger and boredom—with East-West coalition negotiations, which have failed both to achieve German unity and to produce any real measure of security for the peoples of central Europe. The understanding which is dawning on the German people, that Soviet Russia has the power to prolong the division of Germany for as long as it wants to, and the realization that the West as a whole is less than enthusiastic about the prospect of reunifying Germany, can at some juncture be turned into a purposeful drive by the West Germans to make a bilateral settlement with the Russians, dealing with them directly and via Pankow.

One of these two broad courses of action will eventually be adopted by West Germany. There are no genuine alternatives. The nonrecognition policy has been unsuccessful and is proving to be self-defeating; the Western "position of strength" which has prevented a further advance of Soviet power in Europe cannot resolve the existing political problems; a policy of "rolling back" the Iron Curtain to "liberate the captive peoples" could lead only to a suicidal war; unilateral disarmament of West Germany would invite Communist domination of the Federal Republic and the rest of Europe. The Germans will not accept partition as a "final solution"; nor would this be a basis for a stable peace. If the Western powers were simply to accept the partition of Germany as a basis for a *modus vivendi* with Soviet Russia, they would invite friction within the alliance and provoke the Germans into independent and possibly rash policies.

From the U.S. point of view, then, which of the two proposed West German Eastern policies is the more desirable—or the least troublesome? Clearly, any tendency toward bilateral agreements between Bonn and Moscow would weaken western Europe, impair the security of the United States, and might consign the Polish, Czech, and Balkan peoples to an even worse fate. A German-Soviet deal is obviously inimicable to U.S. interests, and steps must be taken to prevent it. This cannot be done simply by keeping the Federal Republic from attaining nuclear parity, or by trying to prevent Bonn from exercising a greater freedom of action in relations with Moscow. The situation calls for strong U.S. support of

an "active" West German Eastern policy leading towards a reëngagement of relations with Poland and Czechoslovakia, Yugoslavia and the Balkan satellite states. Bonn must realize that the
longer it holds back recognition of Polish sovereignty over the
Oder-Neisse territories the less its interests will be served when
recognition is finally given. The West German government must be
left under no illusions regarding Western support of any major
changes in the existing Polish-D.D.R. boundary. If Bonn were now
led to recognize that border in principle (which would still leave
room for minor "adjustments" of the frontier in peace treaty negotiations, or in bilateral talks between Poland and Germany), and
if the principle of *Heimatrecht* were replaced by an appeal to Warsaw and Prague to consider taking back any refugees whose *Heimatgefühl* made them want to return, and if these moves were coupled
with the resumption of diplomatic relations and nonaggression
pacts guaranteed by both the United States and Soviet Russia, then
Bonn would have an Eastern policy which might, over a period of
years, gain it support for an amicable settlement of the partition
problem. As soon as West Germany has recognized the Oder-Neisse
boundary and gives assurances regarding the return of expellees
and refugees, it can be made to feel free to hold broad discussions
with the Soviet government on all outstanding political problems
between the two countries. The Western powers would still maintain their responsibility for reuniting the country, and the Germans
would then be in a position to initiate discussions and to make
proposals to solve their national problem, provided only that the
final military status of Germany is left to be decided by the major
Western powers, as well as by Soviet Russia and the Germans
themselves.

Eight

■

A POLITICAL STRATEGY FOR THE WEST

The root cause of the German problem is the conflict of interest between Soviet Russia and the Western powers over the future of Europe. The Soviet government supported by the vast majority of Russian people is devoted to the Communist cause which would extend Soviet domination beyond its present line of furthest advance. The Western powers are determined to prevent any further Communist advance in Europe and have set themselves the task of "peaceful liberation" of eastern Europe.

The economic and technological successes of Communism, and the political consolidation of the European Soviet bloc, have reinforced the Soviet leaders' belief in the triumph of the Marxist-Leninist system over capitalism. Nevertheless, Communist doctrine and practices are undergoing an evolution in keeping with certain political realities and new technological developments. The doctrine of the inevitability of war between the two blocs has been superseded by a belief in the victory of Communism through peaceful competition, because the development of Soviet military power, Khrushchev says, has diminished the danger of a capitalist military attack. In actual fact, it is the balance of nuclear destructive might which has temporarily diminished the danger of a major conflict. The danger of a local limited war continues to exist in some parts of the world, though not in central Europe, and there can be no assurance short of enforced control of armaments agreements that a serious imbalance in the military and strategic field favoring Soviet Russia would not tempt Moscow to start a major war. Although the most imminent danger of large-scale nuclear war is a "mistake" committed by one side in the midst of an uncontrolled political-military conflict, such as the Suez crisis of 1956, the possibility of calculated aggression by Soviet Russia at some future date cannot be ruled out.

The growth of Russian power since the 1920's has turned Communism into a global challenge, taking advantage of the racial and nationalist revolution sweeping Asia, the Middle East, and now Africa. However, for Moscow as for the West, central Europe remains the single most decisive arena. The Soviet leadership has not divorced itself from the Leninist doctrine that Germany is the pivot of revolutionary successes in Europe. Soviet domination of east central Europe during World War II represents a major advance for the Communist cause, which now has gained a strategic foothold in the European capitalist camp in East Germany.

The emplacement of Red Army military contingents in East Germany, with which Moscow justifies the stationing of its troops also in Poland and Hungary to guard supply and communications lines, is the single most important immediate cause of the partition of Germany and Europe, and is a constant source of danger to the West. The Western powers have responded to this danger by defensive military and political alliances of which NATO is the most important. The inclusion of West Germany in NATO, and the policy of insisting upon leaving a unified Germany the choice of joining NATO, indicate that although German reunification is ostensibly the West's primary goal, the cause of reunification has in fact been sacrificed to maintaining the strongest possible military combination to guard against Soviet aggression. The assertion that West German membership in NATO and the unification of Europe are the best means of bringing about German unity reflects wishful thinking at best and, at worst, chicanery. The West cannot impose terms on Soviet Russia. Similarly, the belief that a unified

Germany must be free to ally itself militarily with the West in order to prevent Soviet aggression after reunification has taken place is misleading. A united Germany's membership in NATO would not change Russia's aims and would not be a more effective safeguard against a successful Russian advance across Europe than a strong Western defense establishment, including German armed might, not under a unified (NATO) command. But the most telling criticism of the Western proposal for a reunited Germany in NATO is that the proposal itself prevents the development of negotiating terms which, over the long run, could stand a chance of achieving the West's major political aims in Europe: German unification and the "peaceful liberation" of eastern Europe.

The Soviet Union has no intention of submitting to reunification terms which would tie a united Germany to the West militarily, and there is no reason to believe that it will change its position in this regard in the foreseeable future. Moscow insists on terms for German unity which will give the Communists an opportunity to win all of Germany for their cause. The Soviet leaders feel themselves so strong today that even a guarantee of German military neutrality may not suffice to permit reunification on political terms that the West, including the West Germans, wants. Western preparedness to negotiate reunification on the basis of a united Germany's military neutrality is, therefore, not by itself sufficient to end partition. The preparedness to permit German military neutrality is only part of a resourceful policy the West must pursue to convince the Soviet leaders that reunification on this basis is to their best interest. First of all, the conditions must be created in which German unity as a free but militarily neutral state is accepted by the Soviet leaders to be in Russia's best interest.

Soviet and Western policies in Europe are similar in certain important respects. The Allies have chosen what appears to them to be the safer path of strengthening the Atlantic area economically and politically within the framework of a tight military alliance.

They demand German unity and "liberation" of the "captive nations," but have devised no means of achieving either aim. The Western powers have built their policy and pin their hopes on maintaining the status quo, though they do not like it, protest against it, and will not officially recognize its existence.

Soviet policy in Europe is avowedly also based on a preservation of the so-called status quo; but Moscow's policy, no less than NATO's, bears earmarks of ambiguity—or as some commentators would have it, of deceit and hypocrisy. Because they have not hesitated to say so, we know that the Communists believe they have the historic duty of burying capitalism. They will undoubtedly spare no effort in propelling the Western governments toward their grave, using any methods as long as they do not excessively endanger the Motherland of the Revolution and its existing Communist empire. At the same time, Khrushchev insists that the Western nations should recognize the status quo in Europe, that is, the fact of Communist domination of eastern Europe, including East Germany. The West's refusal to comply, says Khrushchev, is evidence of the aggressive and *revanchiste* designs of the NATO powers against the Soviet bloc. They—especially Bonn and Washington —prolong the Cold War. Khrushchev has said that when the West recognizes the status quo in Europe and accepts it, a reciprocal withdrawal of troops can follow, foreign bases can be liquidated, and there can be "peaceful competition" to see which system predominates over all of Europe. Just as some in the West are convinced that western Europe unification will cause a dissolution of the Communist bloc, Khrushchev claims that the economic and social successes of the Communist bloc, led by the Soviet Union, will prove the superiority of Communism and draw the western European states into the Communist orbit. Khrushchev, then, bases his policy on the status quo because he believes it will inevitably evolve in his favor. He is as much for German unity as any Western leader, but believes that the time is not yet ripe for reunification on the terms Moscow favors. Thus, both sides base their policies on the status quo—on German partition—hoping and believing that it will evolve in their favor. The chief difference is that Khrushchev wants the status quo recognized by the West because that will speed its evolution in Communism's favor, while the Allies do not want to recognize the status quo in eastern Europe because this will help to consolidate Communist rule and—even more important—because such a step might alienate West Germany.

The stalemate in Europe is only partly due to the balance of mutual nuclear deterrence, which enforces limits on the methods that can be adopted in the conflict. Both sides consider their part of Germany unexpendable on strategic, economic, and political grounds. Both sides count upon time and successes of their own systems to win the struggle in the end.

The prolongation of the status quo in Europe, however, with or without open Western endorsement, plays into the hands of the Communists. The changes that will continue to take place despite the continued partition of the Continent will create more and more complex problems for NATO and tend toward the dissolution of the alliance. And although the Communists will certainly have their share of problems in the rapidly developing economic and social life of eastern Europe, as long as the Red Army encases the bloc from its vantage point in East Germany and Communist governments maintain themselves throughout the area, none of these will lead to a disintegration of the bloc, or to revisionist activity which cannot be tolerated or easily crushed. The very prolongation of the division of the Continent gives Moscow a decisive advantage. The longer the Communists remain in control in eastern Europe and show no signs of diminished authority, the easier will be the process of political and economic consolidation of the Soviet bloc. Even now, many eastern Europeans are resigned to the system, and others, impressed by the higher standard of living they enjoy, by rapid technological advances, and by Soviet military power, are becoming loyal supporters of their regimes. The Soviet leaders are counting upon the German demand for unity to grow;

they believe that as West Germany gains greater military and political power, Germany's alliance with the West will conflict with her demand for unity and will cause a crisis that will be resolved by Germany choosing unity on terms Moscow likes. West Germany may not succumb that easily to Communist terms, but Bonn will certainly become more powerful while partition continues, and the stronger it becomes, the more acceptable it is to Moscow as a negotiating partner.

The mistaken belief that time is on the side of the West is a concomitant of the West's concentration on defending itself, especially militarily, against the threat of Communist aggression. It is no exaggeration to say that a defensive complex, sometimes amounting to an inferiority complex, has grown up in the West and has virtually paralyzed creative international political thought. In part, this is due to an excessive concern with Soviet ideology, a fascination with Communist aims and the bravado with which these are publicized. The audacity of the Communists, their confident belief that they are riding with the tide of history, and also their moral turpitude, or what the West regards as moral turpitude, appals and horrifies Western peoples; they are convinced that their only choice is between desperate resistance and a crusade to eliminate Communism. Since a crusade would mean a suicidal war, the West has dug in grimly to offer desperate resistance.

If it is true that time and the prolongation of the status quo in Europe are the allies of the Communist cause, then the choice of desperate resistance is indeed a dreadful one, for it will permit the Communists to turn a situation which, at present, does not spell "inevitable victory" into an almost certain success for themselves. If the Western powers continue to maintain a wholly defensive position in Europe, permitting political consolation, economic growth, and social development in the Communist bloc while the Western alliance is put to ever more severe tests over such issues as the diffusion of nuclear weapons, national jealousies, the establishment of competing trade blocs, and—above all—the growth of the German demand for unity, Moscow's chance of expanding its influence in Europe is bound to improve.

To the extent that the West's concentration on military defense is produced by a misconception of the role of Communist ideology —or any ideology—in international politics, it is up to the democratic leadership of the Western nations to bring about a more sophisticated level of understanding. There is a particular need for this in the United States, but hardly less in West Germany. The American and German people must realize that although there may be imminent crisis in relations with Moscow, the Communist challenge is a timeless one. It will not subside even if major agreements resolving specific problems are reached. Khrushchev may occasionally impose deadlines and ultimata, as he did over Berlin in 1958, but if these are rescinded the Communist threat does not end—it is merely postponed, as in the case of Berlin—or brought to life elsewhere, perhaps by different methods. In order to support adroit political policies and sustain a continued armaments effort, the American people must be steeled against expecting cultural exchange, summit meetings, visits by heads of states, or other forms of achieving "mutual understanding" to work sudden changes in the basic conflict of aims and interests with Russia. The mistaken belief that the Soviets are rigid ideologists invariably acting with single-minded attention to the letter of Marxist-Leninist dogma leads to excessive hopes of converting the Communists to "our" fundamentally decent outlook on life, thus ending all East-West strife, or to the equally dangerous embittered feeling that there is no sense discussing or negotiating any problem with the Soviet leadership since they are going to continue to work for aims antithetical to our interests anyhow. Ideologies—and ideologists— must be strictly subordinated in the West in the process of devising constructive policies to achieve Allied aims. The Communists are adherents of a fanatic (because it is fatalistic) ideology; but they are realists when it comes to the dynamics of power. Naturally, the

Soviet leaders seek to maximize Russia's power; of course they would like to take Berlin; there is no doubt that they wish to "communize" all of Germany, the rest of Europe, and the United States as well. But they know that none of these cherished goals is attainable now, even if they were willing to take the appalling risk of starting a major war. The Soviet leaders have also concluded that the Western powers are not in a position today to dislodge the Communists from the countries they were able to dominate after World War II. Therefore the slogans of "liberation" annoy but do not bluff the Russians, because they see that the West is not prepared to risk taking aggressive military action and is in fact not probing for or exploiting the weaknesses and shortcomings in the Soviet bloc system. The Soviet leadership has not had to deal with any effective Western pressure to force a withdrawal of the real source of Russian power in East Germany and Poland: the Red Army.

The Western peoples must uphold their ideals and principles, but they must also become more realistic, meaning responsible, in disposing of national power. Moscow believes that the triumph of Communism is "inevitable," that time is on its side. The Soviet leadership will face specific issues, as they come, not in "good faith," if that means giving up Russian and Communist interests, but realistically, which means with a keen appreciation of the relative power of the contending parties. This offers a great opportunity for successful negotiations, from the Western standpoint, provided that policies to maximize Western power—and not only military power—are devised to insure that acceptable agreements are reached.

The propaganda line demanding "liberation of the captive nations" is an ideological gambit without political merit. Propaganda will not improve the conditions of those who live under Communist totalitarianism, but it *can* mislead them—and the American peoples themselves—about the extent to which the Western powers can and will help the satellites to achieve a greater measure of self-determination. Raising the wrath of Jehovah against the Soviet leaders will do nothing to bring this about, nor will it restore to eastern Europe prewar conditions which so many of the "liberation" and "captive nations" propagandists want, but which would be wholly unacceptable to most eastern Europeans. The East German workers, for example, have embraced some of the "socialist advances" of the post-1945 period, though not the regime or its methods. Western ideologists believe that Moscow's differences of opinion with Washington must be due not to conflicts of interest, but to the malevolence of the Russian leaders. Fortunately these ideologists in the West, and also comparable figures in the East, are so far more arrogant than powerful. Still, the dangers of a Western "liberation" crusade taking place must be adjudged at least as great as a Marxist-Leninist Holy War being started by Mr. Khrushchev. Not only is Khrushchev more of a pragmatist in facing specific issues than the insistent propagandists who ply their wares in Washington, Bonn, and Munich, so far as the European peoples are concerned Marxism-Leninism is a dead issue. In fact, the ideological conflict itself is virtually dormant in Europe. Communist theory has not been digested by the Poles, the East Germans, or other satellite peoples who, willingly or unwillingly, accept its economic and social practices. In western Europe Communist dogma has lost its appeal; even the industrial workers have written off its tenets as juvenile and inapplicable to their position in a modern industrial society. The social democratic parties have finally realized this, and although they seek to retain some trappings of their Marxist heritage, they strive to divorce themselves from its substance. The conflict *in Europe* is not a struggle for men's minds, but a power struggle between competing blocs of nations and economic systems.

In this power struggle, Americans who have reconciled themselves to power realities in accepting America's partnerships with non-Communist totalitarian governments, such as the Franco and

Salazar regimes, could adopt a similar "realism" toward Gomulka and Tito, and even toward Khrushchev and Mao.

There is no turning back the clock in eastern Europe. What has happened cannot be undone. But the Western powers can, if they choose, try to influence future developments in that area, though not without adopting new policies. The West's "position of strength" has had an undeniable and crucial success. It frustrated any military advances in Europe that Stalin, Malenkov, or Khrushchev may have contemplated. But the West's military strength, its economic advances, and its political unity have not been utilized in order to achieve its political aims in central and eastern Europe.

The overriding requirement today is a political strategy to effect a Soviet military withdrawal from central Europe. This is a complex and almost certainly a long-term undertaking; it is the only alternative to the West's present tacit acceptance of a dangerous situation. If the Red Army's withdrawal from Eastern Germany will not be unilateral, neither would it follow from unilateral Western disarmament, nor from a greater development of Western military strength. It can follow only from an intensification of political pressure in favor of such a withdrawal, and then only on the basis of Western reciprocity. A reciprocal withdrawal is the only possible policy which stands a chance of bringing German unity and a more dependable European security arrangement into the realm of possibility.

The Western powers could take a decisive step in the right direction by adopting the principle of disengagement in their European policy. Of course a public pronouncement to this effect would not, by itself, change anything. Indeed a mere declaration of the principle of disengagement could, and almost certainly would, undermine the confidence of the western European governments, especially of the Adenauer government, in U.S. intentions, and raise Soviet hopes that American military power and political influence can be swept from the Continent with a few insignificant concessions. Therefore, although the acceptance of the principle

of disengagement by the West is important, there would need to
be a simultaneous declaration of the political conditions and military safeguards which must be met if the principle is to be put into
practice, first in general terms, and in discussion with Moscow
explicitly.

A useful first step, which could be proposed for immediate
adoption when the principle and conditions have been enunciated,
but even before disengagement negotiations are under way, would
be an arms- and troop-level freeze in East and West Germany,
with an exchange of inspection teams to assure that the agreement
is carried out.

The crucial questions in any East-West disengagement negotiations are the disposition of Soviet and of Western, especially of
U.S., forces in Europe; the timing and procedure for reëngaging
the two Germanies politically; and guarantees against a reëntry of
forces into the territories from which they are withdrawn. The
size and equipment of the national forces remaining in a neutral
central European zone would also have to be agreed upon.

It would have to be stated at the outset of any discussion of disengagement plans, that in the present situation it is unlikely that
the Soviet leadership will be willing to settle any European problems in accordance with minimum Western terms. The Soviet
government, in all probability, will continue to insist on the liquidation of all "foreign bases" on the Continent, and perhaps in Britain,
the Middle East, and North Africa as well. If that turns out to be
the fact—and there is no way of knowing this until these questions
have been discussed—the Russians will be motivated both by the
weakness and by the strength of their present position. The major
weakness is that of the Ulbricht regime. Pankow and Moscow do
not believe that the Ulbricht government can maintain itself during a period of reëngagement with West Germany if all Soviet
forces are withdrawn. On the other hand, Khrushchev is apparently
confident that, sooner or later, he can achieve the liquidation of all
foreign, that is American, bases in the European area in exchange

for a Red Army withdrawal from the center of the Continent, and as long as he believes this he will naturally hold out for maximum terms. In other words, Khrushchev wants and can only risk a total disengagement. With U.S. forces withdrawn from the entire European area he would be confident that the East Germans would continue to suffer the Ulbricht regime. But as long as U.S. forces remain within striking distance of central Europe, he could not have such confidence—even though Western forces made no move to aid the East German rebels in 1953 or the Hungarians in 1956. The Russians would probably also reject the limited disengagement which has been proposed by James Warburg and others, namely, a U.S. withdrawal behind the Rhine and a Soviet withdrawal behind the Oder.

In the light of the present balance of power in Europe, and taking into account Soviet fears and expectations, it is very doubtful that the Soviet government would agree today to disengage on terms the West could accept. But this is not a reason for failing to propose disengagement. What the appraisal—if it is verified—shows is that the present equal balance of power in central Europe, and the Communist's belief that it will certainly shift in their favor, does not permit any immediate solution of existing political problems, the essence of which is the partition of Germany. Since there can be no greater degree of security for either side unless such solutions are found, all efforts to "reduce tensions" are also bound to fail. If negotiated settlements of outstanding political problems cannot be reached in the present military and political stalemate then changes must await a substantial swing in the balance of power to favor one side or the other.

The Soviet government is obviously conniving at such a shift, and it believes that time is one of its chief allies. A decisive military advantage, which might be attained through a major technological breakthrough, cannot be made to yield political gains, as the United States learned during the period it had a monopoly of atomic weapons. If a productive change in the balance of power is to be achieved it must be based on superior political power. In regard to the problem of German partition, this means that political pressures must be brought to bear on Moscow which will make the Soviet leaders agreeable to negotiating a settlement which meets with the approval of most Germans and does not impair the security of the major Western powers. How are such pressures to be generated?

A look at the recent past may give a clue as to the proper course for the West to follow. It is plausible to argue that the NATO powers missed an opportunity to negotiate satisfactory political solutions to the German problem in the fall and winter of 1956-1957. During the Polish and Hungarian revolts, and for several months thereafter, the Soviet government seemed to be weakened, and may have felt that its authority in the satellite area had diminished even further than was actually the case. If the Western powers had been on record in favor of disengagement, or if they had proposed it at the time, and if the concessions regarding the role of free elections and the treatment of East German officials as agents, which were made subsequently under the pressure of the Berlin crisis, had been offered to Moscow during this period when they would have been more significant, then negotiations might have followed. Instead, the NATO powers in 1956 affirmed their maximum demands—a unilateral withdrawal of the Red Army, German reunification through free elections, and continued German NATO membership—which the Soviet leaders were not weak enough to have to accept and were not even prepared to discuss.

It would be wise therefore for the Western powers to state terms now which, even if rejected, may later become acceptable to the Russians. A declaration that a reciprocal military withdrawal and the exclusion of a united Germany from NATO would be agreeable to the West, or at least not unacceptable under all circumstances, could be useful. Precisely how the Soviets would react cannot be foretold. But even assuming that Moscow will today reject a conditional disengagement proposal, the proposal would still have merits. The West would gain an obvious propaganda advantage, and the German people would have fresh evidence regarding Moscow's responsibility for the partition of their country. Even more important, if a disengagement proposal is kept in discussion, a situation may arise in which the Russians would accept it. Such developments cannot be predicted. Yet it is possible to say what new situations would not be desirable, and it is also possible to indicate what kind of situation the Western powers can hope to create to cause the Soviet Union to accept a conditional disengagement plan.

A repetition of the Hungarian revolt crisis is obviously *not* desirable. The Red Army would undoubtedly crush an overt revolt in the satellites with the same brutal efficiency shown in 1956. A reimposition of Stalinist rule, at least in the country affected, would follow. It would also be undesirable to weaken the conditions attached to the initial disengagement proposal. The West must not be tempted to offer concessions or to make unilateral sacrifices of its basic military position. They would probably stiffen Soviet opposition; Soviet leaders would expect the West to make more and more concessions. Neither inciting revolts nor "appeasement" would gain Soviet acceptance of a reasonable Western negotiating proposal.

An effort must rather be made to subject Moscow to pressures from within the bloc itself for a withdrawal of the Red Army from central Europe—as part of a reciprocal withdrawal of forces—and for granting greater freedom of action to the satellite states. The long-run interests and aspirations of the satellite states are entirely in harmony with such an effort, but their governments, including the Gomulka regime, are today virtually powerless to work toward this end. They can be helped to gain greater freedom of action by the West, especially by West Germany, even as they are today driven into Moscow's arms by Western—and particularly by Bonn's—policies.

The chief task of West German diplomacy in the immediate future is to reduce the fear of Germany in eastern Europe, particularly in Poland, and to create conditions there which favor the reunification of Germany on a basis acceptable to the majority of its people. Bonn must reëngage relations with its neighbors to the east and give concrete assurances that it has neither claims nor designs on any territory east of the D.D.R.'s frontiers. The only meaningful assurance to this effect from the point of view of the eastern Europeans would be West German recognition of the present borders as final. It would be desirable also for Bonn to elaborate its current demand for *Heimatrecht* to show that it does not insist upon repatriation as a right, but is merely representing the emotional *Heimatgefühl* of many expellees and refugees. The Bonn government can make it clear that it is agreeable to solving the repatriation problem by offering compensation on a per capita basis, to Poland and Czechoslovakia, for readmitting a restricted number of returnees from West Germany. The prospects of large-scale credits and favorable trade terms can be held out to the satellites as alternatives to Soviet commercial terms. The restitution payments to the state of Israel and other claims agreements currently being negotiated by West Germany with her Western neighbors can serve as a model for offers of indemnity, in the form of credits, to the Poles, Czechs, and other eastern Europeans for Nazi crimes and wartime destruction.

Over-all, the Germans could strive to impress the eastern European peoples with their peaceful intentions in order to heal the festering wounds left by the Nazi occupation. Any such effort obviously requires a resumption of diplomatic relations between Bonn and the eastern European governments.

The argument that Bonn cannot recognize Polish sovereignty over the Oder-Neisse territories, except in exchange for Warsaw's support of German reunification on Western terms, is self-contra-dictory. The Poles today are solidly against German unity, even to the point of preferring Russian troops in East Germany and in Poland itself to a common frontier with a reunited Germany that has designs on territory and property under Polish control and the means of forcing its claim on Poland. While it is true that there is no certainty that the Poles would become less fearful of a re-united Germany even if Bonn recognized the Oder-Neisse line, their fears might at least be reduced over a period of years during which they would become less dependent upon Moscow for their security.

The Poles, too, will have to face facts. They cannot rid themselves of Russian domination *and* prevent German reunification. They must realize that the Rapacki formula as it stands will remain un-acceptable to the West, and they must become aware of the fact that a divided Germany struggling for unity and independence is a greater source of danger to peace over the longer run than a united Germany that has forsworn all territorial claims.

The United States is in a position to encourage and support German moves toward improving relations with Poland and Czechoslovakia. Washington can offer to guarantee a nonaggression pact among these nations and offer to insure the integrity of Po-land's current Western frontier with Germany. Such guarantees could help to ease the fears of Germany in Warsaw and Prague. They would be further strengthened if the Soviet government joined in the agreements.

There is, of course, no certainty that a reactivation of Bonn's Eastern policy along these lines, combined with proposals for a reciprocal withdrawal of forces and the creation of a limited arms zone in central Europe, would put effective pressure on the Soviet leadership both within the hierarchy and from the satellite govern-ments to induce a Red Army withdrawal from East Germany. But there would be reasons to hope that such initiatives might lead in this direction, while current Western policies offer no hope whatever of German reunification on Western terms. Current Western policies run the risk that the West German desire for unity will encourage Bonn to seek bilateral arrangements with Moscow. Whether or not Moscow would, in the end, strike such a bargain is uncertain; but there is no doubt that a major aim of the Soviet government is to bring the Germans into a position where this will be their only alternative. It follows that any policy which gives Bonn the opportunity to deal independently with Moscow, or leaves open this avenue as the only resort, is the most dangerous one the United States and the West can follow.

Washington could also urge the West Germans to take the initiative—in fact to adopt an entirely new attitude—toward the D.D.R. This may become absolutely necessary if an irreparable split between the two Germanies is to be prevented and if pressure is to be brought to bear on Moscow to permit unification on terms the West can accept. The question, whether or not two Germanies actually exist, is chiefly academic. Soviet power behind the Pankow regime cannot be ignored. If Soviet policies are permitted to call the tune in central Europe, the Western powers, including Bonn, will sooner or later simply be forced to accept the existence of a second Germany. Pankow cannot be ignored indefinitely.

At present, Bonn has no choice but to treat the D.D.R. as anathema. No West German government can appear to sanction Communist totalitarianism over a segment of the German people and must therefore refrain from official dealings with Ulbricht— the most villainous of Communist villains in German eyes. At the same time, Bonn maintains trade and other technical contacts and relations with East Germany. These are mutually beneficial, and are justified by the Adenauer government on the ground that they improve the living conditions of the enslaved East Germans. But as long as a withdrawal of Red Army forces from the D.D.R. is not even in the discussion stage, Bonn will refuse to deal with Pankow about reunification or about any other principally political subject. Once a reciprocal troop withdrawal from Germany is under discussion between Russia and the United States, Bonn would have an interest in adopting a more diversified policy.

There are only three roads to reunification which could be acceptable to West Germany. The first is annexation, which could only take place if Soviet power collapsed, which is unlikely. The second is a bilateral understanding with Moscow, a risky undertaking. The third and most plausible means of achieving German unity is a broad East-West agreement providing for a growing together, or reëngagement, of the two Germanies over a longer period of time. This third way requires an increasing relationship between the two parts of the country on every level, beginning with the current "technical relations" and building up gradually to political relationships.

It can be argued that even if the NATO powers do not adopt the principle of disengagement, the Federal Republic must find some way of balancing its vehement opposition to communism in East Germany with tactics aimed at retarding East Germany's integration into the bloc. Bonn can adopt new tactics to retain a semblance of a relationship with East Germany without recognizing the Pankow regime, and indeed it has tried in the past to do this, although it has never pushed these tactics hard or far enough. The logical corollary of campaigns to increase interzonal travel, improve conditions in the D.D.R., and to remove the barbed-wire barrier between East and West, is a bold and vigorous campaign challenging the system and accomplishments of the D.D.R. West Germany could invite not only cultural exchange, more trade, and travel, but could propose open political debates and competition between the two Germanies. Why, for example, should the SED not be permitted to campaign in West German elections if the CDU, SPD, and FDP are also permitted to hold rallies, distribute literature, and run for office in the D.D.R.? There would of course be a danger of Communist infiltration into the Federal Republic; but that danger also exists today. Ulbricht's henchmen would undoubtedly try to embarrass West German politicians, but the risk of embarrassment is worth running in order to demonstrate to the East Germans the spirit of freedom in West German politics. By taking up Khrushchev's challenge to "peaceful competition," the West Germans could give their East German compatriots new courage to resist Communism. Convincing demonstrations of the vitality and strength of the democratic system can score successes for the cause of German unity that cannot be achieved in any other way as long as there are no political interchanges between the two Germanys.

The very predictability of the West's impact on the East Germans and other East Europeans in political competition of this kind will make Pankow most reluctant to accept the challenge; but since Khrushchev is apparently convinced of Communism's inherent superiority and eventual success, the Russian leader may force the East Germans to accept the West German challenge. If the West German parties are united and relentless in calling for political exchanges and competition, the Communists can reject their proposals only at the expense of a major propaganda defeat in the eyes of all those who have heard Khrushchev's boasts about the superiority of Communism in any "peaceful competition" with the West.

The over-all purpose of adopting the principle of disengagement in Western policy and of encouraging a vigorous new West German policy toward Warsaw, Prague, and the D.D.R., is to create conditions in which Communist expansionist aspirations will be frustrated to the point where the Moscow government will have to reconcile itself to withdrawing its troops from central Europe in exchange for a withdrawal of Anglo-American forces, and convincing guarantees of Russian and eastern European security against aggression. At the same time, these initiatives would also serve to prevent a situation from developing in which a bilateral Russian-German bargain would become West Germany's only hope of gaining Moscow's approval for reunification.

◆

If the major powers attempted to "neutralize" the divided German states, Bonn would either be forced to agree to Communist terms for reunification or, and more likely, concentrate on developing a nuclear capability of its own which could only be prevented by foreign powers if they were willing to use force—that is, to reoccupy the country.

The military dangers of "neutralizing" Germany point up the political conditions which the West must attach to any disengagement proposal. The Western powers cannot afford to drop the goal of German reunification if only because the Germans themselves are determined to achieve it. A reciprocal withdrawal of troops, and new security machinery in central Europe, cannot improve the chances of peace unless there are simultaneous steps planned toward reëngaging the two Germanies. Some form of dual-state association must be envisaged, leaving the two countries with their own governments and policies for a specified period during which all forms of interstate relationships—economic, social, cultural— are intensified, leading to simultaneous elections in the two parts of the country to a national assembly in which representation can be apportioned according to a predetermined ratio, based on such factors as population and the number of prewar *Länder*. This process of reëngagement would take a longer time, perhaps ten to fifteen years, and could only culminate in free elections.

The activation of Bonn's Eastern policy is particularly urgent. Should Adenauer, or his successor, continue to resist this course, the Western powers must point out that they have no alternative but to recognize, albeit reluctantly, the existence of the D.D.R. as an established fact and probably as a permanent fixture in Europe. The reason for this is clear. The major Western powers cannot uphold their responsibilities in West Berlin after the Soviet government passes control over the access routes to the city to Pankow unless it has some dealings with the East German regime. Since neither the United States nor Britain would tolerate being blackmailed by Pankow or, on the other hand, risk a major conflagration over the city as long as the alternative of recognizing East Germany *de facto,* or even *de jure,* exists, the Western powers will take up relations with Pankow at least to the same extent that Bonn maintains them.

Bonn's refusal to deal with the satellite states and to recognize the existing boundaries, while insisting upon German reunification, can only be interpreted as a means of holding out for a future bilateral German-Russian settlement which would be intolerable to its Western allies. The loyalty, humanity, sincerity, and honesty of the West German leadership are not in doubt. But such personal virtues have little bearing on a nation's interest, and will not prevent the Germans from following whatever policies appear to be most advantageous. U.S. policy must work to reduce the chances and remove the opportunities for Bonn to adopt policies that are in conflict with the best interests of the West as a whole, on the assumption that, in the end, interest and not sentiments will play the decisive role in shaping West German policies. The United States has accommodated itself to good relations and partnerships with undemocratic states and untrustworthy—even unscrupulous —leaders, based on common interests; it should have no difficulty in developing realistic policies toward a democratic Germany, led by honest and upstanding men.

While the Allies must try to break the political deadlock in order to achieve their aims in central Europe, they also have the urgent task of preventing the Soviet government from breaking the stalemate with military or technological break-throughs or a successful mobilization of the new nationalism against the West. The Western powers must shape their relationships to increase the power and viability of their policies *vis-à-vis* Soviet Russia.

It has been asserted that a policy of disengagement is incompatible with the requirements of Western defense. Would the adoption of the principle of disengagement by the West result in a weakening of the NATO alliance—or in conditions which would prevent the strengthening of NATO, meaning a western European capacity for self-defense and a credible American assurance of U.S. participation in the defense of Europe? And is there any alternative or version of the revised Rapacki plan which, if it were implemented by Soviet Russia and the Western powers, would leave the non-Communist world with sufficient military power to deter or defend against Soviet aggression?

Dealing with these problems in order, it must be noted that there are those who contend that if the United States initiates a proposal for a reciprocal withdrawal of forces and the creation of a free, neutral, reunited Germany, the Germans would immediately doubt America's resolve to defend them. This, it is said, would undermine the West's defense structure and possibly lead to German neutralism or submission to Communism. Moreover, it is maintained that if the United States supports a disengagement proposal, this would be a signal for the American people and their friends that the United States is returning to an isolationist policy. These fears are based on a remarkable distrust of public opinion in the United States and Germany. Yet American isolationism of the 1930's is dead; those who apply the term as one of approbation to any policy recommendation they do not approve are themselves responsible for misleading the United States' allies regarding the reliability of American assurances.

Fears of the impact U.S. support of disengagement might have on West Germany are also exaggerated. Provided that there is mutual trust between Bonn and Washington and West German understanding of Western policies, there is no reason why people should jump to the conclusion that the United States intends to withdraw unilaterally because it is willing to participate in a reciprocal withdrawal under specific conditions, or that the United States will cancel its obligations to defend the Federal Republic and West Berlin unless these are replaced by at least equal security assurances.

Bonn must realize, however, that the United States does not

intend to commit troops to West Germany permanently. Indeed, the West Germans themselves will want them withdrawn when it suits German interests. The Bonn government should welcome rather than fear a reasonable statement from Washington of the conditions in which the U.S. divisions would be withdrawn, especially in view of Soviet missile developments and greater American reliance upon intercontinental and underwater strategic weapons.

What of the impact of a disengagement policy on the West's capability for defense against aggression? Can NATO exist without the Federal Republic? Can West Germany, the United States, Britain, and France deter armed aggression or defend themselves against it if a disengagement plan is implemented?

Detailed answers to these questions depend upon the precise form of the military disengagement that is adopted. But one thing is certain: West Germany's membership in NATO is not crucial to the defense of Germany and the West in all circumstances. Bonn's divisions would continue to stand east of the Rhine, at least up to the Elbe line, and behind them would be the combined forces of the western European powers and, at least initially, up to five or six American divisions. It would not be practical here to try to formulate the precise steps that might be taken to implement a reciprocal military withdrawal agreement, but the reciprocity aspect needs to be emphasized. Thus, whether the first step is a freeze of military strength on both sides of the Elbe line within a specified zone, a reduction of forces on both sides, or a withdrawal of nonindigenous forces to behind the Oder and Rhine, both sides must be affected equally and there must be inspection machinery to guarantee that the agreements are carried out. Subsequently, a withdrawal of Soviet forces behind Russia's frontiers can be matched by the return of some U.S. ground forces across the Atlantic, while the rest are quartered in France, if that proves politically feasible, and in Britain or the Low Countries, or possibly in Spain. A complete withdrawal of U.S. ground forces from the

European area can only take place when control of armaments agreements providing for suitable inspection machinery have been implemented.

Although it is most unlikely that broad control of armaments or disarmament agreements will precede the settlement of the major political disputes which are the cause of the arms race, the Western powers can agree to the creation of a denuclearized and limited arms zone starting in East and West Germany and gradually broadened to include Poland, Czechoslovakia, and Hungary, without impairing their essential defensive position, provided that a first disengagement step has been taken. This could be either a reduction of forces or a withdrawal to the Oder and Rhine lines. The West's defense will continue to be insured, as it is today, by the deterrent base network in Europe and elsewhere, with only the loss of West German territory as a potential site for retaliatory bases. This territory is of no use for retaliatory purposes in any event since the range and accuracy of Soviet missiles would neutralize any deterrent stationed that close to the Communist orbit. The deterrent bases in Europe will therefore have to be located on the periphery of the Continent, in Britain, the Mediterranean area, and under water. France, having achieved nuclear status, must be permitted to share in the control of the deterrent in Europe, exercising equal authority with the United States and United Kingdom in deciding when the weapons are to be used. The deterrent bases in Europe cannot be dismantled until all strategic firing sites are liquidated in agreements negotiated by the nuclear powers and ratified by other powers, to enforce through inspection machinery reductions in all forms of armament. The familiar Communist demand for the liquidation of "all foreign bases" must continue to be firmly rejected as long as these serve an essential defensive military purpose or a vital political-psychological one in uniting the Western powers and supporting West Germany against Soviet pressure, whether or not Bonn is a member of NATO with equal standing.

Neither the military defense nor the political tasks of the Western allies require formal changes in the structure of NATO. The NATO Council, supplemented by normal diplomatic channels, suffices to permit consultation among the Allies, intergovernmental coöperation, and, when necessary, collaboration on all problems of mutual interest in the European area. No formal changes in NATO procedure or additional multilateral bodies are required to encourage consultation, coöperation, and collaboration, which are the best means of maintaining unity in the face of the Communists' divisive tactics. Differences in the interests of NATO states, which arise from the diverse responsibilities some have undertaken and others have had thrust upon them, cannot be eliminated by imposing unity through organizational innovations or the creation of directorates composed of the leading NATO members. Instead of leading toward greater unity, these could aggravate the tensions and the divisions in the alliance. In a tightly knit, uniform alliance, the smaller NATO states would increase their power and influence by drastically limiting and even gaining control over the freedom of action of the major powers. For example, the United States cannot permit its NATO membership to commit it to the support of France in Algeria, or to Britain in the Middle East, without also giving Luxembourg the right to tell Washington what it should and should not do in Taiwan. Furthermore, a uniform alliance would inhibit for the common benefit of all the exercise of power by any one member. If the only negotiations any NATO member can conduct with Moscow must be based on positions to which every member is bound by preceding inter-Allied negotiations, this diplomacy is almost certain to be fruitless. Coalition diplomacy, as practiced over the past ten years, robs the West of the viability it needs in dealing with the Soviet government and prevents the United States, in particular, from utilizing its full strength for the benefit of its allies in dealing with Moscow. The package-plan compromises which coalition diplomacy forces the West to adopt in all major negotiations with the Soviet government, reveal rather than obscure divergent interests among the Allies, which the Communists have learned to exploit to their own advantage.

An effective alliance is a useful one. No alliance can be useful in serving the interests of its members unless it is built upon mutual interests. The NATO nations have a mutual interest: they have combined to defend themselves against aggression. However, the alliance is less effective than desired, and may become weaker still, because it has become more of a hindrance than a help in achieving the member states' political aims. NATO gives an appearance of solidarity without the substance of genuine coöperation. In negotiations with the Soviet bloc regarding the major European issues, the principle of unanimity has replaced the coöperative principle which has not succeeded. The task in NATO is to increase and perfect consultation and coöperation among the members to give the alliance the genuine strength that will make it useful in achieving the interests of all the members instead of continuing on the road to uniformity and unanimity which restrict the power of the major states and give the smaller members an influence far greater than can be justified by either their actual power or their immediate interests.

These criticisms of NATO also apply to the organizational forms of Western economic coöperation. Since the disappointing experience with EDC, the United States has restricted its activities in support of European economic coöperation, and eventual political unity, to cheerleading from the sidelines, giving valuable assists here and there, but leaving all initiatives, and the settlement of all disputes, to the states concerned. Although the judgment that the European nations themselves must take the lead in establishing the forms and institutions of economic coöperation is sound, the United States has a strong interest in preventing the development of competing economic blocs which could reduce rather than raise the volume of trade between Europe and the United States, and also between continental Europe and Britain, Scandinavia, and the underdeveloped countries. The United States has an interest in preventing the development of a tight-knit economic unit on the Continent which would compound the political problems involved in reuniting eastern and western Europe. Because of these interests, Washington could use its influence to mediate the disagreements between the Common Market and Free Trade Area groups, perhaps reviving the OEEC as a vehicle for combining the best features of both organizations into a single Free Trade Area which is sufficiently flexible to permit limited agreements among some of the members, such as the Common Market. The disputes between the Common Market and Free Trade Area proponents have definite political implications, both for the security of the West as a whole, and for negotiations with the Soviet bloc. If these disputes are allowed to continue, the Continental Six may continue with a fateful experiment to form a Third Force, which is bound to have untoward consequences for the United States.

The dangers in this situation are well known in Western Germany. No important political group in the Federal Republic is willing to accept De Gaulle's leadership of a Third Force, although there are some forces that believe Bonn can dominate any western European bloc that may be set up. In working toward a compromise solution between the Common Market and Free Trade Area along the lines suggested above, Washington would have the sympathetic support of most West German commercial interests which are becoming increasingly worried about the political consequences of an exclusive western European market and about Germany's in-between position in the economic contest led by France and Britain.

West Berlin is the chief emergency exit for refugees from the Soviet bloc; it also provides a window on the East and a "showcase of freedom" for the West. Strategically, West Berlin is the weakest link in the chain of Western political and military commitments on the Continent. This fact was pointed up by the Berlin crises of 1948 and 1958. Both times the West was able to forestall Soviet attempts to drive the Allies out of the city, but to do this the powers were forced to take drastic action and to threaten even more drastic action. A momentous airlift was needed to save Berlin in 1948-1949 and public assurances of military support coupled with threats of unlimited warfare were issued to prevent Moscow from seizing the city in 1959. The costs and risks the Allies were forced to take in support of West Berlin's independence are a true measure of the symbolic value of the city's role in Western policy and revealed the handicaps the West has to overcome to make good its pledges of support to the Berliners.

The garrison of French, British, and American forces is clearly incapable of defending Berlin against attack from the surrounding Russian and East German forces. Therefore the only defensive strategy the West can employ for Berlin is to convince the Soviet government that an attack on the city would constitute a *casus belli* which would probably develop into a global conflict. Evidently the present Soviet regime has learned that it cannot seize West Berlin except at an exorbitant cost, and understands that West Berlin is not only a symbol of the Western cause but an acid test of America's commitment to the defense of the Continent. West Berlin is indeed an anomaly in central Europe today, but the West could "sacrifice" the city and withdraw from that highly exposed position only at the cost of Europe's confidence in the United States and the Europeans' confidence in themselves. Moscow's apparent reaction to learning these facts is, as one would have expected, to pursue a more cautious line on Berlin and to redouble its efforts to dislodge Western power from the city.

The West was able to stave off the threatened Communist seizure of Berlin in 1959-1960 for two reasons. First, because it was able to impress Khrushchev with the high premium it placed on maintaining the city's independence, and second, because Khrushchev became more reluctant over the course of time to carry out his threat of signing a peace treaty with the D.D.R. permitting the Pankow regime to obtain ultimate control over the access routes

to the western sectors of the city. Khrushchev's reluctance to sign
the treaty is understandable. Doing so would have reduced Soviet
control over the city and the Pankow government, and it would
have complicated potential negotiations about Germany with the
Western victors of World War II. At least for the moment Khrushchev still hopes to extract Western recognition of the D.D.R.
through applying pressure on the West in Berlin before, and possibly without ever, giving the Pankow regime control over the
western access routes to the city.

Thus the crisis over Berlin is a continuing one. It was literally
built into Europe by the agreement to withdraw American troops
from Saxony and Thuringia in exchange for sectors of occupation
in Berlin, and by failing to get written guarantees of access to the
city. A resolution of this continuing crisis is inconceivable except
in the context of an over-all solution to the problem of divided
Germany which would restore Berlin as the capital of a unified
country. Meanwhile crisis conditions will wax and wane according
to the pressures the Communist powers put on the beleaguered
city, which will henceforth probably be chiefly economic and political rather than military.

There can be no "interim solutions" to the Berlin problem; but
assuming that German reunification and, with it, a resolution of the
Berlin problem, lie in the indefinite future, the West can attempt
to take some steps to relieve the danger of a conflict starting over
the city's status. One of the three possible courses of action the
NATO powers can take is to try to maintain the status quo. This
is what Adenauer and De Gaulle advocate. Their proposal, which
even the fall-back position prepared for the Paris summit conference of 1960 did not substantially modify, is that the West insist
on maintaining the present number of troops in West Berlin, that
there be no negotiations regarding the espionage and propaganda
activities carried on by Western and Eastern organizations in
Berlin, and that the Soviet government must be held accountable
for granting British, French, and American forces unrestricted

communications and transportation ties with the city. This stringent position is justified by those who take it on the grounds that the West could only lose from agreeing to negotiate about any of the conditions on which it presently upholds the independence of West Berlin.

A second course of action is one that the British government endorsed until the summit conference fiasco of May 1960, and which found some sympathetic support in American government circles until shortly before the Paris conference. The British proposed that the West attempt to gain new written guarantees of access to West Berlin from the Soviet government by negotiating with the Russians to eliminate the espionage activity carried on from both East and West Berlin and by agreeing to reduce the size of the Western garrison in West Berlin, on the understanding that some Western troops would, however, continue to be stationed there. The Adenauer government strongly objected to this approach because it feared the repercussions in Berlin and East and West Germany of any withdrawal of troops from the city, and also because the Soviet government would probably only agree to a reduction of Western forces on the assumption that this was a first step toward their total withdrawal.

The third approach is hypothetical for it would have the West agree to the Soviet proposal of creating a "free city of [West] Berlin" and this has all along been unacceptable to all of the Western powers, since the so-called "free city" would really be in a state of limbo pending its incorporation in the Soviet orbit. Other versions of the Soviet proposal which would substitute *Bundeswehr* or U.N. troops for American, British, and French forces in Berlin are equally unacceptable to the West. The maintenance of, especially, American troops in West Berlin is of the utmost importance at present, since their withdrawal or even any major reduction in their ranks would dishearten the Berliners, leading them to believe that the American commitment to the city was being withdrawn or softening. The inevitable consequence would be an exodus of ci-

vilians from West Berlin; those who would remain would undoubtedly be less willing to hold out against further Soviet and
Pankow blandishments.

Until definite progress toward German unity has been made,
there can be no compromise in the Western demand to maintain
American troops in West Berlin. And at the same time, the Soviet
attempt to drive a wedge between Bonn and its Western allies
over the status of Berlin, whether it is a part of the Federal Republic, under British, French, and American occupation, or both,
must be countered with firm public statements assuring the West
Berliners of the continued responsibility of the Western allies for
the independence and welfare of the city.

On the other hand, the Western powers can negotiate with the
Soviet authorities to eliminate the espionage and general hazing
activities which are carried on from both East and West Berlin. The
people and government of West Berlin would certainly welcome
such an agreement. Furthermore, the West must be prepared to
change its position in Berlin in the course of negotiations to reunify Germany. In the event that a reciprocal withdrawal of forces
from East and West Germany becomes the subject of negotiations,
the future disposition of Allied forces in West Berlin must also be
reconsidered. Should Moscow be willing to withdraw its forces from
East Germany, the Western powers can also consider withdrawing
from Berlin. Indeed, to maintain Allied forces in West Berlin once
these are withdrawn from the Federal Republic would pose virtually insurmountable logistical problems of supply and communi-
cation. If, therefore, negotiations for a military and political disengagement in central Europe make headway, the Allied powers
can and should contemplate transferring their obligations to insure
the security of West Berlin to U.N. forces and the Security Council. The people of Berlin would also be able to place confidence
in the world organization at that time, since the complexities of
decision-making by the U.N. would not then, as they would in the

present circumstances, force the Berliners to run the risk of being overrun by Communists while U.N. deliberations are paralyzed.

The essential military posture required of the West in the absence of satisfactory political and disarmament agreements with the Soviet Union is becoming clearer. There is, it appears, no choice to be made between conventional weapons and tactical and strategic nuclear armaments. A balance of the three must be maintained by NATO, though not necessarily in every theatre of European operations. Tactical nuclear weapons must be maintained in central Europe to offset the Western weakness in conventional armaments and to guard against any encroachment by satellite troops. The *Bundeswehr* and the French Army, when it is returned from North Africa, could form the bulk of the twenty-five to thirty division conventional force needed by NATO. As long as no denuclearized and reduced arms zones have been created in Europe, the western European forces will have to be supported by three to five American divisions who also maintain control over the nuclear warheads for the major tactical atomic weapons in the possession of the Continental allies, including West Germany.

If she continues on her present course, France will undoubtedly develop her own tactical atomic weapons. This will naturally strengthen Bonn's arguments for taking possession of the warheads to arm its supply of tactical weapons. As signatories of the London and Paris Agreements of 1954, Britain and the United States could prevent the *Bundeswehr* from coming into possession of the warheads and should do so. The reason for this is not that Bonn, once it has owned atomic weapons, would be in a position to involve its allies in an attack on Soviet Russia, which is what Moscow fears, but rather that once the *Bundeswehr* has a nuclear capability it could not be denuclearized without Bonn's consent. In effect, then, West German acquisition of a nuclear capability would handcuff the United States, Britain, and France in negotiating a solution of the German problem in the context of a new European security arrangement. Bonn would continue to insist that its Western allies are responsible for reunification and, at the same time, would exercise an effective veto power over the terms on which the West might achieve this in negotiations with Moscow.

We have already seen that there is no military or strategic basis to justify emplacing the strategic weapons on the Continent, so that the issue of West German possession or control over a deterrent need not arise on military grounds. There are, however, also political factors to be considered in this connection. Instead of creating the larger conventional forces which, in the conditions of an East-West nuclear stalemate, are required to defend against limited attacks, the Continental powers—following Great Britain—have been working to acquire control over both tactical and strategic atomic weapons. The arguments of the Europeans to justify this drive are ambiguous. On the one hand, they insist that U.S. divisions must remain in West Germany to assure American involvement in any conflict with Communist forces and, on the other hand, that the presence of five to six U.S. divisions on the Continent is not a sufficient guarantee of America's commitment, and that they must therefore have control over a nuclear stockpile and a strategic retaliatory capability. Despite the ambiguity, these arguments have been gaining support and, unless they are resisted by Washington, will soon succeed in giving the Continental allies the best of both worlds, that is, the retention of American ground divisions to substitute for the larger conventional forces the Europeans do not want to pay for, and acquisition of tactical nuclear weapons and at least control over the strategic weapons, if not possession of an independent retaliatory capacity, which would reduce the relative bargaining power of the United States and United Kingdom within NATO and toward Moscow.

It is readily understandable that France, the Federal Republic, Italy, and their Continental neighbors should strive to attain the stronger and more secure status of nuclear powers. On the basis of national pride alone they cannot be expected to forego atomic armaments if other and smaller nations, such as Sweden and Switzerland, develop a nuclear capability. But while the motives for the drive to become members of the nuclear club may be honorable the achievement would not be compatible with the best interests of either the NATO alliance or the United States. The reasons for this are military and political.

Running the risks involved in giving West Germany and other European powers a nuclear capability could be justified if this added vitally necessary military defensive strength to NATO or stood a chance of forcing Moscow to negotiate acceptable agreements regarding Germany with the West. However, a French, West German, or other new nuclear capability is not required for the defense of the West. Nor will the spread of nuclear capabilities have positive political results. All the evidence points in the opposite direction. The Soviet government, it has been pointed out, is not afraid of German arms and will not make concessions to the West in order to prevent the *Bundeswehr* from acquiring nuclear weapons. Moscow could not ignore this development. Khrushchev fears the combination of U.S. and German armaments; he is apprehensive of Bonn's ability to involve the United States in a conflict with Soviet Russia. The Soviet government would therefore react to Bonn's acquisition of control over nuclear weapons with a new drive to split the Federal Republic from its allies. Previous efforts to isolate West Germany have been aimed chiefly at the British, French, and American governments, and have been unsuccessful. Once Bonn acquires nuclear weapons and, with these, the ability to pursue a more independent foreign policy, Moscow's efforts may be directed at the West German government where they would have a better chance of succeeding, especially if Moscow—recognizing Bonn's growing power and freedom of action—were willing to make some concessions on the reunification problem.

The Federal Republic's acquisition of nuclear weapons would therefore bring the nightmare of U.S. and Western policy-makers generally a step closer to reality; and it must be said that, in those circumstances, one could hardly blame the Germans for whatever deal they decide to make with Moscow to achieve German unity.

It should be clear, then, that in evaluating proposals for disengagement and for a more active West German policy toward the D.D.R. and eastern Europe generally, both of which do entail risks, Bonn, Washington, and their allies must weigh the new proposals against the risks in continuing along the present course, in which Bonn's acquiring nuclear weapons eventually is a virtual certainty. And in weighing the respective risks of the possible policies, the United States must base its judgments on the national interests of its allies, rather than on some vague but fashionable conception of "loyalty" to the "Western cause."

A crucial juncture has been reached. In recent years the American government, with support from leading spokesmen of the Democratic Party outside of Congress, has been following a course which could greatly restrict the United States' power of decision in the future. Despite the meetings at the summit between Khrushchev and Eisenhower, Washington has, in fact, been guided in its policies by the wishes and whims of its Continental allies. Those in Britain who wanted to foster a policy of disengagement on the part of the United States, regardless of whether progress was made simultaneously toward German unity, have not succeeded in persuading the Administration. Secretary Dulles' enemies, who were quick to seize upon President Eisenhower's initiative in exchanging visits with Khrushchev as proof of a "reversal" of the Dulles policies, have been woefully disappointed. American policy has continued along the same course charted by Acheson and Dulles; there has been wavering, but no departure from the policy of a position of strength. France has acquired a nuclear capability. Washington has granted West Germany and other powers the right to gain experience with the use of nuclear weapons, which is a definite step in the direction of giving these powers control over nuclear warheads for tactical and medium-range missile weapons. Through this and other agreements, these powers are gaining the insight needed to manufacture tactical and strategic weapons. The cost of producing the delivery systems for these weapons is still a bar to independent manufacture for a number of powers, but the costs are being reduced with every technological innovation. In time, the engineering components will become accessible, possibly on the open market, or on an international black market. Steps can, of course, be taken through W.E.U. to inhibit Bonn from undertaking independent manufacture of nuclear weapons, but over the longer run it will not be possible to maintain West German membership in NATO if the Federal Republic is discriminated against in this crucial field. The effort is nevertheless worth making. If Moscow refuses to accept a realistic disengagement proposal providing for German unity on terms which the West approves, it would still be better to risk straining the NATO alliance in the short run by trying to hold the Federal Republic in it without giving it a nuclear capability than to risk the destruction of the alliance over the longer run through unilateral German action based on the power of the atom.

This holds true not only for West Germany. Even in the absence of productive political negotiations with Moscow, and Soviet Russia's growing military power, it would not be to the interest of the United States to add new members to the nuclear club or to make the use of its deterrent power subject to the agreement or initiative of other nations.

The virtual certainty that one or both of these developments will be forced on Washington at some future date if East-West negotiations do not succeed in solving the German partition problem, reinforces the arguments for a series of policy initiatives which envisage German unity and the creation of a neutral central European zone. The United States cannot afford to weaken the West's military defensive potential. It can afford even less to permit the eroding of the alliance resulting from the refusal of some of its members and forces in the United States itself to reconsider German NATO membership and the redeployment of the West's military forces.

The possibility of German military neutrality, whether through East-West negotiation or a German intiative leading to reunification, has raised a number of fears in the West. Officially, the Western powers have rejected the establishment of a militarily neutral Germany on the grounds that the NATO alliance would be critically weakened if West Germany withdrew; this in effect rules out German reunification. It is inconceivable that the U.S.S.R. would permit East Germany, and therefore a united Germany, to become associated with a Western military alliance in any form whatsoever. This seemingly hypocritical Western position, professing to aim for German unity but demanding it on terms which are clearly unacceptable to Moscow, has been justified on the ground that the Federal Republic's membership in NATO is more valuable to the West than German reunification, and also because the proposals for German unity that have been made so far, including various disengagement plans, are either potentially workable but unacceptable to the East or West, or potentially acceptable to both sides but unworkable. In the face of a harsh Soviet policy, the argument runs, it would be dangerous for the United States to propose German unity on the basis of German military neutrality since the Soviet government would probably reject the West's corollary security conditions, while the proposal itself would undermine what the West has been trying to achieve in the Federal Republic. This reasoning is not convincing.

In the first place, there can be no certainty about the Soviet reaction to a Western disengagement proposal until it has been discussed with Moscow. Such discussions need not be public. Initial explorations can be made privately and informally, through diplomatic channels. The military risks involved in proposing a reciprocal troop withdrawal and German armed neutrality are no greater than those that are run by current Western policies. And if a disengagement plan were implemented, the risks of establishing a denuclearized armed zone in central Europe would have to be weighed against the danger of adding members to the nuclear club, taking into account, too, that a disengagement of forces would effect the withdrawal of the Red Army and make German reunification feasible, while present policies, if they are continued, stand no chance of achieving Western political aims in compensation for keeping up a defensive effort which will entail increasing military risks.

Objections to proposing disengagement have been raised also on anticipated political repercussions in West Germany. Some observers believe that the greatest danger of a bilateral deal between Bonn and Moscow would arise if the United States were to depart from its established position of requiring NATO membership as a condition for German unity. As has been pointed out, a West German government with increasing military power and political independence would be sorely tempted to negotiate bilaterally with Moscow if that seemed the only chance for achieving unity, and that temptation would exist whether or not Bonn is a member of NATO, but would seem to have a better chance of success—from the German point of view—if West Germany gained nuclear parity with the major Western powers. In other words, the risk that Bonn will sooner or later deal with Moscow directly exists whether or not an attempt to negotiate disengagement is made. The risk that such negotiations will put Bonn's Western allies at a disadvantage is greater if West Germany has the standing of a power capable of offering Moscow something in return for reunification—and that standing requires the possession or control of a nuclear capability. And secondly, the chance that Bonn will try to deal with Moscow independently and be willing to make sacrifices to achieve national unity will be diminished if proposals are under discussion between East and West which emit a ray of hope for the achievement of German unity by agreement among the major powers.

A second political objection to advancing a disengagement proposal is that the West would thereby undermine the government of Chancellor Adenauer. Since Adenauer's policy is based on West Germany's adherence to NATO, it is argued that the acceptance of any plan which would exclude a reunited Germany from the Western defense alliance would amount to a major defeat for Adenauer and his party. This argument overlooks this fact: although the Western powers have so far maintained a preference for West German NATO membership over the achievement of German unity, they have all along had to contend with the possibility that Moscow would propose the creation of a neutral united Germany, or that Adenauer's successors would propose this to Moscow, and that such a solution would meet with the basic aspirations of the German people who would put up an irresistible demand for accepting it. If that had happened, or were now to happen, the United States, Britain, and France could not prevent the Germans from excluding themselves from NATO. Is it really necessary for the United States to demonstrate its confidence in Adenauer, and to aid him in winning the 1961 elections, to the point of giving him and his eventual successors and the Soviet leadership exclusive possession of this powerful initiative? Yet both the German and American people stand to gain more from the possible success of a reciprocal withdrawal of troops in central Europe and the gradual reunification of Germany and Europe than they risk losing in the possible defeat of the CDU at the polls. And although the adoption of a disengagement policy by the West would mark a reversal of Adenauer's policy, it is by no means certain that this would work against him in the national elections. He could interpret the new Western initiative as a bold stroke for the achievement of German unity and take credit for it in the election campaign. The military security conditions the West would attach to any plan for a reciprocal withdrawal of troops could be emphasized by the Chancellor to show that the implementation of the proposal would not diminish the security of the German people.

There is another category of objections to negotiating German unity through a reciprocal withdrawal of forces. There are those who fear that if a reunited Germany is not tied to NATO it would become dangerously susceptible to undemocratic forces in its internal development and also attempt to carry on a *schaukel-politik*—playing off the East and West against each other—thereby presenting a new danger to its neighbors. These apprehensions are usually backed by recalling the experiences of Weimar and Nazi Germany. But how much similarity is there between Germany's position after 1918 and today?

Nazism has not been repudiated in Germany, as has been pointed out earlier, but there is nevertheless almost no chance that it will be revived. This does not mean that democratic practices and institutions in West Germany or in a united Germany are certain to mature, or if they do prosper, that they will necessarily conform to the patterns of democracy in the Anglo-Saxon countries, but the decade of Adenauer's leadership shows that the German people will uphold political and civil liberties at least as long as these prove to be compatible with strong and orderly national government. The development of free institutions is a good sign for the future. The exemplary performance of a difficult duty by the first President of the Federal Republic, Heuss, has given that office a degree of prestige and importance which, if it is continued, will reduce the chance that there will be a resurgence of chauvinistic symbols. The trade unions, an active and reasonably responsible press, and the development of numerous private organizations operating in the field of civic and communal education for political responsibility are among the other leading institutions which could be relied upon to support democracy in Germany even in the face of adverse economic and political circumstances. A new generation of teachers in the schools, and the gradual growth of a new attitude among school and university students, too many of whom are still prone to regard a professor as virtually infallible, will help to strengthen the spirit of free inquiry and intellectual honesty in the country. If the CDU and SPD remain as dominant parties, each united by common interests rather than either ideological fervor or fear of their leaders, and if both parties are able to dominate the interest groups which, until now, have too often been able to command allegiance to their views, the political party system in the Federal Republic stands a good chance of developing into a genuine democratic system, offering the electorate accountable and responsible government and the choice of real alternatives.

Many developments justify confidence in the vivacity and endurance of democracy in Germany. But the decade of *"Kanzler-Demokratie"* also has its debit side, chiefly in the failure to produce respect for democratic habits and responsible citizenship among the broad mass of the German people. The propensity of the German people to shove off responsibility to "higher-ups" has been reinforced by Adenauer's benevolent autocracy. He has done little—some Germans say nothing—to encourage active participation in politics, community responsibility, and involvement in the decision-making process by the average citizen. The sharp campaigning tactics of the Chancellor, his preference for conducting national policies, and especially foreign policy, virtually on his own, without consulting the leaders of his own or other major parties, are partly responsible for the abysmal weakness of the SPD. It is certain that at present the SPD could not form a government on its own; it would have to form a coalition, even in the most favorable political circumstances following a national election. The virtual monopoly of national power by one party is a danger to any democracy. That danger will not be diminished in the Federal Republic as long as the CDU leadership encourages bigotry against the democratic left in right-wing and conservative sections of the society.

Over-all, then, one cannot dismiss the criticism that democracy in West Germany is little more than skin-deep. It was nurtured in the stupendous economic successes of the postwar period and is associated with success. In the event of prolonged economic setbacks, or if Bonn fails over a longer time to achieve German unity, democracy and its institutions may be associated with failure. This need not portend a revival of Fascism, but it could cause rapid changes in the form of government into something which many Britons and most Americans could not reconcile with their conceptions of democracy.

Freedom is not absolute in any country. The restrictions on personal freedoms Germans may be prepared to accept in order to safeguard or achieve national interests are traditionally more rigorous than those most Americans and Englishmen tolerate. But the question of how Germany's institutions will evolve is really highly speculative. It does not lend itself to precise answers. The evolution of German government will depend on the nature of the problems and needs confronting the society, and one is therefore justified in asking under what circumstances democracy in Germany stands the best chance of success.

The partition problem plays a crucial role in this connection. The reunification issue is a source of undiminished irritation in West German politics, and shows no sign of abating. Because of international political factors which are mostly not under German control, the issue causes more discussion than action. Because of the very nature of the issue, it leads to charges and countercharges, accusations and counteraccusations, which threaten to undermine the very foundation of the country's social and political structure. Social Democrats and Free Democrats accuse the Adenauer government of failing to make genuine efforts to achieve unity; in turn the Chancellor and other CDU leaders accuse the opposition of a different kind of treason, alleging that they are prepared to sell out West Germany's freedoms to achieve unity. There seems to be no room for moderation where the reunification issue is concerned. Normally moderate elements on the left and right have reacted to the exchange of charges between the government and opposition by proposing the formation of an all-party "national front" to achieve unity. A "national front," or Grand Coalition as the Germans call it, on foreign policy issues would not only limit discussion, but could also be easily exploited by the Soviet government. Moscow has much practice in playing on the national sensibilities of a people.

However, the picture is not one-sided. The achievement of German unity, even on current Western terms, would not be an unmixed blessing for German democracy. Whatever the form of the reëngagement process between the two Germanies, there would be unprecedented social, economic, and political problems to overcome. The tender shoots of democracy in West Germany may be crushed by the expediency necessary to achieve unity. The East Germans, moreover, have had no experience with any form of democracy since the ill-starred Weimar experiment. Their suffering under Nazism and Communism may have given them a longing for personal freedoms matching anything to be found in the Bonn Republic; but the desire to have freedom cannot be equated with the ability to undertake the social and political responsibilities which the preservation of freedom requires. The East German people have no experience of the responsibilities of citizenship in a free society. Moreover, the East German workers have become used to a measure of employment and social security under the Communist system which they will not want to give up, but which are irreconcilable with the practices of the West German economic system. Even in the most favorable circumstances it will be difficult to reconcile the security motive of the East Germans with the West Germans' profit motive. A solution may be possible only by enforcing stronger government controls than those in which democracy thrives.

Looked at entirely from the point of view of these technical problems, with their profound political implications, one might indeed conclude that the safest course is to refrain from urging German reunification. But are the dangers of German unity really greater than a prolongation of partition? Is it possible for Bonn's allies and East Germany's captors to desire a *modus vivendi* on which both sides could rely for a longer time if the agreement is based on the existence of two Germanies? Such a "solution" is surely unworkable. It would require Bonn's allies to repress German agitation for unity, resulting in possible violence. The growth of the demand for unity would subject the East-West *modus vivendi* to more strain, with each side accusing the other of scheming to break the agreement in order to win both Germanies to its side. Moreover, a *modus vivendi* based on partition would amount to a Western sacrifice of its principles and aims of helping the central and eastern European peoples to achieve a greater measure of freedom. More than recognizing Soviet Russia's dominant position in eastern Europe, the West would give its seal of approval to the Russians' extension of their sphere of exclusive influence.

These arguments against an East-West *modus vivendi* based on the "neutralization" of Germany are generally accepted in the West. But the NATO governments, and some leading opposition spokesmen in the member countries, including the United States, go even further than that. They equate the "neutralization" of two Germanies with the creation of a unified but militarily neutral Germany, arguing that if a united Germany is not in NATO there is a great danger that she will be swallowed up or forced into collaboration with Soviet Russia. In either event, there would be a drastic change in the balance of power which would be disadvantageous to the West.

These arguments generally fail to take several important factors in the present situation into consideration. First, the chances of a bargain between Germany and Russia are at least as great as long as the partition problem exists as they would be if a united Germany were militarily neutral. In the present situation the Germans would stand to gain from such a deal. A united Germany would have nothing to gain and much to lose by becoming involved in a one-sided agreement with Moscow.

Second, there have been sweeping changes in the balance of power since 1922 and 1939, which make a repetition of German aggression or adventurous foreign policy experiments very unlikely. Even as a reunited country Germany will not rank with the "great powers," and her people know this. And even though the Federal Republic has become the most powerful European nation except for Russia, neither West Germany nor a hypothetical reunited Germany could rely on its own military establishment alone for security. Whether it is a member of NATO or neutral, Germany would still be dependent upon the military strength of its neighbors and on guarantees from the "great powers" to preserve her security. Economically, too, Germany's interdependence with her European neighbors is an irrevocable fact. The West Germans will need and want to maintain close ties with France, Italy, the smaller European powers, and the United States. On the other hand, one must not expect a united Germany to abrogate the commercial ties currently binding the D.D.R. to the Soviet bloc. A united Germany would naturally attempt to obtain better terms of trade by using the alternatives of Western and other foreign markets which the Pankow government cannot today dare to bring into bargaining with Moscow. But in exchange for more favorable terms of trade one might well expect even West German industry to want to increase its commercial relationships with Russia and the rest of eastern Europe, as long as these prove to be beneficial. The Federal Republic's Western economic ties would not be cut off; they would undoubtedly be supplemented—some Germans use the term "balanced"—by a further development of trade relations in the East. This is by no means undesirable from the Western point of view. Germany is, after all, the key to European unity, not only of the "Little (western) Europe," but of Europe proper, which does not end at the Iron Curtain. Beneficial trade agreements between western Europe and eastern Europe are one of the most direct means of helping the satellites to achieve greater strength and independence, and may possibly also help to bring Soviet Russia into a constructive relationship with all of Europe by giving it a stake in the economic and social welfare and stability of non-Communist nations.

Military neutrality would not in any way disengage Germany from her Western heritage. The basic cultural and social ties which bind the Germans to the West today, the real source of German unity with the West, will not be impaired by Germany's withdrawal from NATO. And since the establishment of German unity in some acceptable form would have the effect of eliminating the objections to West Germany's application for membership in the U.N., one would expect the Germans to become responsible members of a world organization on whose further development as an effective security agency so much hope rests.

The chance that Germany will follow an adventurous foreign policy seems to be greater as long as the country is divided than if it were united. But assuming that a united Germany would have only the most peaceful intentions, if it were not allied militarily to the West, is there not a chance that the Soviet Union will be able to impose pressures on it to form a close association with the Communist world? Certainly that danger exists as long as Moscow pursues imperialist policies, whether by principally nonviolent means or through direct military action. But the danger of Soviet pressure on a neutral Germany can be exaggerated, especially if one fails to take into consideration the changes that will have been worked in the location of troops on which the West would have to insist as a condition for the creation of a neutral united Germany. The Red Army would not be on German soil, and if disengagement is carried beyond a first step, not on Polish, Czech, or Hungarian soil either. While it is true that the Red Army would have a shorter distance to travel to reënter Germany than Western forces that have been withdrawn from the Federal Republic, reëntry poses more problems for Moscow than are generally cited. One can be sure that the Poles would not invite the Russians back; there would be logistical problems to overcome; and, most important,

Moscow would have to assume that the West would treat the reëntry of Soviet forces as a *casus belli*.

In theory, the Germans might not have the confidence in their allies' determination to retaliate against a Soviet reëntry and might therefore give in to Soviet pressure. To be sure, this theoretical danger would remain, just as there is no foolproof guarantee today that the Red Army will not reënter Austria or Yugoslavia, or invade the Federal Republic. There simply are no foolproof guarantees of any kind in relations among nations: total security, like total victory, is an illusion. There is no sure strategy for peace or success; but we can be certain that without new efforts to achieve our aims defeat and failure are assured, while with them hopes are raised and progress is, at least, possible.

INDEX

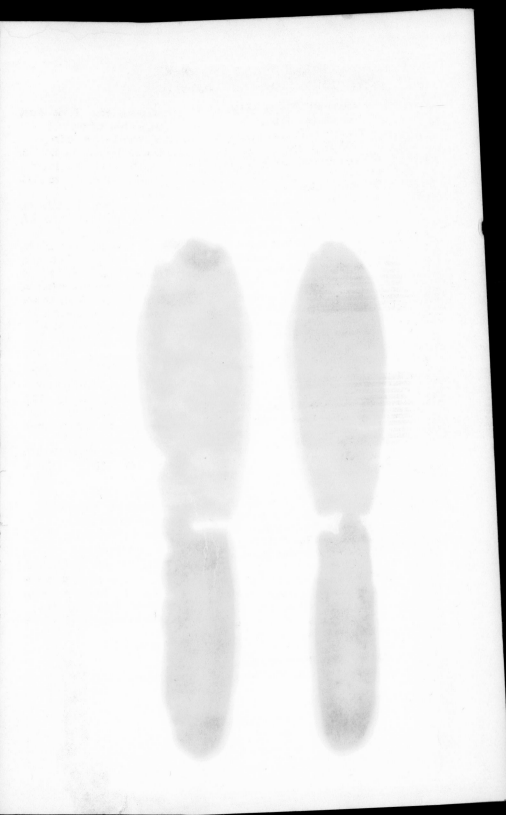

5/20/61

42916   DD
                               259.4
                               F78

FREUD, GERALD
    GERMANY BETWEEN
TWO WORLDS.

DATE DUE	
NOV 16 1993	

GAYLORD   PRINTED IN U.S.A.

Pocket
inside

Boundary of Germany in 1938
(before the Hitler acquisitions)

Germany after the
Second World War

Former German territory

0 — Miles — 100

North Sea

DENMARK

Copenhagen

Kiel Canal

Kiel

Lübeck

Rostock

Hamburg

Neubrandenburg

Elbe R.

Emden

Bremer-
haven

Bremen

Weser R.

EAST

NETHERLANDS

Amsterdam

Hanover

Helmstedt

AIR CORRIDORS
AND SUPPLY ROUTES
TO W. BERLIN

Magdeburg

GERMAN

Münster

Essen

Dortmund

RUHR

Rhine R.

Kassel

Brussels

BELGIUM

Cologne

Bonn

WEST

RHINELAND

Leipzig

Karl Marx Stadt
(Chemnitz)

Dr

LUXEMBOURG

Wiesbaden

Mainz

Frankfurt-
on-Main

Main R.

SAAR

GERMANY

Heidelberg

Nuremberg

Pilse

Strasbourg

Baden-
Baden

Stuttgart

Danube R.

Regensburg

Augsburg

FRANCE

Munich

Basel

Innsbruck

A

SWITZERLAND

ITALY